CLASSICS ADAPTED
for
ACTING and READING

Other books by

LEWY OLFSON

DRAMATIZED READINGS OF FAMOUS STORIES
RADIO PLAYS FROM SHAKESPEARE
DRAMATIZED CLASSICS FOR RADIO-STYLE READING
(Two volumes)

CLASSICS ADAPTED
for
ACTING and READING

A collection of one-act dramatizations
of famous stories and books for
royalty-free performance and reading

By **LEWY OLFSON**

Publishers PLAYS, INC. *Boston*

Library of Congress Catalog Card Number: 79–118941
ISBN: 0–8238–0003–2

For

MOTHER *and* DAVE

CONTENTS

Part One—PLAYS FOR ACTING

Part Two—PLAYS FOR READING

Preface

The use of dramatizations to support and enrich the traditional teaching of literature has long been regarded as a valuable technique by English teachers. Acting out episodes from great novels and stories introduces students to a wide range of literary experiences; piques their interest and whets their appetites for further reading; adds the dimension of creative participation to classroom study; and directly involves youngsters in what they are studying to a degree that passive reading alone cannot achieve. The plays in this volume, all of them based on well-known and dearly-loved books, plays, and stories, were designed to provide such enrichment experiences.

There are two types of play included: the traditional one-act play, and the more informal reading-aloud play. Each has its special uses; together, they offer a variety of dramatic experiences.

The traditional one-acts—called here "Plays for Acting"—lend themselves to regular production by students. So used, they require memorization of lines, thoughtful development of characters, and a series of regular rehearsals. If selected for presentation in a play tournament or at other public performances, some thought must be given to scenery and costumes and make-up as well. To encourage such full-scale production, these scripts have been kept as technically simple as possible. In most cases, a few pieces of furniture are all that is really necessary to set the scene; lighting, sound, and other special effects are minimal.

This is not to suggest that more informal classroom use may not well be made of the plays. Scripts in hand, students can act the plays out at the front of the room—or even read the parts from their desks, with one student reading important stage directions. The imaginative teacher will find a number of applications for these plays.

The reading-aloud plays, on the other hand, have specifically been designed for informal classroom use. Requiring no rehearsal and no memorization, they are ideal change-of-pace activities for the regular English class. Of course, they lend themselves to more elaborate treatment, too. With a few rehearsals and the addition of recorded music, they can be tape-recorded for broadcast over the school public address system, or for addition to the school's collection of spoken arts tapes. They can be presented at assemblies as staged readings. They can be broadcast over the community radio station. Here again, their utilization need be limited only by the teacher's imagination.

To insure students' continuing interest in using a number of these scripts, the plays included cover a wide range of literary styles, periods, and genres. Here are high comedies and light farces, adventures and romances, drama and melodrama, bright fantasy and dark tragedy. Comprising sixteen plays in all, this volume provides a stimulating, varied, yet balanced assortment from which the teacher can choose the plays most likely to meet the needs and interests and talents of his own students.

Helping students regard great world literature with genuine enthusiasm and delight is one of the major objectives of our schools' English programs. The plays in this book can help generate that excitement.

—Lewy Olfson

PART ONE

Plays for Acting

Rip Van Winkle

by Washington Irving

Characters

BROM DUTCHER
VAN BUMMEL
NICHOLAS VEDDER
DAME VAN WINKLE⎫
JUDITH GARDENEIR ⎬ *played by the same actress*
RIP VAN WINKLE
TWO LITTLE BOYS
TWO LITTLE GIRLS
THREE DUTCH SAILORS
HENDRICK HUDSON
TWO WOMEN
TWO MEN
RIP VAN WINKLE, JUNIOR

SCENE 1

TIME: *Late summer afternoon, mid-eighteenth century.*
SETTING: *The yard before the Inn. A Union Jack is flying from a flagpole; a sign over the Inn door has a portrait of King George the Third.*
AT RISE: BROM DUTCHER, NICHOLAS VEDDER *and* VAN BUMMEL, *three men of the town, sit in the Inn yard,*

3

casually smoking their pipes. After a moment, the sound of thunder is heard, far off. The men gaze lazily at the sky.

DUTCHER: Ach! Thunder it is . . . and on such a lovely day, too!

BUMMEL: Not a cloud in the sky! Do you think it will storm?

DUTCHER: When there's thunder, a storm is sure to follow.

VEDDER: What makes you so sure it is thunder? (*Sound of thunder is heard again, far off.*)

DUTCHER: Only listen to it! What else could it be?

VEDDER: Who knows? Perhaps it is Hendrick Hudson and his men, playing at ninepins in the Catskill Mountains!

DUTCHER (*Laughing*): You believe in those fairy tales, do you, Nicholas Vedder? Ach, I thought it was more sensible you were!

VEDDER: You may laugh if you like. I say it is Hendrick Hudson's men, and I say there will be no storm.

DUTCHER: What do you say, Van Bummel?

BUMMEL: I agree with Nicholas, Brom Dutcher. I say it will not storm.

DUTCHER: I'll make a bet with you!

BUMMEL: Go on!

DUTCHER: I'll bet we have a storm within the hour. If I am right, you must each buy me another glass of wine.

VEDDER: And if you are wrong? If there is no storm . . . ?

DUTCHER: Then the treat is on me! Agreed?

VEDDER *and* BUMMEL (*Laughing*): Agreed! (*Sound of thunder again, far off.*)

VEDDER: I think, Brom, you had better begin untying your purse! It is Hendrick Hudson, sure as I am standing here.

DUTCHER: We'll see. I say there will be a storm! (*From off right comes* DAME VAN WINKLE's *voice calling.*)

DAME VAN WINKLE (*Off-stage*): Rip! Ri-p! Rip Van Winkle!

VEDDER: Heaven help us, it's Dame Van Winkle!

DUTCHER (*Clapping his hands over his ears*): Listen to the fury of that woman's tongue!

DAME VAN WINKLE (*Off*): I'll catch you yet, you lazy good-for-nothing!

VEDDER: That voice of hers goes through a man like a bolt of lightning!

BUMMEL: Her poor husband gets nothing but thunder from that one—morning, noon and night! And what a drenching with words!

VEDDER (*Looking off*): And now, *we're* in for it! She's coming this way!

DUTCHER (*Laughing, holding out his hand*): I told you there would be a storm, and sure enough, Dame Van Winkle is coming to provide it! Pay up what you owe, gentlemen!

VEDDER (*Protesting*): Now wait, Brom Dutcher.

BUMMEL: We thought you meant a *real* storm.

DUTCHER (*Laughing*): If *that* one doesn't cause a real storm with her tongue, I'd like to know what does! I'd rather be caught in the ocean in the middle of a typhoon than have to listen to the storm of the tongue of Dame Van Winkle! (*As the men laugh,* DAME VAN WINKLE *enters.*)

DAME VAN WINKLE (*Sharply*): And just what are you good-for-nothings laughing about?

MEN (*Soberly*): Good day, Dame Van Winkle.

DAME VAN WINKLE: Is it? I haven't noticed! Now then, where is my husband?

VEDDER: How should we know, Dame Van Winkle?

DAME VAN WINKLE: I thought sure I'd find him down here, wasting his afternoon at the King's Arms with the rest of you lazybones!

DUTCHER: Your husband has not been here all day!

DAME VAN WINKLE: And I suppose you *have* been here all day, Brom Dutcher! Well, it may be all right with *your* wife if you spend the day in idleness and gossip, but for my part, I wish to see *my* husband hard at work!

BUMMEL (*Laughing*): Rip Van Winkle hard at work? That's a good one!

DUTCHER: He's the most idle man in the village!

DAME VAN WINKLE: You needn't tell me that, for it's well enough I know it! If I can lay my hand on him just once, *he'll* know something, too, I can tell you.

BUMMEL (*Consolingly*): Now, now, Dame Van Winkle. Don't take on so. Sit down for a moment and rest yourself.

DAME VAN WINKLE: Rest myself! With me married to that shiftless, lazy, irresponsible wretch, Rip Van Winkle, the only rest I'll get is in my grave! (*Calling off left, loudly*) Rip Van Winkle! (*Starts moving left*) I'll find him yet, if I must hunt in every corner and attic and haystack of this village! Rip! (*Sees him coming*) Ah, here comes the good man now . . . with a flock of dirty, yelling children at his heels. Rip Van Winkle, you come here this minute!

VEDDER (*To the other men*): Now the poor chap is in for it!

BUMMEL: I wouldn't want to be in his shoes, I can tell you.

DUTCHER (*Shaking his head*): Ach! Poor old Rip Van

Winkle! (RIP VAN WINKLE *enters. A little girl holds his hand and three other children are at his heels.*)

DAME VAN WINKLE: Ah, so here you are at last, husband!

RIP (*Sheepishly*): Yes, wife, here I am.

DAME VAN WINKLE: It is high time, too, I can tell you. As though you have nothing better to do than to go romping off on a spree with a bunch of children!

RIP: But they're very nice children, wife. Children, say hello to Dame Van Winkle.

CHILDREN (*In a monotone*): Good day, Dame Van Winkle.

DAME VAN WINKLE: Now, husband, I want you to come home with me this instant! The roof to the shed must be fixed, and I want it done before it begins to rain.

RIP: Yes, wife, I'll do it first thing tomorrow morning.

DAME VAN WINKLE: Tomorrow! Tomorrow! Everything with you must wait until tomorrow.

RIP: But I promised the children that I would take them fishing today.

DAME VAN WINKLE: You make promises to the children and your own family must suffer! I tell you that you will come home with me right this minute!

RIP (*Dejectedly*): Yes, wife.

FIRST BOY (*Plaintively*): Oh, Rip, does that mean you won't take us fishing?

DAME VAN WINKLE (*Going towards exit, angrily*): Yes, that's exactly what it means! (*Turning before she goes out*) Are you coming, husband, or must I grab you by the scruff of your neck?

RIP: I'm coming, wife.

DAME VAN WINKLE (*As she exits*): See that you do!

FIRST GIRL: Rip . . .

RIP (*Gently*): Yes, little Katrina?

FIRST GIRL: Will you show me where the chicken bit you, Rip?

RIP (*Laughing*): What do you mean? I had to sell all my chickens long ago, and the goats, too! I have not been bitten by a chicken!

FIRST GIRL: But my mother said you were the most hen-pecked man in town!

RIP: Oh she did, did she?

BUMMEL (*Laughing*): Katrina has you there, Rip!

RIP: Oh she has, has she?

VEDDER: Everyone knows it, Rip. You must admit that it's true!

RIP: I'll show you a thing or two, Nicholas Vedder! Children!

CHILDREN (*Eagerly*): Yes, Rip?

RIP: Children, we are going fishing!

CHILDREN (*Dancing with glee*): Hurrah! Hurrah for Rip Van Winkle!

RIP: I'll show you gentlemen that I still have a mind of my own!

DUTCHER (*Laughing*): That's all well and good for now, Rip. But what about later—when Dame Van Winkle gets hold of you?

VEDDER: It won't go easy with you then, my friend.

BUMMEL: How that woman's tongue runs on!

RIP: Yes, yes, what you say is true. A woman's tongue is the only tool that gets sharper with constant use. But it can't be helped! What must come later, will come. Meantime, I promised the children I would take them fishing—and I was ever a man of my word! (*Sound of thunder, far off.*)

SECOND BOY: It's going to rain! That always means extra good fishing!

SECOND GIRL: Rip, I'm afraid! I'm afraid of the thunder!

FIRST GIRL: Me, too, Rip! I'm afraid!

RIP (*Going to them, gently*): There's nothing to be afraid

of, Katrina, Gretchen. It's only Hendrick Hudson and his men—high up on the mountain tops.

FIRST BOY: You mean the same Hendrick Hudson that discovered the Hudson River long ago?

RIP: The very same.

FIRST GIRL: But he's—he's dead!

RIP: Some people say he's dead—but I know better!

SECOND GIRL: Really?

SECOND BOY: Tell us, Rip!

RIP: They say that Hendrick Hudson, long ago, climbed to the top of the Catskill Mountains with all of the sailors from his ship.

SECOND BOY: His ship was the "Half Moon". I learned that in school.

RIP: Right! Well, old Hudson and all of his men have lived on and on until this day, high in their mountain homes.

FIRST GIRL: Has anyone ever seen them?

RIP: That's hard to say for sure, Katrina. Generally, they hide themselves in the mist whenever they hear anyone coming. But once every twenty years, it is said, they allow themselves to be seen—and good things come to the man who is lucky enough to see them.

SECOND GIRL: What has all of this to do with the thunder?

RIP: I'm just coming to that part.

DUTCHER: Ah, go on with you, Rip—telling the children a lot of fairy stories!

RIP: They aren't fairy stories, Brom Dutcher!

SECOND BOY: Rip never tells lies, do you, Rip?

RIP: Of course I don't!

FIRST BOY: Go on with your story, Rip!

RIP: It is said that the old Dutch sailors love to play ninepins more than anything else in the world! And whenever one of their bowling balls hits one of the

pins, it makes a loud noise which is echoed and re-
echoed throughout the surrounding mountains and
valleys.

FIRST GIRL: And that is the noise we hear!

SECOND BOY: The thunder is the noise of the bowling
balls!

RIP: Right! So you see, there is nothing to fear. (*Sound
of thunder, louder than before. From this point to the
end of the scene, the lights fade very slowly.*)

FIRST GIRL: One of the sailors has made a hit!

SECOND GIRL: Perhaps it is old Hendrick Hudson himself!

RIP: But children, look! The sky is beginning to darken.
Perhaps it will rain after all. You'd better be going
home.

CHILDREN (*Disappointed*): Oh!

FIRST BOY: Couldn't we go fishing anyway?

SECOND BOY: The fish always bite best when it's raining—
and we need you to show us the best places!

RIP: What would your parents say if you came home in
the dark, all dripping wet? They would forbid you to
have anything to do with me—and that would be the
end of all our fun! No fishing, no kite-flying, no wood-
carving—no anything, ever again! No, children, you'd
better run home now. We'll go fishing tomorrow.

FIRST BOY: Do you promise, Rip?

RIP: Of course I promise. And I keep my promises, don't
I?

SECOND GIRL: Yes, yes, you do! Oh, I think you're the best
man in the whole world!

CHILDREN: Hurrah for Rip Van Winkle! (*They go out,
calling, ad lib.*) Goodbye, Rip! See you tomorrow. (*Etc.*)

RIP (*Happily*): How I love children!

BUMMEL (*Laughing*): To hear your wife tell it, it's little
love you have for your *own* two children.

RIP: For Judith, my daughter, and young Rip, my son? Why, of course I love them!

VEDDER: Your wife thinks otherwise—always complaining that you don't provide food and clothes for them.

DUTCHER: And she is even more upset with you for teaching your young son your bad habits.

RIP: What bad habits? I haven't any! What can she mean?

DUTCHER: She says that young Rip is lazy . . .

VEDDER: Just like you.

DUTCHER: She says he doesn't listen to a word she says . . .

VEDDER: Just like you.

RIP: And I tell you that young Rip will grow up to be a happy man—just like me!

BUMMEL: *If* he doesn't marry a nagging wife, as you had the misfortune to do.

RIP (*Sighing*): A misfortune it was indeed, gentlemen. When I married that woman, she was as sweet and pretty as my own dear daughter, Judith. But how the passing years have changed her!

BUMMEL: I hope Judith doesn't change. She is a lovely girl! (*Sound of thunder, nearer and longer.*)

RIP (*Looking up at the sky*): A hit! Good for you, old Hendrick Hudson! (*Sighing*) Ah . . . that's the life! Playing ninepins from dawn to dusk with a company of hearty sailors . . . and no wife along!

BUMMEL: Do you really believe in that old wives' tale, Rip? About Hudson and his men, I mean?

RIP: I do indeed—and it is no fairy tale, you can believe that! It's good old Hendrick Hudson, with the crew of his fine boat, the "Half Moon".

VEDDER: Well, Hudson or no Hudson, it will rain soon, to be sure. Come inside the Inn, gentlemen, where we won't get wet.

DUTCHER: And where *you* can pay off on the bet you lost!

(*Laughing as he enters the Inn*) Hendrick Hudson indeed!

VEDDER: Will you join us for a glass of wine, Rip? My treat?

RIP: Some other time perhaps, Nicholas. But thank you kindly for the offer. I'd better be getting back to my house now.

VEDDER (*Going into the Inn*): Better run, then, before the rain catches you!

BUMMEL: There's not so much hurry as all that, eh, Rip? If the rain doesn't catch you, your wife will! (*Laughing, he goes into the Inn. Sound of thunder, nearer, mixed with sound of wind.*)

RIP (*Turning up his collar*): It's going to rain, sure enough! (*Whistles*) Wolf! Wolf! Time to go home! Wolf! Where is that dog, I wonder? Well, I don't blame him for not wanting to go home. Poor dumb animal! Even *he* feels the fury of my wife's tongue!

DAME VAN WINKLE (*From far off, but shrill nonetheless*): Rip! Rip Van Winkle! Come home this minute, you hear? Ri-p!

RIP (*His hands covering his ears*): Ach! That voice would turn cream sour in the churn! I can tell by the edge in it, there's a real tongue-lashing waiting for me at home! (*Suddenly making up his mind*) Well, then, let it wait. I'd rather go for a walk on the mountainside! Wolf! Wolf! Come, dog! Come! We're going for a walk up on the mountain! (*Gazing at the horizon*) Ah, Hendrick Hudson, it's lucky you are to have such a beautiful mountain for a home! I hope you don't mind if I drop in soon to pay you a visit! (*Slowly* RIP *begins to move off, as the lights fade and the curtain falls.*)

*   *   *

Scene 2

Time: *Later, the same afternoon.*

Setting: *Before the curtains. On a mountain top.*

Before Rise: *From off left comes a booming voice, calling "Rip Van Winkle!", echoed on every side. The voice repeats itself, with echoes. Then thunder is heard. From right comes a short, bearded* Sailor, *carrying a large barrel on his shoulder. He makes his way slowly to the center of the stage, pauses, turns around and looks off right.* Rip *enters from right. He stops when he sees the* Sailor.

Rip: Ho there! Wait up, friend! Was it you that called me? (*The* Sailor *shakes his head "No."*) No? That's funny! I thought sure I heard someone call me by name! (*Sound of thunder.*) Ah, perhaps it was the thunder! Why, what an odd suit you have on there, my friend! It looks like the clothes the men are wearing in that old Dutch painting the schoolmaster has hanging in his house! Say, you aren't very talkative, are you? (Sailor *motions* Rip *to follow him.*) What's that? You want me to follow you? Don't mind if I do. I'm always glad of a little company, and I wasn't going anywhere in particular. Let me give you a hand with that cask. Since we're going in the same direction, I'll help you carry it! (*Takes barrel. From off left come two* Sailors, *the first carrying a bowling ball, the second a tray with mugs on it. Then* Hendrick Hudson *enters.*) More of you! Was it one of you gentlemen that called my name?

Hudson (*Slowly, majestically*): It was I, Rip Van Winkle!

Rip: How do you come to know me?

Hudson: That does not matter. We must be quick; the game of ninepins has already started.

RIP: The game of—the game of—

HUDSON: Ninepins, Rip Van Winkle.

RIP: Then you are Hendrick Hudson! This is the crew of the "Half Moon".

HUDSON: Yes, it is I . . . with my crew of ghostly sailors. Set down the cask you carry, and take some refreshment with us, my friend. (RIP *sets down the barrel and the* SAILORS *fill the mugs, passing them around.*)

RIP: I knew the stories they told me were true! I told the others!

HUDSON: Drink, my friend. Drink, Rip Van Winkle!

RIP: Thank you. I am thirsty from my long climb up the mountain. (*Drinking*) What a wonderful brew! What a tasty refreshment!

HUDSON: Come, my men, we must get on with our playing. (*One of the* SAILORS *carries out the cask, followed by* HUDSON *and the others.*)

RIP: Wait for me, men. Wait for me! How strange! I—I can't move! My feet are stuck firm to the ground!

HUDSON (*From off left*): Come, Rip Van Winkle! The game of ninepins has begun!

RIP: How—how tired I am. (*Yawning*) I can't seem to move. My eyes—my legs—how heavy they are! (*Sinks to the ground*) How tired I am!

HUDSON (*Off*): Come, Rip Van Winkle! (*Becoming more distant*) Come, Rip Van Winkle!

RIP: I'll just lie here for a few minutes and rest. That's what I'll do. I'll just rest awhile, here on the grass. I'll be able to catch up with the others later on. I'll . . . just . . . rest. (*He lies down on the ground and falls asleep. The lights fade to a blackout for about a minute. In the darkness we hear the thunder rolling in the background. When the lights come up,* RIP *is still asleep, but he has a long beard, and his coat is in tatters.*)

See Production Notes for arranging this change. RIP, *rubbing his eyes, and raising himself on one arm*) Where —where am I? Ah yes . . . I remember now! But where is Hendrick Hudson? Is the game of ninepins over so soon? I don't hear them! And what's this? Daylight? Surely I have not slept here all night! Oh, that drink— that wicked brew! What excuse shall I make to Dame Van Winkle? (*He gets up, stiffly. From here to the end of the play, he moves like an old man.*) Oh, how stiff in the knees I am! How my back aches! These mountain beds do not agree with me. The dampness and night air have given me a case of rheumatism, I'll be bound! (*Rubs his back and legs.*) How my wife will scold! I dread that tongue of hers already! But there's no help for it, I see. I might as well begin my climb down the mountain. With this stiffness in me, it will take me half the day! (*Moves to exit, turns and shakes his fist off left*) Ah, this was a mean trick to play on a friend, old Hendrick Hudson! (*Shaking his head, he goes off right.*)

* * *

SCENE 3

TIME: *Twenty years after Scene 1.*

SETTING: *The yard before the Inn. The first American flag has replaced the Union Jack; the sign over the Inn door now has a picture of George Washington on it, with his name inscribed underneath.*

AT RISE: *The stage is empty for a moment, and then* RIP *shuffles in and looks around.*

RIP (*Wonderingly*): What? Nobody around? How strange! It is the first time I can remember passing the Inn without seeing Brom Dutcher and Nicholas Vedder, drinking ale and smoking their pipes! Ach, perhaps it is Sunday! But is it Sunday? Yesterday was not Saturday. Or was it? My mind seems clouded. I have difficulty remembering. *(From off-stage we hear the voice of* JUDITH GARDENEIR*)*

JUDITH *(Off)*: Rip! Rip! Where is that child?

RIP *(Shaking his head, sadly)*: Well, that is one thing, at least, that I have no difficulty in remembering: my dear wife's voice! And she's calling me, as usual! But why does she call me a child? *(Philosophically)* Ah, perhaps it is a new insult she has thought up! *(*JUDITH *enters. At first she doesn't see* RIP.*)*

JUDITH *(Calling)*: Rip!

RIP: You called me, my dear?

JUDITH *(Startled)*: I beg your pardon, sir. I did not call you.

RIP: I thought you called . . .

JUDITH: I am looking for my little boy. *(Calls)* Rip!

RIP *(Not understanding)*: And you have nothing to say to *me?*

JUDITH: What should I say to you, sir? I do not know you.

RIP: What? Not know me? Am I not your husband?

JUDITH *(Laughing)*: You? My husband? No, old gentleman, my husband is Van Gardeneir.

RIP: Van Gardeneir? But your face . . . your voice. My mind is fuddled. I cannot remember. *(Musing)* Hendrick Hudson. . . .

JUDITH *(Gently)*: Sit here, old sir. Rest a moment. Perhaps your thoughts will clear.

RIP: Now, at least, I know you are *not* my wife! *She* never spoke a kind word to me in all our married life!

JUDITH: Some women have sharp tongues. I hope I am not one of them.

RIP: No, no, indeed. You are a lady! But—where am I? Where is my wife?

JUDITH: One moment, sir. I'll fetch the men from the Inn. Perhaps they will be able to help you. (*She goes into the Inn.*)

RIP: Ah yes, the men from the Inn. Once I see old Nicholas and Brom again . . . but what is this? That's not a picture of King George! What does the lettering say? The man's name is George, all right—but his last name says "Washington." (*Repeating the name, thinking*) Washington . . . Washington . . . I do not know anyone in the village with that name. And why have they put a red and white nightcap on top of the flagpole? How strange everything is! What has happened?

JUDITH (*Leading three men and two women from the Inn*): This is the man I told you of, good friends. He seems to be a bit confused.

FIRST MAN (*To* RIP, *heartily*): Well, old gray-beard, what seems to be the trouble?

RIP: Old gray-beard? Me? (RIP *puts his hand to his chin, feels his beard with amazement.*) Why, I—I *have* a beard! How did this happen?

FIRST WOMAN: He doesn't know how he got his beard! The man must be mad!

SECOND MAN: He *looks* mad to me!

RIP: Mad? No, I'm *not* mad!

SECOND MAN: What's your name, old fellow?

RIP: My name is Rip Van Winkle.

RIP, JR. (*The third man*): That's nonsense! *I* am Rip Van Winkle!

RIP: Impossible!

FIRST MAN: The old one *must* be mad!

FIRST WOMAN (*Pointing to* RIP, JR.): Of course! *This* is Rip Van Winkle! We all know him!

RIP: If you are me—then I don't know *who* I am!

RIP, JR.: That's plain!

SECOND MAN: Are you Federal or Democrat?

RIP (*Confused*): Federal? Democrat? What do those words mean?

SECOND MAN: On which side do you vote?

RIP: Vote? Alas, gentlemen, I am a poor quiet man, a native of this place, and a loyal subject of the King, God bless him!

FIRST MAN: The King!

FIRST WOMAN: He's a Tory—a spy!

SECOND MAN: Hustle him away!

JUDITH: Gently, gently, good neighbors! Give the poor man a chance to speak! You can see his thoughts are clouded, and that he is harmless.

RIP: Thank you, good woman. I assure you that I mean no harm; I have come merely to find some old friends of mine who used to frequent this Inn.

FIRST MAN: Well—who are they?

RIP, JR.: Name them!

RIP: Where's Nicholas Vedder?

SECOND WOMAN: Nicholas Vedder! Why, he is dead and gone these eighteen years!

RIP: Nicholas dead? Then where is Brom Dutcher?

FIRST MAN: Oh, he went off to the army in the beginning of the war; some say he was killed at the storming of Stony Point—others say he was drowned in a squall at the foot of Antony's Nose. I don't know—he never came back again.

RIP: And where is Van Bummel, the schoolmaster?

SECOND MAN: He went off to the wars, too, was a great militia general, and is now in Congress.

RIP: All gone! Does no one here know me? I am Rip Van Winkle!

RIP, JR.: But *I* am Rip Van Winkle!

RIP (*Sadly shaking his head*): I see. (*To* JUDITH) And you are not Dame Van Winkle? You are not my wife?

JUDITH: No indeed, sir. I am Judith Gardeneir—and Rip Van Winkle's sister.

RIP (*Suddenly understanding*): His sister! Ah, that explains it! Who was your father, good woman?

JUDITH (*Sadly*): Ah, poor man, his name was Rip Van Winkle also, but it's twenty years since he went away from home, and never been heard of since. Whether he was killed by accident, or carried away by Indians, nobody can tell. I was then but a little girl.

RIP: One question more, good woman. Where is your mother?

JUDITH: Alas, she too has died—but a short time ago. She broke a blood vessel in a fit of anger at a New England peddler.

RIP: That sounds like her! Judith—young Rip—don't you know me? I am your father! I am Rip Van Winkle!

RIP, JR.: What? Can it be?

JUDITH: Impossible!

RIP: Look at me—closely. Don't you know me?

JUDITH: Why, yes! Now that I look carefully—oh, Father, it is you, come home at last! (*She embraces him.*)

RIP, JR.: Good neighbors, it is indeed my father! Home after twenty long years! Welcome home, Father!

FIRST WOMAN: Welcome home, old neighbor! You used to play with us when we were children!

SECOND MAN: How we all loved you, Rip!

JUDITH: But where have you been all these years?

FIRST MAN: Tell us!

RIP: It is a strange tale. You may not believe it! Yesterday, I left this Inn yard . . .

SECOND MAN: Yesterday, Rip?

RIP (*Shaking his head, smiling*): I *thought* it was yesterday. But I see now it was twenty years ago.

JUDITH: Go on, Father.

RIP: It was a clear day—but there was thunder, nonetheless. In those days we often heard thunder—even on the brightest of days. From nowhere it would seem to come, suddenly and without warning!

SECOND WOMAN: That often happens to this day.

RIP: Such a day it was then. Your mother, my children, was angry with me—and rather than face her angry tongue, I decided to go for a walk in the mountains.

FIRST MAN: Who can blame him? We all know what Dame Van Winkle's tongue was like!

RIP: When I got to the top of the mountain, I met Hendrick Hudson himself!

MEN *and* WOMEN: What?

RIP: I knew you would not believe it, but every word I speak is true. There was old Hendrick Hudson, with his crew of sailors, dressed in their old Dutch clothes, playing ninepins. They asked me to join them.

SECOND WOMAN: And did you join them?

RIP: I did indeed—for very hospitable they were. They offered me a drink of ale from a huge cask they had . . . and when I had drained the flagon . . .

FIRST WOMAN (*Impatiently*): Yes, yes?

RIP: I was suddenly transfixed. My whole body became stiff with tiredness. Thinking to refresh myself, I lay down upon the ground for a nap. And when I woke, it was this morning.

SECOND MAN: You mean you slept for twenty years?

RIP: So it would seem.

FIRST MAN: A strange tale it is, indeed.

RIP: Strange it may be, but true it is!

FIRST WOMAN: I believe that. It's many the tale I've heard of old Hudson and his ghostly crew!

JUDITH: And glad I am that you have come home, Father. Now that Mother is gone, you must come and live with me!

RIP, JR.: No, no! As I'm to be married soon, Father must live with me!

RIP: You are to be married, son?

RIP, JR.: Indeed I am, Father.

RIP: I hope, for your sake, that your wife is as soft-spoken a woman as your sister is. I would not for all the world wish the next Dame Van Winkle to be like the last!

RIP, JR.: Nor would I, Father. I think we have all learned a lesson from you on that score.

MEN *and* WOMEN: Three cheers for Rip Van Winkle! Hip, hip, hurrah! (*Sound of a sudden burst of thunder. All look up at the sky.*)

RIP (*Smiling*): And three cheers for Hendrick Hudson! The game of ninepins has begun again! (*General laughter as the curtain falls.*)

THE END

Production Notes

RIP VAN WINKLE

Characters: 13 male; 6 female.

Playing Time: 25 minutes.

Costumes: Consult any illustrated edition of "Rip Van Winkle" for costume suggestions. Note: In Scene 1, Rip appears in a jacket, under which he wears a tattered old shirt. In the pocket of his jacket, he carries a fake beard, wired so that it will slip over his ears. During the blackout in Scene 2, Rip slips the beard on, takes off the jacket, and pushes it under the curtain, out of sight. One of the actors waits behind the curtain for the jacket; he has enough time to carry it to the wings before the start of Scene 3.

Properties: Pipes for Brom Dutcher, Nicholas Vedder and Van Bummel; large barrel; bowling ball; tray with mugs.

Setting: The yard before the Inn. At upstage center is the door to the Inn. In Scene 1, a sign over the door has a portrait of King George the Third. In Scene 3, the sign has a picture of George Washington, with his name inscribed underneath. In Scene 1, a flagpole at one side of the stage flies the Union Jack; in Scene 3, the first American flag has replaced the British flag. Several benches are in the yard.

Lighting: The lights fade in Scene 1 as indicated. There is a blackout in Scene 2.

Sound: Thunder, as indicated.

Jane Eyre

by Charlotte Brontë

Characters

MRS. FAIRFAX
JANE EYRE
MR. EDWARD ROCHESTER
MR. MASON
MANIAC, *off-stage voice*

SCENE 1

TIME: *A warm spring morning. The early 1800's.*

SETTING: *The drawing room of Thornfield Hall, a stately mansion.*

AT RISE: JANE EYRE *is standing center, in her wedding gown. She is a sweet, if slightly plain, girl, but at the moment she is radiant.* MRS. FAIRFAX, *the elderly housekeeper, is admiring her.*

MRS. FAIRFAX: Never have I seen a more beautiful bride, Miss Eyre! Never in all my days!

JANE: That is hard to believe, Mrs. Fairfax. I have never been beautiful in my life.

MRS. FAIRFAX: Oh, go on with you! Take a look at yourself in the mirror! (*As* JANE *goes to the mirror and looks at herself*) Now tell me the truth: were you not born to wear that dress? Does it not become you?

JANE: Perhaps it is vanity to say so, Mrs. Fairfax, but the gown does look well on me.

MRS. FAIRFAX (*Laughing*): Listen to the girl! It looks well on her! Goodness, Miss Eyre, you are a perfect vision! How the guests at the wedding will gape! "Mr. Rochester has certainly found a bride as handsome as himself," they'll be saying. And I'll tell you a secret, Miss Eyre. They will be right!

JANE: Oh, no, Mrs. Fairfax, I could never be as handsome as Mr. Rochester. He is so fine and elegant! I can hardly believe I am to become his wife. Indeed, I find everything a little hard to believe!

MRS. FAIRFAX: Aye, much has come to pass, Miss Eyre, since you first walked in that door to be governess to the master's ward.

JANE: Yet it seems as though it were only yesterday. I can remember so vividly the fear with which I left the orphanage that had been my home for so many years. With what trembling I approached Thornfield Hall on that windy day! I have come to love this old house with all my heart, but the first time I saw it, it seemed to me to be a frightening place—rather like a prison.

MRS. FAIRFAX: Fancy thinking of our dear old house as a prison! (*From off-stage comes a frightful, maniacal laugh —hysterical and intense.*)

MRS. FAIRFAX (*Running to the foot of the stairs*): She's at it again! (*Calling off*) Grace! Grace! Be quiet, I say! (*The laugh comes again, but farther off, and a door slams.* MRS. FAIRFAX *turns to* JANE.) Why, Miss Eyre! You're as pale as if you had seen a ghost! Sit down, my dear. You shouldn't be frightened on your wedding day!

JANE (*Seating herself, weakly*): I can't help it, Mrs. Fairfax. That dreadful laugh unnerves me every time I hear it!

MRS. FAIRFAX: I don't understand myself why the master keeps Grace Poole on as a servant. When she's quiet, she does the work of three, I'll admit. But when she gets into *that* state—well, it's enough to frighten a body to death!

JANE: I have been able to get used to all the rest, since I have been here. I've adjusted to Mr. Rochester's strange moods; I love his little ward as though she were my own sister; I've even become used to the knowledge that I am soon to be Mrs. Rochester, and mistress over the whole of Thornfield Hall. But that one thing—that horrible, mad laughter of Grace Poole is something I shall never get used to, I think.

MRS. FAIRFAX (*Changing the conversation*): Come, Miss Eyre. Let us think of more pleasant things. On such a day, no clouds should be allowed to pass over your face.

JANE: There are no clouds in my heart, Mrs. Fairfax, and that is what truly matters. I think there was never anyone happier in the world than I am at this moment.

MRS. FAIRFAX: And that you should be, marrying the handsomest, richest and most educated man in the whole of England!

JANE: Sometimes I wonder why such a man would want me—a poor, plain, dull thing. I should have thought Mr. Rochester would have fallen in love with one of the wealthy and beautiful women of the town. Indeed, I thought he was in love with Miss Blanche Ingram!

MRS. FAIRFAX (*Snorting*): Blanche Ingram! Blanche Ingram indeed! Rich she may be, but Mr. Rochester is too fine a man to want a woman for the money she may have. And beautiful—well, perhaps she has a certain amount of style. But there isn't a brain in that Miss Ingram's head! The master could never tolerate a stupid woman. And as for virtues, she has none of yours.

JANE: My virtues, Mrs. Fairfax?

MRS. FAIRFAX: Your kindness and your humility, Miss Eyre. Your good sense and your honest heart. Those are jewels worth far more to a man of Mr. Rochester's character. What does it matter if you are not rich?

JANE: I count myself rich indeed, being rich in his love; for that is all that matters to me, Mrs. Fairfax, and all that ever will.

MRS. FAIRFAX: Spoken well, Miss Eyre—and that's the sort of sentiment you'd never hear from Blanche Ingram. I want never to hear that woman's name again!

JANE (*Laughing*): Very well, Mrs. Fairfax. From now on, the only woman's name I shall mention is Mrs. Edward Rochester! Mrs. Edward Rochester!

MRS. FAIRFAX: That is as it should be. But time is fleeting! Your bridegroom will be here soon! Hadn't you better begin putting on your wedding veil?

JANE: I—I have no wedding veil.

MRS. FAIRFAX: What? No veil? But the master had one made especially for you in Paris. I saw it myself.

JANE: Yes . . . I know. But you see . . . last night, as I slept in my room in the west wing, I had a strange dream.

MRS. FAIRFAX: A dream, Miss Eyre?

JANE: At least I *thought* it was a dream. In the middle of the night, I heard that awful sound—Grace Poole's laugh—and saw a figure in the shadows by my bureau. I could hear Grace lift my wedding veil from its box, try it on, and then rip it into shreds. Then I fell asleep again.

MRS. FAIRFAX: Well, as long as it was only a dream . . .

JANE: When I awoke this morning, there was the bridal veil Mr. Rochester had given me—in shreds.

MRS. FAIRFAX (*Horrified*): I don't believe it! Grace would never do such a thing!

JANE (*Crossing to a table and lifting some torn net*): Here is the veil, Mrs. Fairfax—or at least what is left of it. See for yourself.

MRS. FAIRFAX (*Imploringly*): Oh, Miss Eyre—dear Jane Eyre—I'm sure there is some explanation for it. Don't let it spoil your wedding day! (MR. ROCHESTER *comes down the stairs and enters the room. He is a stern, handsome man, in formal dress.*)

ROCHESTER (*Crossing to* JANE *and taking her hands in his*): My dear Jane Eyre.

MRS. FAIRFAX (*Horrified*): Mr. Rochester! Don't you know it is bad luck for the bridegroom to see his bride before the marriage ceremony?

JANE (*Smiling*): That is only a superstition, Mrs. Fairfax! There is no truth to it! What harm could possibly befall us? I am the happiest woman in the world.

ROCHESTER: And I am the happiest man! Oh, Jane, Jane, you are the pride of my life.

JANE: Oh, sir, you make me blush with your compliments!

ROCHESTER: Blush away, then! The rose color becomes you! To think you will shortly become my wife!

JANE: I find it hard to believe myself, sir. Do you truly love me, and want me to marry you?

ROCHESTER: I do. And if an oath is necessary to satisfy, I swear it.

JANE: Then, sir, my heart is full.

ROCHESTER: My little wife, you must call me Edward.

JANE: Dear Edward.

ROCHESTER (*Putting his arm around her*): Are you happy, Jane?

JANE: Oh, yes, Edward. Yes, yes, yes!

ROCHESTER: You are very beautiful, my dear.

JANE: Oh, do not say so, sir.

ROCHESTER: You are a beauty in my eyes, and I will make the world acknowledge you as one. I will attire my Jane in satins and lace, and she shall have roses in her hair, and I shall cover her with priceless jewels.

JANE: Oh, sir! Never mind jewels. Jewels for Jane Eyre sound unnatural and strange. I would rather not have them.

ROCHESTER: Nonsense! I will myself put the diamond chain around your neck. I will clasp the bracelets on these fine wrists, Jane, and load these fairy-like fingers with rings.

JANE: No, no. Do not address me as if I were a queen. I am your plain, prim governess.

ROCHESTER: No, Jane, I tell you, you are lovely. Magnificent!

MRS. FAIRFAX: I was telling Miss Eyre earlier, sir, that she was the prettiest bride I've ever seen, but she would not believe me.

ROCHESTER: But she must believe you, Mrs. Fairfax. As your husband, Jane, I command you to believe that you are the prettiest woman in the world!

JANE: You are not my husband yet, Mr. Rochester, and if we stand here chattering all day, you may never be.

ROCHESTER (*Laughing*): Quite right! Always the practical one, eh, Jane? Mrs. Fairfax, is the luggage brought down?

MRS. FAIRFAX (*Indicating it*): Yes, sir.

ROCHESTER: Is the carriage ready?

MRS. FAIRFAX: They are preparing it in the stables, sir. It will be ready and waiting when you leave the church. (*The maniacal laugh comes from off-stage.* JANE *runs to* ROCHESTER.)

JANE: Oh, sir, I am frightened.

ROCHESTER (*Strangely*): Frightened, Jane? While I am beside you?

JANE: It's that laugh—that horrible laugh of Grace Poole's. It strikes terror to my heart.

MRS. FAIRFAX: Can you blame the girl for being afraid of it, Mr. Rochester? I have been in this house many more years than she, and I have not become used to it. Indeed, you yourself, sir, are the only one in the whole of Thornfield Hall that does not fear Grace Poole.

ROCHESTER (*Coldly, calmly*): There is nothing to be afraid of in the person of Grace Poole. Granted that she is odd in her behavior at times; but I know her story, and I can assure you that she is not to be feared.

JANE: All the same, sir, I shall be happier once we are away from here on our wedding trip—even for a little while. (*The doorbell rings off-stage.*)

MRS. FAIRFAX: Now, who can that be?

ROCHESTER: It will be the minister, I expect. He will want to ride to the church with us, and it is almost time. Let him in, Mrs. Fairfax.

MRS. FAIRFAX (*Going out left*): Yes, Mr. Rochester.

ROCHESTER: There now, Jane. Are you feeling better?

JANE: Oh, yes, sir. Just the thought of being your wife makes all my fears and worries vanish.

MASON (*From offstage*): No matter. I must see him at once. (MASON *enters, followed by the anxious* MRS. FAIRFAX. MASON *is an intense-looking young man, at the moment quite agitated.*)

ROCHESTER (*Angrily*): Mason! What are you doing here?

MASON: You know quite well, Mr. Rochester, why I have come. But it is not to speak with you; it is to speak with Miss Eyre.

JANE: With me, sir? But I do not know you.

MASON: Permit me to introduce myself. I am Mr. Mason, an old friend of Mr. Rochester's.

ROCHESTER (*Coldly, steadily*): Whatever you have to say, Mason, must wait until later. At the moment, Miss Eyre and I must be off to the church where we will be married.

MASON: What I have to say can *not* wait, Rochester, as you well know. After I have spoken, you will *not* be married.

MRS. FAIRFAX: What is this?

JANE: What do you mean, sir—not be married?

ROCHESTER: Mason, I forbid you to speak another word. Come, Jane. Let us go to the church. (ROCHESTER *takes* JANE's *arm and begins to move toward the door, but* MASON *bars the way.*) Out of our way, Mason, before I knock you down.

MASON: One word with Miss Eyre.

ROCHESTER: Not a syllable! Come, Jane.

JANE: Wait. Let him speak, Mr. Rochester.

MASON: Aye, Mr. Rochester, let me speak. It will be easier to say what I must say here; and if you do not allow me to do so, I shall be forced to follow you to the church. And there, when the minister pronounces those solemn words, "If any knows of any impediment why these two may not be lawfully joined together in matrimony, let him speak now or forever hold his peace," I shall be forced to declare the existence of such an impediment. (JANE *becomes faint and* MRS. FAIRFAX *rushes to her side.*)

MRS. FAIRFAX: Quick, Mr. Rochester, some wine! (*He hurriedly pours a glass, which* JANE *refuses, as* MASON *speaks.*)

MASON: I am sorry, Miss Eyre, to be the bearer of such unhappy tidings.

ROCHESTER: Do not listen to him, Jane. The man is mad!

JANE (*Weakly*): No. No. I must hear him out. What is the nature of this—this impediment, Mr. Mason?

MASON: It exists in the person of another woman. Mr. Rochester has now a wife to whom he is lawfully married, living here at Thornfield Hall.

JANE (*Sinking into a chair*): Another wife! Can it be true?

MRS. FAIRFAX: That is impossible, sir! I have lived here for many years and have never heard of such a wife!

JANE: Mr. Rochester!

MASON: Yes, Miss Eyre! Ask him!

JANE: Mr. Rochester, does Mr. Mason speak the truth?

ROCHESTER (*Angrily*): Yes, yes, the truth! Enough of this travesty! He tells the truth!

JANE: Who . . . who is the woman?

MASON: She is my sister, Miss Eyre: Bertha Mason Rochester.

MRS. FAIRFAX: How is it, then, that I have not heard of her? She lives here at Thornfield, you say?

ROCHESTER (*Violently*): I took care that none should hear of it—or of her, under that name. Enough! There will be no wedding! Bigamy is an ugly word—yet I meant to be a bigamist! You say you have never seen Mrs. Rochester, Mrs. Fairfax. Come then, and see her now. She's a maniac—an insane woman—under the care of Grace Poole, locked away in a room on the third floor. It's *she* that you hear laughing and screaming at night, *she*! (*Calling off left, bitterly*) Grace, prepare *my wife* for a visit from Mrs. Fairfax! (*To the others*) This man, Mason, who calls himself my friend: he tricked me into marrying her fifteen long years ago, even at a time when he knew her blood was tainted. Go! Take them, Mason, to see this horrible woman! Go, all of you! See the mad-woman that I call wife! Go! (*There is a slight pause, as* ROCHESTER *turns his back to the others.* MRS. FAIRFAX *and* MASON *turn and go softly up the stairs. Another pause.* ROCHESTER *turns, quietly.*) Well, Jane? You do not go with the others?

JANE (*Stunned*): No, sir.

ROCHESTER: Have you no word of reproach for me? Nothing bitter—nothing poignant? You know I am a scoundrel, Jane.

JANE (*Numbly*): Yes, sir.

ROCHESTER: Then tell me so—roundly and sharply. Don't spare me.

JANE: I cannot. I am tired and sick. I want some water.

ROCHESTER (*Giving her the wine glass*): Here is wine, Jane. Drink it. Oh, Jane, Jane, come to me.

JANE: There is no room for me now.

ROCHESTER: Why? No, I'll spare you the trouble of answering. I'll answer for you. Because I have a wife already, you would reply.

JANE: Yes.

ROCHESTER: A wife in name, yes. But in nothing else! You have heard her! Is this a wife? I ask you. Jane, dearest Jane, I love you. Do you believe that?

JANE: Yes, sir. I will always believe it. And I love you.

ROCHESTER: Then you must understand what I want of you. Just this promise: Mr. Rochester, I will be yours.

JANE (*Rising, looking at him steadily*): Mr. Rochester, I will *not* be yours. (*She moves slowly toward the doorway, left.*)

ROCHESTER: Are you going, Jane? Leaving me?

JANE: Yes, sir. I cannot stay. I shall leave in the morning.

ROCHESTER (*Tortured*): Jane!

JANE: Will you go now, sir? Go to the church and tell our guests that—that there will be no wedding.

ROCHESTER (*Pleading*): Jane . . . (*Seeing it is no use, he exits left, slamming the door.*)

JANE (*Taking a step toward the door, her hands out-stretched*): Mr. Rochester! Edward . . . ! God bless you, my dear master. God keep you from harm and wrong— direct you, solace you and reward you well for your past kindness to me. (*Weeping, lifting her eyes upward*) Dear God, be not far from me, for trouble is near: there is none but You to help me! (*Curtain*)

*   *   *

SCENE 2

TIME: *Several years later.*

SETTING: *The drawing room. The windows are now boarded up and the furniture is covered.*

AT RISE: MRS. FAIRFAX, *looking much older, is seated on the sofa, sewing. After a moment, the doorbell rings.*

MRS. FAIRFAX (*Starting*): Who on earth can that be? And so late in the afternoon. (*She goes off left and is heard speaking from offstage.*) Good heavens, is it you, Miss Eyre?

JANE (*From offstage*): It is indeed, Mrs. Fairfax. (MRS. FAIRFAX *re-enters, followed by* JANE, *who is wearing a traveling cloak.*)

MRS. FAIRFAX: I can hardly believe it is really you, Miss Eyre, come at this late hour to this lonely place . . . and after all these years.

JANE: It is really I, Mrs. Fairfax, after all these years.

MRS. FAIRFAX: Is it still "Miss Eyre?"

JANE: Yes, it is. You know that I have had room in my heart for only one man; and though my love was put away that terrible day, it has not died, Mrs. Fairfax, nor will it ever. But tell me: what has happened to Thornfield Hall in my absence?

MRS. FAIRFAX: Ah, well may you ask that, Miss Eyre. It was a dreadful tragedy.

JANE: That I can easily believe. When I turned the bend in the road a few minutes ago, I fully expected to see the magnificent old home that I remembered so clearly, with its spreading wings and lofty spires. When I saw instead this ruined, blackened and scarred shell of a house, my heart leaped into my throat.

MRS. FAIRFAX: Oh, Miss Eyre, it was a terrible thing. Aye, a terrible thing. We had a great fire here, not a month after you left; it swept through the whole west wing of the house, until all that was left was a pile of ash and rubble. Only this wing remains.

JANE: Forgive my next question, but I cannot help wondering if the madwoman—Mrs. Rochester—had any hand in the fire.

MRS. FAIRFAX: You've hit it at once, Miss. It's quite certain that it was she, and nobody but she, that set the blaze. One night, when Grace Poole was asleep—you remember Grace Poole, do you not?

JANE: I do, indeed. But tell on!

MRS. FAIRFAX: As I say, Grace was asleep one night. The mad one stole the keys out of her pocket, let herself out of her room and ran down the hall.

JANE: Yes?

MRS. FAIRFAX: She headed straight for your room . . .

JANE (*Starting*): My room!

MRS. FAIRFAX: I mean the room that had been yours when you were governess here. In that room the madwoman started the fire.

JANE: How terrible! Why do you suppose she chose that room?

MRS. FAIRFAX: Mad though she was, Miss Eyre, I think she knew enough to sense the great love Mr. Rochester had for you. I suppose that was why. She wanted to destroy you—just as she had once destroyed your wedding veil.

JANE: Ah, yes. My veil.

MRS. FAIRFAX: At any rate, in no time at all, the whole wing was ablaze.

JANE: Was Mr. Rochester at home when the fire broke out?

MRS. FAIRFAX: Yes, indeed. In fact, after you left, Miss Eyre, he was so heartbroken he never left the house from that day on, but lived alone here without seeing anyone. But perhaps I've said too much.

JANE: No, no, Mrs. Fairfax. Go on!

MRS. FAIRFAX: The master went up to the attic when all was burning above and below, and got the servants out of their beds and helped them down himself, through the smoke and all. Then, he went back to get his mad wife out of her room. By that time she had got out on the roof, and we who were on the ground could see her waving her arms above the battlements and shouting out until they could hear her a mile off.

JANE (*Anxiously*): Go on, go on!

MRS. FAIRFAX: Mr. Rochester crawled through the skylight onto the roof where she was standing, her long black hair flying against the flame. We heard him call to her as he inched toward her over the roof. Just as he was within an arm's reach of her, she yelled and gave a spring, and the next minute she lay on the pavement of the courtyard.

JANE: Dead?

MRS. FAIRFAX: Aye, dead as the cobblestones on which she had fallen. Oh, it was horrible!

JANE: And afterwards? Were there . . . were there any other lives lost?

MRS. FAIRFAX: No, but perhaps it would have been better if there had been.

JANE (*Horrified*): What do you mean?

MRS. FAIRFAX (*Shaking her head sadly*): Poor Mr. Rochester. I little thought ever to have seen it.

JANE: What is it, Mrs. Fairfax? What are you hinting at? You say he is alive?

MRS. FAIRFAX: Aye, he is alive, but like a dead one. After Mrs. Rochester fell, the master tried to make his way out of the flaming house. As he came down the west staircase, there was a great crash. He was taken out of the ruins, poor man—blinded for life. Both his eyes have been useless from that day.

JANE (*With a gasp*): Blind!

MRS. FAIRFAX (*Shaking her head*): Aye. Poor, poor man! (*From off right comes* MR. ROCHESTER's *voice, loud and clear.*)

ROCHESTER (*Offstage*): Mrs. Fairfax! Why have you not called me for my tea yet? It's past the regular time!

MRS. FAIRFAX (*Calling to him*): Coming, sir, in a minute. (*To* JANE.) I'll fetch his tea now, Miss. Shall I tell him you're here?

JANE: No, Mrs. Fairfax. Not yet. I want a moment to think.

MRS. FAIRFAX (*Going out left*): Very good, Miss Eyre.

JANE (*Thinking aloud*): Blind! How horrible for him! And yet—how like him, to try to save the madwoman who had ruined his life. The madwoman who wished him death! How like him! (*Looking at herself in the mirror*) You love him still, Jane Eyre. You love him still. (MRS. FAIRFAX *enters, carrying a tray with tea things.*)

MRS. FAIRFAX: I hope he will not be angry. It is later than usual.

JANE: Knock on his door, Mrs. Fairfax, and tell him his

tea is ready. Then leave us alone, please. I will give him his tea.

MRS. FAIRFAX: Very well, Miss Eyre. (*She goes to the door, right, and knocks on it.*) Mr. Rochester, your tea is ready. Shall I bring it in or will you have it in the drawing room?

ROCHESTER (*From off right*): I will come to you. You may serve me in the drawing room.

MRS. FAIRFAX: Very good, sir. (*She smiles at* JANE *and exits, left.* JANE *picks up the tray from the table on which* MRS. FAIRFAX *had set it. The door, right, opens, and* MR. ROCHESTER *enters, carrying a cane. He moves slowly, using his hands and the furniture to guide him. He sits.*)

ROCHESTER: Now then, Mrs. Fairfax, where is the tea?

JANE (*Setting the tray before him*): Here it is, sir.

ROCHESTER (*Startled*): That voice! Is it you, Mrs. Fairfax?

JANE (*Calmly*): Mrs. Fairfax is in the kitchen, sir.

ROCHESTER: Who is it? Who is it? (*He clasps one of* JANE's *hands.*) Whose hand is this? Answer me! Speak again!

JANE: Shall I pour your tea, sir?

ROCHESTER: Good heavens! What delusion has come over me? What madness?

JANE: No delusion—no madness. Your mind, sir, has always been too strong for delusion, your health too sound for frenzy.

ROCHESTER: And where is the speaker? Is it only a voice? I must touch you, or my heart will stop and my brain burst! Whoever you are, be perceptible to my touch or I cannot live! (*JANE takes his hands in her own and kisses them.*) Her touch! Her kiss! Is it Jane? (*His hand on her head*) This is her brow! This is her hair!

JANE: And this her voice. She is all here; her heart, too. God bless you, sir! I am glad to be so near you again!

ROCHESTER (*Happily*): Jane Eyre! Jane Eyre!

JANE: My dear Edward, I have come back to you!

ROCHESTER: You have come back to me when I need you most.

JANE: Is not that the task of friends?

ROCHESTER: But you do not find the man you expected. I am now no better than a lightning-struck chestnut tree. And what right would that ruin have to hope to be covered by a flowering woodbine, covering with her scented blossoms his ugliness and decay?

JANE: You are no ruin, sir, no lightning-struck tree. You are green and vigorous. Plants will grow about your roots whether you ask them or not, for you have many friends.

ROCHESTER: You speak of friends, Jane. But I want a wife.

JANE: Do you, sir?

ROCHESTER: Yes. Is it news to you?

JANE: Of course. You said nothing about it before.

ROCHESTER: Is it unwelcome news?

JANE: That depends, sir, on circumstances—on your choice.

ROCHESTER: Which you shall make for me, Jane. I will abide by your decision.

JANE: Choose then, sir, the one who loves you best.

ROCHESTER: I will at least choose the one I love best. Jane, will you marry me?

JANE: Yes, sir.

ROCHESTER: Truly, Jane?

JANE: Most truly, sir.

ROCHESTER (*Takes her hand*): God bless and reward you!

JANE: Mr. Rochester, if ever I did a good deed in my life, if ever I thought a good thought, if ever I prayed a sincere and blameless prayer—I am rewarded now. To be your wife is, for me, to be as happy as I can be on earth.

ROCHESTER: Once, I was filled with bitterness that you

would not have me. Now, I thank God for it! I see that this is the better way! I thank God for keeping you for me, my dearest—my beloved—my Jane Eyre. (*They embrace as the curtain falls.*)

THE END

Production Notes

JANE EYRE

Characters: 2 male; 2 female; offstage voice.

Playing Time: 30 minutes.

Costumes: In Scene 1, Jane wears a bridal dress; in Scene 2, she wears a plain gown and traveling cloak. Mr. Rochester wears formal dress in Scene 1; in Scene 2, he should be dressed in plain dark clothes. Mr. Mason and Mrs. Fairfax wear clothes of the period. Mrs. Fairfax should seem much older in Scene 2. (Consult any illustrated edition of *Jane Eyre* for costume suggestions.)

Properties: Scene 1: Torn net veil, decanter of "wine" and glass. Scene 2: Sewing for Mrs. Fairfax, tray with tea things, cane for Mr. Rochester.

Setting: The drawing room of Thornfield Hall. The room is elegantly furnished with tables, chairs, heavy drapes, etc. A mirror is on one wall. Upstage center is a staircase. There are exits at left and right. In Scene 1, some luggage is onstage. In Scene 2, the windows should be boarded and the furniture covered.

Lighting: No special effects.

The Importance of Being Earnest

by Oscar Wilde

Characters

ALGERNON MONCRIEFF
LANE, *a butler*
JACK WORTHING, *alias Ernest*
LADY BRACKNELL
GWENDOLEN FAIRFAX
CECILY CARDEW
MISS PRISM
DOCTOR CHASUBLE
MERRIMAN, *a butler*

SCENE 1

TIME: *A spring afternoon, late nineteenth century.*

SETTING: *The drawing room of Algernon's apartment, London.*

AT RISE: ALGERNON, *a handsome young man in his mid-twenties, is stretched out on a sofa, eating a tea sandwich.* LANE, *the butler, is just going to the door to open it.*

LANE (*After opening the door, turns and announces*): Mr. Worthing. (*As* LANE *goes out,* JACK *enters. He is a very pleasant young man, a few years older than* ALGERNON. *He is sometimes called Ernest.*)

JACK (*Advancing* to ALGERNON): Algy, my good fellow, how nice to see you.

ALGERNON (*Shaking his hand*): How are you, my dear Ernest? What brings you up to town?

JACK: Oh, pleasure, pleasure. What else should bring one anywhere?

ALGERNON: Where have you been since last Thursday?

JACK: In the country.

ALGERNON: What on earth do you do there?

JACK: When one is in town, one amuses oneself. When one is in the country, one amuses other people. It is excessively boring. But why all these cups, Algy? Are you expecting someone to tea?

ALGERNON: Merely Aunt Augusta and Gwendolen.

JACK (*Pleased*): How perfectly delightful!

ALGERNON: Yes, that is all very well. But I am afraid Aunt Augusta won't quite approve of your being here.

JACK: May I ask why not?

ALGERNON: My dear fellow, the way you flirt with Gwendolen is perfectly disgraceful. It is almost as bad as the way Gwendolen flirts with you.

JACK: But I am in love with Gwendolen. I have come up to town expressly to propose to her.

ALGERNON: I thought you had come up for pleasure. I call that business.

JACK: How utterly unromantic you are.

ALGERNON: Oh, it's very romantic to be in love. But there's nothing romantic in a definite proposal. (JACK *puts out his hand to take a sandwich.* ALGERNON *at once interferes.*)

ALGERNON: Please don't touch the cucumber sandwiches.

They are ordered specially for Aunt Augusta. (ALGER-
NON *takes one and eats it.*)

JACK: Well, *you* have been eating them all the time.

ALGERNON: That is quite a different matter. She is my aunt.
(*He proffers a different plate.*) Have some bread and butter. The bread and butter is for Gwendolen. Gwendolen
adores bread and butter.

JACK (*Munching*): And very good bread and butter it is,
too.

ALGERNON: Well, my dear fellow, you need not eat as if
you were going to eat it all. You behave as if you were
married to her already. You are not married to her
already, and I don't think you ever will be. I don't give
my consent.

JACK: *Your* consent!

ALGERNON: My dear fellow, Gwendolen is my first cousin.
And before I allow you to marry her, you will have to
clear up the whole question of Cecily. (*He rings a small
bell on the tea table.*)

JACK: Cecily? What do you mean, Algy, by Cecily? I don't
know anyone by the name of Cecily. (LANE *appears in
the doorway.*)

LANE: You rang, sir?

ALGERNON: Yes, Lane. Bring me the cigarette case Mr.
Worthing left in the smoking room the last time he
dined here.

LANE: Yes, sir. (*He goes out.*)

JACK: Do you mean to say you have had my cigarette case
all the time? I was very nearly offering a reward.

ALGERNON: I wish you *would* offer one. I happen to need
cash.

JACK: There is no good offering a reward now that the
thing has been found. (LANE *enters, carrying the cigarette case, which he hands to* ALGERNON.)

LANE: The cigarette case, sir. (*He exits.*)

ALGERNON (*Looking at it*): No need for you to offer a reward, Ernest, for I see, now that I look at the inscription, that the case isn't yours at all.

JACK: Of course it's mine.

ALGERNON: But this case is a present from someone named Cecily, and you said that you didn't know anyone of that name.

JACK: Well, if you want to know, Cecily happens to be my aunt.

ALGERNON: Then why does she call you her uncle? Here's the inscription: "From little Cecily, with her fondest love to her dear Uncle Jack." Besides, your name isn't Jack. It's Ernest.

JACK: My name, dear Algy, is really Jack.

ALGERNON: But how can it be? You've always told me your name was Ernest. I've introduced you to everyone as Ernest. You answer to the name of Ernest. You are the most earnest-looking person I ever saw in my life. It's perfectly absurd your saying that your name isn't Ernest. It's on your card. Here is one of them. (*Taking card from case*) Mr. Ernest Worthing, B.4, The Albany. I'll keep this as a proof that your name is Ernest if ever you attempt to deny it to me or to Gwendolen or anyone else.

JACK: That's my town card. At the Albany, here in town, I'm Ernest. But in the country I'm always Jack. And the cigarette case was given to me in the country.

ALGERNON (*Exasperated*): Will you kindly explain yourself?

JACK: Give my cigarette case to me first. (*He does so.*) Thank you. Now listen closely to what I am about to say. In his will, old Mr. Cardew, who adopted me when I was a little boy, made me guardian to his granddaughter, Miss Cecily Cardew. Cecily, who addresses me as her uncle, lives at my place in the country under the charge of her admirable governess, Miss Prism.

ALGERNON: Where is this place in the country?

JACK: That is nothing to you. You are not going to be invited.

ALGERNON: Even so, how does that explain why you are Ernest in town and Jack in the country?

JACK: In order to be a good guardian to Cecily, I must adopt a high moral tone regarding everything while I am in the country. This becomes rather boring at times, and so in order to get up to town, I have always pretended to have a younger brother by the name of Ernest, who lives in the Albany and gets into the most dreadful scrapes. But the fact of the matter is, I think I shall soon have to kill off Ernest altogether.

ALGERNON: But why, my dear fellow? He seems a most useful sort.

JACK: I suspect my ward, Cecily, is becoming rather too interested in Ernest. So I shall just get rid of him and be Jack in the country and Jack in the city, too. It's rather a bore, but that's the whole truth, pure and simple.

ALGERNON: The truth is rarely pure, and never simple. (LANE *enters, followed by* LADY BRACKNELL *and* GWENDOLEN FAIRFAX. LADY BRACKNELL *is an overbearing dowager;* GWENDOLEN *is a lovely girl of twenty.*)

LANE: Lady Bracknell and Miss Fairfax. (*He goes out.*)

LADY BRACKNELL: Good afternoon, dear Algernon. I hope you are behaving very well.

ALGERNON: I'm feeling very well, Aunt Augusta.

LADY BRACKNELL: That's not quite the same thing. Ah, Mr. Worthing, good afternoon.

ALGERNON: How are you today, Gwendolen?

GWENDOLEN (*Coyly*): How do I look?

JACK: You're quite perfect, Miss Fairfax.

ALGERNON: Will you have tea, Aunt Augusta?

LADY BRACKNELL: First things first, Algernon. I asked you to prepare the program for my musicale this evening.

ALGERNON: I have laid the music out on the piano. You can select whatever you prefer. Won't you come into the music room?

LADY BRACKNELL: Will you excuse us, Mr. Worthing? Gwendolen, while I am gone I expect you to think constructive thoughts.

GWENDOLEN (*Meekly*): Yes, Mamma.

ALGERNON: This way, Aunt Augusta. (ALGERNON *ushers* LADY BRACKNELL *out of the room.* GWENDOLEN *seats herself on the sofa with poise, and stares sweetly ahead.* JACK *is obviously at a loss as to what to say.*)

JACK (*Falteringly, after a pause*): Charming day it has been, Miss Fairfax.

GWENDOLEN: Pray don't talk to me about the weather, Mr. Worthing. When people talk to me about the weather I always feel quite certain they mean something else.

JACK: I do mean something else. I would like to take advantage of Lady Bracknell's absence—

GWENDOLEN: I would advise you to do so. Mamma has a way of coming back into a room so suddenly.

JACK (*Nervously*): Miss Fairfax, ever since I met you I have admired you more than any girl . . . I have ever met since . . . I met . . . you.

GWENDOLEN: Yes, I am quite aware of that fact. And even before I met you, I must confess, I was far from indifferent to you. We live, as you know, in an age of ideals. My ideal has always been to love someone by the name of Ernest. There is something in that name that inspires confidence. The moment Algernon mentioned to me that he had a friend named Ernest, I knew that I was destined to love you.

JACK (*Taken aback*): But you don't really mean to say that you couldn't love me if my name wasn't Ernest? Personally, darling, to speak quite candidly, I don't care much about the name Ernest. In fact I don't think it suits me at all.

GWENDOLEN: It suits you perfectly. It is a divine name. It has a music of its own. It produces vibrations.

JACK: I think there are lots of other much nicer names. I should say that Jack, for instance, is a charming name.

GWENDOLEN (*Considering*): Jack? No, there is very little music in the name Jack. It does not thrill. It produces absolutely no vibrations. No, darling, I truly feel I must marry someone by the name of Ernest. It is the *only* really safe name.

JACK (*Going down on his knees before her, impetuously*): Gwendolen, I must get christened at once . . . I mean, we must get married at once.

GWENDOLEN (*Coyly*): But you haven't proposed to me yet.

JACK: Well, then, may I propose to you now?

GWENDOLEN: I think it would be an admirable opportunity. And to spare you any possible disappointment, Mr. Worthing, I think it only fair to tell you that I am fully determined to accept you.

JACK (*Rapturously*): Gwendolen!

GWENDOLEN: Yes, Mr. Worthing? What have you to say to me?

JACK: Gwendolen, will you marry me?

GWENDOLEN: Of course I will, darling. Really, how long you took! (LADY BRACKNELL *enters. She takes in the situation at once and explodes.*)

LADY BRACKNELL: Mr. Worthing! Rise, sir, from your knees. Such a position is most indecorous.

GWENDOLEN (*Happily*): Mamma, I am engaged to Mr. Worthing.

LADY BRACKNELL: When you become engaged, Gwendolen, your father and I will inform you of the fact. Now I have a few questions to put to Mr. Worthing. While I am making these inquiries, you, Gwendolen, will wait for me in the carriage.

GWENDOLEN (*Protesting*): Mamma!

LADY BRACKNELL (*Imperiously*): In the carriage, Gwendolen.

GWENDOLEN (*Smiling at* JACK *as she moves to the door*): Yes, Mamma. (GWENDOLEN *goes out.* LADY BRACKNELL *seats herself majestically.* JACK *squirms.*)

LADY BRACKNELL: Now, then, Mr. Worthing, do you smoke?

JACK: Well, yes, I must admit I smoke.

LADY BRACKNELL: I am glad to hear it. A man should always have an occupation of some kind. How old are you?

JACK: Twenty-nine.

LADY BRACKNELL (*Approvingly*): A very good age to be married at. Now, as to your parents.

JACK: I have lost both my parents.

LADY BRACKNELL: Both? That seems like carelessness. Who was your father?

JACK (*Embarrassed*): I'm afraid I really don't know. The fact is, Lady Bracknell, I was . . . well, found. In the cloakroom of a station on the Brighton Line, by a gentleman named Mr. Thomas Cardew. He gave me the name of Worthing because he happened to have a first-class ticket to Worthing in his pocket. Yes, I was found, Lady Bracknell, in a large black handbag.

LADY BRACKNELL (*Indignantly*): I'm sure that you can

hardly consider that an assured basis for recognition in good society.

JACK: May I ask, then, what you would advise me to do?

LADY BRACKNELL (*Rising imperiously*): I would strongly urge you, sir, to try to acquire some relations as soon as possible. You can hardly imagine that I would allow my only daughter to marry into a cloakroom, and form an alliance with a parcel! Good afternoon, Mr. Worthing. (*Majestically,* LADY BRACKNELL *sweeps out the door.*)

JACK (*Calling out, miserably*): It's all right, Algy. You can come in now.

ALGERNON (*Entering from the music room*): What's the matter? Didn't it go off all right? You don't mean to say that Gwendolen refused you?

JACK: Oh, Gwendolen is as right as a trivet. Her mother is unbearable.

ALGERNON: Did you tell Gwendolen the truth about your being Ernest in town and Jack in the country?

JACK: My dear fellow, the truth isn't the sort of thing one tells a nice young lady like Gwendolen. And besides, as I say, I plan to get rid of Ernest by the end of the week. He shall die of a chill in Paris.

ALGERNON: Won't your poor little ward, Miss Cecily, feel his loss a good deal?

JACK: Oh, I doubt it. Cecily is not a silly romantic girl, I'm glad to say. She has a capital appetite, goes on long walks, and pays no attention at all to her lessons.

ALGERNON: I would rather like to see Cecily.

JACK: I will take very good care you never do. She is excessively pretty, and she is only just eighteen. (LANE *enters.*)

LANE: Miss Fairfax. (*He goes out as* GWENDOLEN *enters.*)

ALGERNON: Gwendolen, upon my word!

GWENDOLEN (*Rushing to* JACK): Ernest, we may never be married. Mamma has just told me all, and from the expression on her face I fear we never shall. But although she may prevent us from becoming man and wife, nothing she can possibly do will ever alter my eternal devotion to you.

JACK: My own darling!

GWENDOLEN: The story of your romantic origin has naturally stirred the deeper fibres of my nature. The simplicity of your character makes you exquisitely incomprehensible to me, and your Christian name, ·Ernest, has an irresistible fascination for me.

JACK: Dear Gwendolen!

GWENDOLEN: It may be necessary to do something desperate. I shall write you daily. There is a good postal service outside of London, I suppose. If you will just give me your country address . . . (JACK, *not wishing* ALGERNON *to hear, whispers to her in a loud stage whisper.* ALGERNON *overhears, and writes the address on his cuff.*)

JACK: I don't want Algy to know, but it's the Manor House, Woolton, Hertfordshire.

GWENDOLEN: What is it again? I can't hear.

ALGERNON (*Blandly*): He said he didn't want me to hear, but it's the Manor House, Woolton, Hertfordshire.

JACK (*Outraged*): Oh bother, Algy! Come along, Gwendolen. I'll escort you to the door.

ALGERNON (*Pleasantly*): Goodbye, Cousin Gwendolen. Goodbye, Ernest. (LANE *opens the door for them from without, as* JACK *and* GWENDOLEN *go out.*) Oh, Lane.

LANE (*Coming into the room*): Yes, sir.

ALGERNON: I'm going visiting tomorrow—to Mr. Worthing's country home.

LANE: Yes, sir.

ALGERNON: I shall probably not be back till Monday. Pack my dress clothes and my summer suits. Oh, I hope tomorrow will be a fine day, Lane.

LANE: It never is, sir. It never is. (ALGERNON *pops a tea sandwich into his mouth as the curtain falls.*)

*   *   *

SCENE 2

TIME: *Afternoon, the next day.*

SETTING: *The garden of the Manor House, Woolton, Hertfordshire.*

AT RISE: CECILY CARDEW, *a sweet girl of eighteen, is discovered writing in her diary. After a pause,* MISS PRISM'S *voice is heard.*

MISS PRISM (*Off-stage*): Cecily! Cecily! Where are you? (CECILY *continues writing, unperturbed.* MISS PRISM, *a prim, elderly maiden lady, dressed plainly, enters.*) Ah, so you're here in the garden. Put away that diary and come to your German lesson. You know your Uncle Jack put particular stress on your German lesson before he left for town yesterday. I really don't see why you waste time on your diary, when you could be spending it on your German lesson.

CECILY: I keep a diary, Miss Prism, in order to enter the wonderful secrets of my life.

MISS PRISM: But memory is the diary we all carry about with us.

CECILY: I believe it is memory that is responsible for those horrible three-volume novels everyone reads nowadays.

MISS PRISM (*Loftily*): Please do not speak slightingly of the three-volume novel. I wrote one myself in earlier days. Alas, I lost the manuscript and so I was never able to finish it. (DR. CHASUBLE, *the portly, elderly rector, enters at the back of the garden.*)

CECILY: That is a shame, Miss Prism. But look, here is dear Dr. Chasuble coming up through the garden.

MISS PRISM (*As he approaches*): Ah, Dr. Chasuble. This is indeed a pleasure.

CHASUBLE: Has Mr. Worthing returned from town yet, Miss Prism?

MISS PRISM: No, we don't expect him until Monday.

CHASUBLE: Well, then, I'll be on my way. Would you care to walk a way with me, Miss Prism?

MISS PRISM (*Simpering*): Gladly. Now study your German, Cecily. (*With a beatific smile, she takes* DR. CHASUBLE'S *arm, and they stroll out.*)

CECILY (*Pushing a book off the table*): Oh, horrid, horrid German! (MERRIMAN, *the butler, enters, followed immediately by a jovial* ALGERNON. MERRIMAN *stands stiffly.*)

MERRIMAN: Excuse me, Miss Cardew. Mr. Ernest Worthing is calling. (ALGERNON *advances, his hand outstretched, as* MERRIMAN *leaves.*)

ALGERNON: You must be my little cousin Cecily, I'm sure.

CECILY (*Shaking his hand*): And you are Uncle Jack's brother, my cousin Ernest, my wicked cousin Ernest. I don't understand how you happen to be here. Uncle Jack won't be back until Monday afternoon.

ALGERNON: What a shame that I must leave, then, on Monday morning.

CECILY: It would be better if you could wait for him, I think. He is anxious to talk to you about emigrating. He said he's sending you to Australia. I shouldn't wonder that he does—you do look awfully pale.

ALGERNON: I expect it's because I'm so awfully hungry.

CECILY: How thoughtless of me. Won't you come in to tea? (*She rises and moves toward the house.*)

ALGERNON: Thank you. You know, cousin Cecily, you're the prettiest girl I ever saw.

CECILY: Miss Prism says that all good looks are a snare.

ALGERNON: They *are* a snare—one every sensible man wants to be caught in.

CECILY: Oh, I don't think I would care to catch a sensible man. I shouldn't know what to talk to him about. (*She leads* ALGERNON *off left. Immediately,* JACK *enters from right, followed by* MISS PRISM *and* DR. CHASUBLE. JACK *is in full mourning, and his manner is almost sepulchral.*)

MISS PRISM: But we didn't expect you back until Monday, Mr. Worthing. But—but what is this? You are in mourning?

JACK (*Sighing heavily*): My poor brother Ernest.

CHASUBLE (*Commiseratingly*): Still leading his shameful, wicked life?

JACK (*Mournfully*): Alas, he is leading no life at all. He's dead—of a chill, in Paris.

CHASUBLE: My sympathies, sir. I shall mention this in Sunday's sermon.

JACK: Ah, that reminds me. I should like to be christened, Dr. Chasuble. This afternoon, if convenient.

CHASUBLE: But have you never been christened before?

JACK: I don't know. At any rate, I should like to be christened this afternoon. Will half-past five do? (CECILY *enters in the highest spirits.*)

CECILY (*Excitedly*): Uncle Jack! How nice to see you back! Who do you think is in the dining room? Your brother Ernest. He arrived just a few minutes ago, and what do you think? He has already proposed marriage to me. Of course I have accepted him. And he's promised to be wicked no more.

MISS PRISM (*In horror*): But Mr. Worthing's brother Ernest is dead, Cecily. (ALGERNON, *enjoying himself hugely, enters, eating a sandwich.*)

ALGERNON: I am no such thing, madam. (*Extending his arms cordially to* JACK) Dear brother Jack!

JACK (*Astonished*): Algernon! (*Catching himself*) I mean Ernest!

CHASUBLE: I think it is so touching to see this family reunion. Come, Cecily, Miss Prism; we shall leave them alone.

CECILY (*Going to* JACK): You *will* forgive cousin Ernest, won't you, Uncle Jack? You must, for my sake. I must confess, ever since I heard you had a brother named Ernest I was determined to love him and be his salvation. There is something in the name Ernest that inspires a woman so.

ALGERNON (*Sputtering*): Do you—do you mean, Cecily, that you couldn't love me if my name were not Ernest?

CECILY (*Sweetly*): But your name *is* Ernest. So what is the matter?

CHASUBLE: Come along, Cecily. We must leave these brothers to their joyous reunion. (CECILY, *smiling sweetly over her shoulder at* ALGERNON, *follows* DR. CHASUBLE *and* MISS PRISM *out of the garden.*)

JACK (*Exploding as soon as they are out of sight*): Algy, you young scoundrel. You must leave at once.

ALGERNON: Don't be silly, Jack. I'm engaged to Cecily and I'm staying.

JACK (*Calling toward the house*): Merriman! (JACK *glowers at* ALGERNON, *who is smiling sweetly.* MERRIMAN *appears.*)

MERRIMAN: Yes, sir?

JACK: Merriman, send for the dogcart. Mr. Ernest is leaving.

ALGERNON (*Airily*): Never mind, Merriman. He's decided to stay after all.

JACK: Oh, no, he hasn't!

ALGERNON: Oh, yes, he has!

JACK (*After a moment, with disgust*): Oh, what's the use? (JACK *throws himself into a seat, disgruntled.* ALGERNON *smiles triumphantly.* MERRIMAN *looks from one to the other in amazement as the curtain falls.*)

*   *   *

SCENE 3

TIME: *Later, the same day.*

SETTING: *The garden.*

AT RISE: CECILY *is writing feverishly in her diary. After a moment,* MERRIMAN *enters, followed by* GWENDOLEN.

MERRIMAN: Miss Gwendolen Fairfax. (*He withdraws.*)

CECILY (*Rising*): Pray let me introduce myself. I am Cecily Cardew.

GWENDOLEN: How do you do, Miss Cardew? I am Gwendolen Fairfax.

CECILY: How do you do?

GWENDOLEN: Are you on a visit here at Mr. Worthing's country home?

CECILY: Why, no. I am Mr. Worthing's ward.

GWENDOLEN (*Taken aback*): His ward! He never told me that he had a ward. Though I must say, I'm not jealous. Ernest is so dependable.

CECILY: Oh, it is not Mr. Ernest Worthing who is my guardian. It is his elder brother, Jack. Oh no, Mr. Ernest is not my guardian—indeed, soon I shall be his. You see, Mr. Ernest and I are engaged.

GWENDOLEN (*Icily*): My darling Cecily, I think there must

be some error. Mr. Ernest Worthing is engaged to me.

CECILY (*Icily*): My dearest Gwendolen, it is you who are mistaken. Ernest proposed to me just an hour ago.

GWENDOLEN: It is certainly quite curious; he asked me to be his wife yesterday afternoon at 5:30. Therefore, I have the prior claim.

CECILY: I should say it was quite clear that he has since changed his mind.

GWENDOLEN: But here he comes now. I'll ask him myself. (JACK *enters. He is delighted to see* GWENDOLEN.) Ernest, dear.

JACK: Gwendolen, darling, this is a surprise.

CECILY: I knew there must be some mistake, Miss Fairfax. The gentleman whom you are now embracing is my dear guardian, Uncle Jack.

GWENDOLEN (*Drawing back in horror*): Jack!

CECILY: Here comes *Ernest* now. (ALGERNON *enters, munching a sandwich.*)

ALGERNON: You know, Cecily, I have never eaten such delicious cucumber sandwiches.

CECILY: May I ask, Ernest, if you are engaged to this young lady?

ALGERNON: To what young lady? (*Seeing her for the first time*) Good heavens, Gwendolen!

CECILY: Yes, to good heavens, Gwendolen. I mean, to Gwendolen.

GWENDOLEN: I knew there was an error, Miss Cardew. The gentleman about whose waist you now have your arm is my cousin, Mr. Algernon Moncrieff.

CECILY (*Horrified*): Algernon!

GWENDOLEN: Well, then, if *you* are not Ernest, and if *you* are not Ernest, who on earth *is* Ernest?

JACK (*Slowly, hesitatingly*): Gwendolen—Cecily—it is very painful for me to say this, but I'm afraid the truth is—

there is no Ernest. (GWENDOLEN *and* CECILY, *both crushed, rush into each other's arms.*)

GWENDOLEN: Poor Cecily!

CECILY: Poor Gwendolen! (MERRIMAN *appears, followed by* LADY BRACKNELL.)

MERRIMAN: Lady Bracknell. (*He withdraws.*)

ALGERNON: Good lord, it's Aunt Augusta.

GWENDOLEN: Heavens, it's Mamma!

LADY BRACKNELL (*Her glance sweeping across the others imperiously*): Mr. Worthing! Why have you spirited off my daughter?

GWENDOLEN: He didn't spirit me off, Mamma. I came of my own free will. Mr. Worthing and I are engaged.

LADY BRACKNELL: You are no such thing. (*Turning to* ALGERNON) Algernon, who is the girl around whose waist your left arm is twined?

JACK: Allow me to present my ward. Lady Bracknell, Miss Cecily Cardew. (CECILY *curtsies.* LADY BRACKNELL *is unmoved.*)

ALGERNON: Cecily and I are engaged.

LADY BRACKNELL: You are no such thing. There must be something invigorating in the air, hereabouts. There seem to be a peculiar number of engagements. (DR. CHASUBLE *enters, followed by* MISS PRISM, *who timidly hides behind him.*)

CHASUBLE: Gentlemen, about the christenings . . .

GWENDOLEN, CECILY *and* LADY BRACKNELL (*In unison*): Christenings?

CHASUBLE: Yes. Mr. Jack Worthing is to be christened Ernest at 5:30. Mr. Ernest Worthing is to be christened —er, I don't know what—at 6:00.

GWENDOLEN (*Radiantly*): You were prepared to make this sacrifice for us?

CECILY (*Delighted*): Darlings!

CHASUBLE: Well, about the christenings. Might they be postponed?

JACK: Whatever for?

CHASUBLE: Well, sir, the fact is—Miss Prism here and I have just become engaged.

LADY BRACKNELL (*Hopelessly confused*): May I have the honor of knowing what is going on here? (*Suddenly sees* MISS PRISM *and explodes*) Miss Prism!

MISS PRISM (*Horrified*): Lady Bracknell!

LADY BRACKNELL (*Slowly, emphatically and menacingly*): Miss Prism, where is that baby? (*The others gasp in amazement.*) Twenty-eight years ago, Miss Prism, you left Lord Bracknell's house in charge of a perambulator containing a baby of the male sex. You never returned. A few weeks later, the police discovered the perambulator standing by itself in a remote corner of Bayswater. It was empty, except for the unfinished manuscript of a dreadful three-volume novel. Miss Prism! Where is that baby?

MISS PRISM (*Humiliated*): I don't know, I admit it. I only wish I did. The plain facts are these. By mistake, I put the manuscript for a book I was writing into the perambulator, and I put the baby into a large, black handbag that I had intended for the manuscript.

JACK (*Urgently*): Where did you deposit the handbag?

MISS PRISM: I left it in the cloakroom of one of the larger railway stations in London.

JACK: What railway station?

MISS PRISM (*Crushed*): Victoria. The Brighton Line.

JACK (*Excitedly*): Excuse me for one moment. (*He dashes wildly off toward the house.*)

LADY BRACKNELL (*Sternly*): I need not tell you, Miss Prism, I suppose, of the weeks—nay, years of anguish your error has caused?

MISS PRISM (*The picture of abject repentance*): I can imagine!

LADY BRACKNELL: Can you indeed? (JACK *enters with a large handbag.*)

JACK: Miss Prism. Is this the handbag? Examine it carefully before you speak. Is this the handbag?

MISS PRISM (*Looking it over carefully*): It seems to be mine. Yes, here are my initials on the clasp. Thank you so much for restoring it to me.

JACK: Miss Prism, more has been restored to you than that handbag. I am the baby you placed in it.

LADY BRACKNELL: Mr. Worthing! Then you are the son of my dear dead sister, and therefore Algernon's elder brother.

JACK: Algy's elder brother! Then I have a brother after all. I always said I had a brother. Miss Prism, Dr. Chasuble, meet my unfortunate younger brother.

GWENDOLEN (*Throwing her arms about* JACK): My own! (*Puzzled*) But what own are you? What *is* your Christian name, now that you have become someone else?

JACK: Good heavens, I almost forgot. Can you not love me but under that one name?

GWENDOLEN: Alas, no. Cecily and I have both resolved to marry men by the name of Ernest.

LADY BRACKNELL: That's it! You were named after your father, Mr. Worthing. His name was General Ernest John Moncrieff.

JACK (*Calmly*): I always told you my name was Ernest, didn't I, Gwendolen?

GWENDOLEN: Ernest, my own. I felt from the first you could have no other name. I forgive you now for all that has gone before.

ALGERNON: Cecily, do you forgive me?

CECILY: Yes, Algernon, I do—if you promise to be rechristened.

ALGERNON: I do, my love, I do. And now—may I kiss you?

CECILY: But of course! (*She stretches out her hand. He bows low and kisses it.* LADY BRACKNELL *is scandalized.*)

LADY BRACKNELL: My dear nephew, you seem to be displaying a dreadful amount of triviality.

ALGERNON: On the contrary, Aunt Augusta, I've only just realized for the first time in my life, the vital importance of being earnest! (*He kisses* CECILY's *hand.* JACK *kisses* GWENDOLEN's *hand.* DR. CHASUBLE *kisses* MISS PRISM's *hand.* LADY BRACKNELL, *horrified, looks at this shocking display with dismay as the curtain falls.*)

THE END

Production Notes

THE IMPORTANCE OF BEING EARNEST

Characters: 5 male; 4 female.

Playing Time: 30 minutes.

Costumes: Late nineteenth century dress.

Properties: Tea set, tea cups and saucers, two platters of tea sandwiches, small bell, silver cigarette case, pencil, diary, pen, books, large black handbag, and small leather case containing calling card.

Setting: Scene 1 is an elegant nineteenth century drawing room with sofa, tea table, chairs, desk, etc. Doors at right and left lead outside and to the music room. Scenes 2 and 3 take place in a corner of a garden. There are pots of flowers, an iron settee, two iron chairs, and a table covered with books. An entrance at right leads to the house, and a gate at left leads to the street.

Lighting: No special effects.

The Transferred Ghost

by Frank R. Stockton

Characters

GHOST OF JOHN HINCKMAN
MRS. GUDGEON, *the housekeeper*
FRANK LETTERMAN, *a bachelor*
MADELINE HINCKMAN, *a lovely lady*
CECIL VILARS, *a crashing bore*

TIME: *A spring afternoon, at the end of the 19th century.*
SETTING: *The drawing room of John Hinckman's country
home. An easy chair, with a folding screen behind it,
is at center.*
AT RISE: *For a moment there is silence. Then the* GHOST
OF JOHN HINCKMAN *peers around the screen. When he
sees that the room is empty, he comes out of hiding,
yawns, stretches broadly, and sinks comfortably into the
easy chair. There is a blissful expression on his face.
Suddenly from offstage comes a woman's voice.*

MRS. GUDGEON (*Off-stage*): I'll set the tea things right
away, sir. (*The* GHOST *is startled, jumps up angrily,
shakes his fist in the direction of the voice, and then
darts behind the screen as* MRS. GUDGEON, *the house-*

keeper, and FRANK LETTERMAN, *a young man of about twenty-five, enter.*) Shall I serve tea here in the drawing room, sir, or will you take it in the garden?

FRANK: I hardly know what to tell you, Mrs. Gudgeon. I'm so used to having Mr. Hinckman give such orders. Now that he's gone away, I'm quite at a loss.

MRS. GUDGEON: He'll only be gone for a day or two, sir, so you needn't feel the burden of responsibility lies too heavy on you. And besides, I don't think any great judgment is required in deciding whether you will take the tea inside or out.

FRANK: It might not seem like a great decision to you, Mrs. Gudgeon, but these last few months I haven't been able to make up my mind about anything.

MRS. GUDGEON (*Smiling wisely*): Love will do that to a man, sir.

FRANK: I beg your pardon?

MRS. GUDGEON: I didn't mean any offense, sir, but it certainly seems obvious that you are in love with Miss Madeline. Tell the truth, now, sir.

FRANK (*Smiling*): As a matter of fact I *am* in love with Miss Madeline, but I don't know how you can say it's obvious! *She* certainly doesn't seem to notice it.

MRS. GUDGEON: Doesn't she indeed, sir?

FRANK: Of course she doesn't. Did you see the way she was fussing over that namby-pamby Cecil Vilars all through luncheon? (*Mimicking her*) "*Dear* Mr. Vilars, have some more butter," and "*Kind* Mr. Vilars, do you take milk or lemon?" (*In his own voice*) And such batting of her eyelashes at him that one would think she were trying to stir up a breeze in the dining room. And yet when *I* asked her to pass the salt, she gave me such a look of coldness that I felt as though I had asked her to perform all twelve labors of Hercules.

MRS. GUDGEON: Pshaw, sir, have you never heard the saying, "Strange are the ways of a woman in love"?

FRANK: Well, Miss Madeline's ways are certainly strange, but if she's in love, I would say it is with Cecil Vilars and *not* with me.

MRS. GUDGEON (*Loftily, about to leave the room*): I suppose you are entitled to your own opinion, sir. I'll fetch the tea now.

FRANK (*Hastily*): No, wait, Mrs. Gudgeon. Come and sit down.

MRS. GUDGEON (*Taken aback*): I—a servant—sit down, sir?

FRANK: Oh, never mind about that. Mr. Hinckman has gone to Bristol, and the way Mr. Vilars was quoting poetry to Madeline out in the garden, it will be hours before they come back to the house. So there's no one to see you but me, and I certainly would *like* to see you sit down.

MRS. GUDGEON (*Sitting*): Very well, sir, if you insist. I must say it does my old bones a bit of good to get a rest, sir.

FRANK: Now tell me, Mrs. Gudgeon—honestly and as a friend—what you were hinting to me just now about Miss Madeline.

MRS. GUDGEON: I wasn't hinting anything, sir. I only said that *my* opinions on whom Miss Madeline might be in love with were different from yours.

FRANK: That is to say—you think she might be in love with *me*?

MRS. GUDGEON: Quite frankly, sir, I think it more than likely.

FRANK: Then why on earth has she never said anything about it?

MRS. GUDGEON: Why on earth, indeed! Why on earth have

you never given her the opportunity to say something about it?

FRANK: You mean—you mean tell her how *I* feel about *her*? Oh, but I couldn't. I'm so quiet, you know, and so shy. Why, I hardly know what to say to her across a luncheon table—let alone talk love to her. And then there's her uncle—

MRS. GUDGEON: What do you mean by that, sir? What does her uncle have to do with it?

FRANK: Well, Mr. Hinckman is such a *stern* old man. I've lived as a guest in his house for many months now, and to this day I'm afraid to death of him. One never knows when and where he's going to pop up next. Every time I try to get up the courage to speak to Madeline about my adoration of her, I always think: "What if Mr. Hinckman should see us together?" And then my courage and my determination crumble like lumps of sugar in a cup of tea.

MRS. GUDGEON: Then today should be a perfect opportunity for you, sir, with Mr. Hinckman gone to Bristol overnight. Now you need have no fear of his popping into the room at some inopportune moment.

FRANK: That's all well and good. But instead of Mr. Hinckman's presence, today I am cursed with Cecil Vilars. If it isn't one thing it's another.

MRS. GUDGEON (*Rising*): I must say, sir, that in my time I've known many *men* who were in love. But never until now have I ever known a *rabbit* who was in love. Mr. Letterman, you're afraid of your own shadow!

FRANK (*Unhappily*): I know. And it's a dreadful trial to me, I can tell you. (MADELINE HINCKMAN *and* CECIL VILARS *enter.* MADELINE *is a sweet young thing of nineteen, an audacious flirt. He is a priggish bore of twenty-three.*)

MADELINE: Ah, here you are, Mr. Letterman!

FRANK (*Instantly a mass of confusion*): Yes, Miss Madeline, I'm—well, I'm—yes, here I am!

MADELINE: I could understand why Mrs. Gudgeon should come back to the house directly my uncle's coach pulled out of the yard, but what was the need of your dashing away so suddenly?

FRANK: I—I—that is, I thought I might be in the way.

CECIL: In the way? On the contrary, dear sir, it would have been a delight if you had stayed. I was reading some of my poetry to Miss Hinckman, and I am always appreciative of a large audience.

MADELINE (*Teasingly*): You missed a real treat, Mr. Letterman. Mr. Vilar's poetry was quite entrancing.

CECIL (*Eagerly*): Did you really think so, Miss Hinckman?

MADELINE: Oh, I did indeed! I especially liked the sonnet about agriculture in the Middle Ages. So refined! Such feeling!

CECIL (*Greatly pleased*): Really? Yes, that is a good one, I must admit. But I'm rather partial to my "Elegy on Galileo's Telescope." Would you like to hear it, Mr. Letterman? (*Beginning to declaim*) "O noble instrument of Italian science . . ."

FRANK (*Hastily*): Perhaps some other time, Mr. Vilars. I—I must be going to my room.

MADELINE: But will you not have tea with us, Mr. Letterman? Bring in the tea things, please, Mrs. Gudgeon. We shall have it here in the drawing room.

MRS. GUDGEON (*Going out*): Yes, Miss Madeline.

MADELINE: Now won't you gentlemen be seated? (*She sits on the settee. Both men dash for the seat next to her. CECIL reaches it first and sits. FRANK fumes and throws himself into chair. She speaks teasingly.*) Why, what a scowl you are wearing, Mr. Letterman. Has something upset you?

FRANK (*Glumly*): Nothing.

CECIL: You certainly are not cheerful, sir. My motto is "Always smile as though a beautiful woman were in love with you."

MADELINE (*Archly*): But perhaps a beautiful woman *is* in love with you, Mr. Vilars. And perhaps Mr. Letterman knows that none loves him. Is not that reason enough to be glum?

CECIL: Do you really think a beautiful woman might be in love with me, Miss Hinckman?

MADELINE: Does it not seem likely? Think, sir! Perhaps you know of one—quite near you—who holds you in the highest esteem.

CECIL (*Suddenly getting her meaning*): Miss Hinckman! By Jove! You mean—you mean—

FRANK (*Jumping up*): This is preposterous! I cannot stay and watch this nonsense a moment longer. You will excuse me?

CECIL (*Rising indignantly*): Nonsense, sir? Do you call Miss Hinckman's declaration of love "nonsense"?

FRANK (*Exploding*): I do indeed! And if you would take one look in the mirror, Mr. Vilars, and listen to your own idle chatter for five consecutive minutes, *you* would see that it is nonsense as well.

CECIL (*Huffily*): Well! I have never been so insulted in my life! Good afternoon, Miss Hinckman. Good afternoon, Mr. Letterman. I see that the soul of an artist is not appreciated here.

MADELINE (*Placatingly*): But Mr. Vilars—

CECIL (*Icily*): Good afternoon. (*He goes out stiffly.* MADELINE *glares at* FRANK, *who becomes intensely uncomfortable under her stare.*)

MADELINE: Mr. Letterman! Whatever moved you to such rudeness to Mr. Vilars?

FRANK: I—I beg your pardon, Miss Madeline, but I could not bear to watch you flirt with that—that fool!

MADELINE: A pretty mess you have made of things, I must say. Now I must run after him and apologize. (*She goes to the door and turns.*) From this day forward, Mr. Letterman, I shall thank you to allow me to flirt with whomever I see fit.

FRANK (*Unhappily*): May I go to my room?

MADELINE: You may go wherever you please. It is *you* who are the fool! (*She goes out haughtily, slamming the door.*)

FRANK (*Wretchedly*): Oh, Madeline, why can't I tell you I love you? Why must I make such a botch of things? (*Miserably he goes up the stairs. Immediately, the* GHOST *peeks around the screen, sees that the room is empty, and comes out.*)

GHOST (*Muttering*): I thought they'd *never* leave! Human beings! Bah! (*He stretches himself, and then sinks comfortably into the armchair, shutting his eyes. A blissful expression spreads over his face. The* GHOST *looks like a real human being—in fact, he looks just like the absent Mr. Hinckman. After a moment,* MRS. GUDGEON *enters, carrying the tea things on a tray. She sees the* GHOST *and is startled.*)

MRS. GUDGEON: Why, Mr. Hinckman! What are you doing here? (*The* GHOST *jumps up and begins shushing her.*)

GHOST: Sh-h-h! Sh-h-h! Please!

MRS. GUDGEON (*Confused*): What is it, Mr. Hinckman?

GHOST (*Furtively looking around, in an agony of embarrassment*): I'm *not* Mr. Hinckman!

MRS. GUDGEON (*Going to tea table and setting to work*): What nonsense! Of *course* you're Mr. Hinckman! Though how you happen to be sitting here in the parlor, when only half an hour ago you left on a journey to Bristol, is more than I can make out.

GHOST (*Trying to interrupt*): Madame—

MRS. GUDGEON (*Continuing to set the tea things*): Imagine, thinking I wouldn't recognize you, after being your housekeeper these past twenty years!

GHOST: Madame—

MRS. GUDGEON: How surprised the others will be when they discover that you've returned so suddenly! I daresay none of them is expecting you, sir.

GHOST (*Explosively*): Madame! Once and for all, let me assure you that I am *not* Mr. Hinckman!

MRS. GUDGEON (*Nonplussed*): Not Mr. Hinckman? Then who are you, sir?

GHOST: Will you promise not to scream when I tell you? I can't *stand* people who scream.

MRS. GUDGEON (*Sensibly*): Of course I shan't scream! (*Still humoring him*) But I insist, sir, on knowing who you are.

GHOST: Well—I'm—that is to say—madame, I am Mr. Hinckman's ghost.

MRS. GUDGEON (*Turning away and picking up almost empty tray*): Oh, well, if that's the case—(*She does a double take, drops the tea tray, which clatters to the floor. She screams. At this, the* GHOST *jumps up and darts behind the screen.*) Help! Help! Somebody! Anybody! Mr. Letterman! Help! (*FRANK comes tearing down the stairs.*)

FRANK: Why, Mrs. Gudgeon! What is it? You look as if you'd seen a ghost!

MRS. GUDGEON: I have, sir, I have!

FRANK: Calm yourself, Mrs. Gudgeon, please. You're shaking like a leaf. Here, sit down in the easy chair.

MRS. GUDGEON (*Becoming hysterical again*): No, no, not the easy chair! That's *his* chair!

FRANK: Please, Mrs. Gudgeon, try to get hold of yourself. What is it?

MRS. GUDGEON: Oh, sir, I hardly know what to say.

FRANK (*Impatiently*): Well, say *something*—anything!

MRS. GUDGEON: Well, sir, I was bringing in the tea things and all—you know, the tray, the teapot, the cups, the saucers, the jam, the—

FRANK: Never mind what you were bringing in, Mrs. Gudgeon. Get to the point!

MRS. GUDGEON: Well, sir, I—I turned around, and *he* was sitting there!

FRANK: He? *Who?*

MRS. GUDGEON: Mr. Hinckman!

FRANK: It couldn't have been.

MRS. GUDGEON: It wasn't! That is, he *looked* like Mr. Hinckman—large as life, sitting in that chair.

FRANK: But Mr. Hinckman left for Bristol half an hour ago. How could he have been sitting there?

MRS. GUDGEON: I don't know, sir. But you yourself said that he has a way of popping up when you least expect him.

FRANK: That's true. But if it *was* Mr. Hinckman, where did he go?

MRS. GUDGEON: I don't know, sir, I'm sure. He just vanished into the thin air. And the worst part of it is, he said he *wasn't* Mr. Hinckman. He said he was Mr. Hinckman's—Mr. Hinckman's *ghost!*

FRANK: Don't be absurd, Mrs. Gudgeon. Mr. Hinckman is alive—and live people don't have ghosts. Besides, I don't smell any sulphur. They say you can always tell when a ghost has been around by the smell of sulphur. I think you've been working too hard, Mrs. Gudgeon. Your imagination is playing tricks on you.

MRS. GUDGEON: But I *saw* him!

FRANK (*Calmly*): You *think* you saw him, Mrs. Gudgeon, and that's quite a different thing. Now you just go to your room and lie down for the rest of the afternoon. Never mind those things. (*Indicates the tea tray on the floor*) I'll take care of this for you.

MRS. GUDGEON (*Going to the stairs*): Frightened me out of ten years' growth, it did, sir! I've never been so upset before in my life!

FRANK: You just take a nap, Mrs. Gudgeon, and when you awaken, you'll have forgotten all about it.

MRS. GUDGEON: I hope you're right, sir. And please, Mr. Letterman—don't say anything about this to Miss Madeline.

FRANK: Mrs. Gudgeon, you know me well enough to know that I can't say *anything* to Miss Madeline.

MRS. GUDGEON: And more's the pity, say I. (*She goes out.*)

FRANK (*Angrily, to himself*): What a dreadful afternoon this is turning out to be! Here I thought that Mr. Hinckman's departure would bring nothing but pleasantness to all. Instead, Madeline is angry with me, the tea things are smashed, Mrs. Gudgeon is seeing ghosts— (*He is down on his hands and knees, picking up the tea things. The* GHOST *comes out from behind the screen and timidly taps him on the shoulder.*)

GHOST: I beg your pardon, Mr. Letterman.

FRANK (*Looks up at him and screams*): Good Heavens!

GHOST (*Cringing*): Oh, *please* don't do that. You have no idea how I hate to hear people scream. It jangles my nerves—and turns my ice water to blood.

FRANK: I—I beg your pardon. I didn't mean to upset you. Would you mind telling me who you are and what you want here? You're causing no end of trouble.

GHOST: Do you know if Mr. Hinckman will return tonight?

FRANK: No, we do not expect him until tomorrow.

GHOST (*Sinking into the easy chair*): You can't begin to know how relieved I am to hear it. After living in this house for two and a half years, I was beginning to think that man might *never* go away.

FRANK: Are you—are you his twin brother?

GHOST: No, I'm not. I'm his—I hope this doesn't alarm you—I'm his ghost.

FRANK (*Taken aback*): His what?

GHOST: His ghost. G-H-O—

FRANK: Yes, yes, I know how to spell it. But it's impossible! I told Mrs. Gudgeon it was impossible. People who are still alive don't *have* ghosts!

GHOST: You're quite right, sir. Ordinarily they don't. And that's the trouble. I was assigned to Mr. Hinckman by mistake. You see, ghost positions are very difficult to get, and when he was taken ill two years ago, it seemed pretty certain that he would not recover. I was young and eager, and so I put in my application to be the ghost of John Hinckman. And I got the job—then, unfortunately, he decided to live after all.

FRANK: What do you mean—"unfortunately"? That's not a very polite thing to say.

GHOST: It's unfortunate for me, of course. How do you suppose you would feel if *you* were the ghost of someone who was still alive? I'm so dreadfully afraid that I might meet him face to face someday, and wouldn't *that* be an embarrassing situation?

FRANK: Yes, I suppose it would. But why on earth are you telling all this to me?

GHOST: For one thing, I'm tired of having nobody to talk to. And for another, I've been watching you for quite a long time, and I think you might be able to do me a favor. There is every reason to believe that Mr. Hinckman intends to live many years more, and my situation is becoming intolerable. My great object at the moment is to get myself transferred.

FRANK: Transferred? What do you mean by that?

GHOST: What I mean is that I want to become the ghost of somebody who is already dead.

FRANK: I should think that would be easy enough. Opportunities must be occurring every day.

GHOST: Not at all. You've no idea what a rush there is for the few good jobs that come along. And of course, most of the jobs are the kind that nobody would care for at all.

FRANK: But how could I help you?

GHOST: Well, you might know of a case where an opportunity for a ghost-ship is not generally suspected, but which might present itself at any moment. If you would give me short notice of it, I'm sure I could arrange a transfer.

FRANK: Good heavens! Do you want me to commit suicide? Or to undertake murder for your benefit?

GHOST (*Shuddering*): What a dreadful idea! How cold-blooded and inhuman you are. No, my request is much more civilized. You were the only person I could speak to, and I hoped that you might have some information which might be of use to me. And, in return, I shall be very glad to help you in your love affair.

FRANK: My love affair! How do you know about that?

GHOST: Good Heavens, man, anyone who stayed in this house five minutes and saw the way you look at Miss Madeline would know at once you were miserably in love with her. I must say, though, that you need some help in managing the business. You're dreadfully incompetent.

FRANK: How well I know it!

GHOST: Shall we strike a bargain, then? If you should hear of a case where a ghost-ship might become available, promise to let me know of it at once. For my part, I shall promise to help you in every way to win the hand of Madeline. Is it agreed?

FRANK: Very well, it is agreed. But quite honestly, I don't see how you can fulfill your part of the bargain. If Miss Madeline should see you, or hear of you—if she should have any idea at all that I am having dealings with a ghost—won't she become more distant and cold than ever?

GHOST: I shall take great care to stand behind her at all times, so that she will not see me. And as for hearing me—there is no danger of that. No one hears me except the person to whom I address myself.

FRANK: If anyone had ever told me that I would require the services of a ghost in proposing, I should have told him that he were mad. And yet, here I am, doing that very thing. I am indeed a desperate man!

GHOST: You needn't speak about it as though it were distasteful. We ghosts are a very civilized group—though, perhaps, a bit high-spirited.

FRANK: One question more. Are you a ghost that comes from . . . (*He points upward and raises his eyes*) . . . or from . . . ? (*He points downward and lowers his eyes.*)

GHOST (*Blandly*): Being a relative newcomer to these parts, I'm afraid I have quite lost my sense of direction. Let us say simply that I come from—elsewhere. But enough of these questions. Madeline is coming.

FRANK (*Instantly nervous*): Oh dear, oh dear! I shall never be able to go through with it, I know it.

GHOST: Don't be silly, old boy. Of course you can do it.

I'll just meander around in the background—and if you seem to need help, I'll do what I can for you.

FRANK (*Clasping his hands before him, fervently*): Heaven give me strength!

GHOST: Strength you shall have, but never mind where it comes from. (MADELINE *enters, sees* FRANK, *and glares at him coldly.*)

FRANK (*Timidly*): A—a good afternoon, Miss Madeline.

MADELINE (*Snapping at him, sitting down and facing dead front*): Is it? I had not noticed the fact.

FRANK (*Taking his courage in his teeth*): It is always a good afternoon when you are here, Madeline. (*He looks to the* GHOST *for encouragement; the* GHOST *nods his silent approval.*)

MADELINE: Thank you, Mr. Letterman. (*There is a long pause.*)

GHOST (*Impatiently*): Good heavens, man, get on with it. Never mind the coldness of the lady. It is all make-believe, I assure you. She dotes on you. Now is the time. You are not likely to be interrupted, so make your proposal. Tomorrow Mr. Hinckman will return—and you wouldn't want Mr. Hinckman around when you were proposing to his niece. You are not overfond of Mr. Hinckman, are you?

FRANK (*Angrily, to the* GHOST): I cannot bear to think of him.

MADELINE (*Turning to* FRANK): Think of whom?

FRANK (*Recovering his wits quickly*): Mr. Vilars! I cannot bear to think of Mr. Vilars!

MADELINE: It is wrong of you to speak of him in that way. He is a remarkably well-educated and sensible young man, and he has very pleasant manners—which is more than I can say for *some* young men of my acquaintance. What I especially admire about Mr. Vilars is that when he has anything to say, he knows just how and when to say it.

GHOST: By Jove, *there's* a hint to you.

FRANK (*Angrily, to* MADELINE): And what has he said?

MADELINE (*Coolly*): He has proposed marriage to me.

FRANK (*Miserably*): No!

MADELINE: Yes! And when I refused him—which of course I did—he told me he was going to kill himself out of anguish.

FRANK (*Excitedly*): Did he really say he would kill himself?

MADELINE: Do you think I am making it up, Mr. Letterman?

FRANK (*Joyfully, to the* GHOST): My friend, put in your transfer.

MADELINE (*Puzzled*): I beg your pardon?

FRANK (*Recovering*): I—I said, "That was a wise answer." To tell him no, I mean.

MADELINE (*Coyly*): I could not very well tell him yes when I am in love with someone else, could I?

GHOST: Now's your chance, man, now's your chance! You've fulfilled your part of the bargain—though I don't suppose I'll have any better luck with that Mr. Vilars than I've had waiting around all this time for Mr. Hinckman. Now listen to me. Propose to her, propose to her! She's waiting for you to do it—longing for you to do it! If you get stuck, I'll help you over the tricky parts!

FRANK (*Uncomfortably*): Madeline, I wish to ask you . . . that is, I . . .

MADELINE (*Gazing at him rapturously*): Yes, Mr. Letterman?

FRANK: Oh, call me Frank, please!

MADELINE (*Lovingly*): Yes, Frank? You wished to say?

(*The* GHOST *has moved in behind* MADELINE, *quite close, and is staring at* FRANK *in eager anticipation.*)

FRANK (*Crossly, to the* GHOST): Confound it, I can't say it with you staring at me like that!

MADELINE (*Prettily confused*): I—I beg your pardon! If I look away—if I cast my eyes down at the floor—does that make it easier for you to say?

FRANK (*Torn between his desire to propose to* MADELINE *and his discomfort at being watched by the* GHOST): Madeline, I—Madeline— (*To the* GHOST.) Confound it, what are you waiting for? I have nothing to say to *you!*

MADELINE (*Leaping up angrily*): What am I waiting for? What do you suppose I am waiting for, you booby? Nothing to say to me indeed! I should think so! What should you say to me?

FRANK (*Miserably*): Madeline, let me explain!

MADELINE: Explain it if you can! You are very rude to-day, sir!

FRANK: I *do* have something to say to you, Madeline, but I find it difficult to say it— (*Glowering at the* GHOST) —because of a—a certain obstacle.

MADELINE (*Coyly*): Is that obstacle in any way connected with my uncle?

FRANK: Yes, in a way it *is* connected with your uncle. Madeline, you must know that I love you—but the obstacle I am thinking of makes it very difficult to say what I have to say.

MADELINE: I have heard that at such moments men are often incomprehensible. Pray, sir, say it the best way you know how, and I shall try to comprehend.

FRANK: I—I—Madeline, I—oh, what's the use? I cannot do it!

GHOST: Once and for all, ask the young lady to marry you. Never mind if I'm standing here. I can't wait around forever, you know. I have to be on my way to put in my application for transfer, and time is running short. I have to be somebody *else's* ghost, you know!

FRANK (*Miserably, to the* GHOST): Oh, I wish to Heaven you were mine!

MADELINE (*Turning to* FRANK, *a huge smile of love on her face*): Darling! At last! I *am* yours! (*She runs to* FRANK, *who, amazed at having been tricked into a proposal, but happy nonetheless, embraces her.*)

GHOST: Well, thank heaven! I've always said that it takes some spirit to get a man to propose! (*He smiles broadly at the audience as the curtain falls.*)

THE END

Production Notes

THE TRANSFERRED GHOST

Characters: 3 male; 2 female.

Playing Time: 20 minutes.

Costumes: Victorian dress.

Properties: Tea tray with pot, sugar, cream, three cups, saucers, spoons and a white tea cloth.

Setting: The Victorian drawing room of a country house. There are three entrances: one to kitchen, one to the outside, and one, via stairs, to the rest of the house. At center is an easy chair, with a small table beside it and a folding screen behind it. Center is a small settee. Right is a small tea table with several straight chairs beside it.

Lighting: No special effects.

The Rivals

by Richard Brinsley Sheridan

Characters

FAG, *a manservant*
THOMAS, *a coachman*
LYDIA LANGUISH
LUCY, *her maid*
JULIA MELVILLE, *her cousin*
MRS. MALAPROP, *her aunt*
SIR ANTHONY ABSOLUTE
CAPTAIN JACK ABSOLUTE, *his son*

SCENE 1

TIME: *The eighteenth century. A spring morning.*
SETTING: *A street in Bath, England.*
BEFORE RISE: FAG, *a young, high-spirited manservant, enters from one side, and* THOMAS, *a coachman carrying a whip, from the other. When they see each other, they rush together and shake hands.*

FAG (*Delightedly*): What? Is it my old friend, Thomas, that I spy? Sure, 'tis he. Thomas!
THOMAS (*Happily*): Bless my soul, it's Mr. Fag, my old fellow servant.

FAG: I'm more than glad to see you, my lad. But what brings you to Bath?

THOMAS: My master—

FAG: Sir Anthony Absolute?

THOMAS: Aye, the same. He thought another fit of the gout was coming to make him a visit, so he had a mind to give it the slip. And whip! We were all off at an hour's warning, persons, parcels, bag and baggage.

FAG: Aye, aye; hasty in everything, or it would not be Sir Anthony Absolute.

THOMAS: And how is *your* master, Sir Anthony's son? How the old gentleman will stare to see his young son here.

FAG (*Casually*): I do not serve Captain Jack Absolute now.

THOMAS (*Surprised*): What's this? Not serve Captain Jack, you say?

FAG: No, no, Thomas, I am employed now by Ensign Beverly.

THOMAS (*Reproachfully*): I doubt, Mr. Fag, that you have changed for the better. There is none better than young Captain Jack.

FAG: But I have *not* changed.

THOMAS (*Confused*): Didn't you say you had left the young master?

FAG: Not really, honest Thomas, but I must puzzle you no further. Briefly, then, Captain Jack Absolute and Ensign Beverly are one and the same person.

THOMAS: The devil they are. Explain yourself, Mr. Fag.

FAG: Hark ye well, then, Thomas. It has all come about through love. My master, Captain Jack Absolute, is in love with a very strange lady. She thinks his name is Ensign Beverly.

THOMAS: But why does he call himself ensign to her, when actually he is a captain?

Fag: This lady—Lydia Languish by name—has very singular tastes, and loves him better as a half-pay ensign than if she knew he was son and heir to Sir Anthony Absolute, a baronet with three thousand a year.

Thomas: That is odd taste, indeed. But is she rich, Mr. Fag?

Fag: Zounds! Why, Thomas, she could pay the national debt as easily as I could my washerwoman. She has a lap dog that eats out of a gold dish. She feeds her parrot with small pearls, and all of her curlpapers are made of bank notes.

Thomas: And does the captain love her? Are they fond of each other?

Fag: As loving fond as two cooing pigeons. But there is an old, tough aunt in the way—one Mrs. Malaprop— though she has never seen my master, for he got acquainted with Miss Lydia while Mrs. Malaprop was on a visit to Gloucestershire. She's a strange one, that aunt, always using words she doesn't understand, saying such things as, "He can tell you all the *perpendiculars*," when of course she means, "He can tell you all the *particulars*."

Thomas: I'm sure that it would be my master's wish— Captain Jack's father, I mean—to see his son well married.

Fag: Pray you, say nothing of this to the old gentleman. Ensign Beverly's identity must be kept in strictest confidence. And now, friend Thomas, adieu. I must find my master and tell him the news of his father's arrival in Bath.

Thomas (*Shaking hands with* Fag *and laughing*): Your secret is safe with me. Farewell, Mr. Fag, farewell. (*They go off in opposite directions as the lights fade.*)

*   *   *

Scene 2

Time: *One hour later.*

Setting: Lydia's *boudoir.*

At Rise: Lydia Languish, *a beautiful young woman, is seated on a small sofa.* Lucy, *her pert and saucy maid, stands before her, holding several books.*

Lydia: And could you not get any of the books I had asked for, Lucy?

Lucy: No, indeed, Miss Lydia, ma'am. I traversed half the town in search of them. I don't believe there's a circulating library in Bath I haven't been at. But all I could get were these.

Lydia (*Sighing*): What a disappointment. I was so hoping for a romance. (*There is a knock at the door.*) Hold! Someone is coming. Quick, see who it is!

Lucy: Yes, ma'am. (*She curtsies and goes out.*)

Lydia (*Nervously running about, hiding the books under the sofa, etc.*): *Peregrine Pickle* can hide beneath the settee. *Humphrey Clinker* I shall put beneath the chair. And *The Tears of Sensibility* must lie beneath this cushion.

Lucy (*Appearing in the doorway*): It is your cousin, ma'am. Miss Melville.

Lydia: Is it possible? Show her in. (Lucy *ushers* Julia Melville *into the room, then leaves, closing the door behind her.* Julia *is slightly older than* Lydia.)

Julia (*Embracing* Lydia): My dear Lydia.

Lydia: Julia! Whatever has conjured you to Bath? Is Sir Anthony Absolute here with you?

Julia: He is. We arrived within this hour, and I suppose he will be here to visit with your aunt, Mrs. Malaprop, as soon as he can.

LYDIA: Then before we are interrupted, let me impart to you some of my distress. My aunt has discovered the entirety of my connection with my beloved Ensign Beverly. She found a note he sent to me, and has confined me ever since. And the greatest misfortune of all is that I had quarreled with him, just before Mrs. Malaprop made the discovery, and I have not seen him since to make it up.

JULIA: What was his offense, dear Lydia?

LYDIA (*In anguish*): Nothing at all. You see, we are so perfectly matched that in all of our romance we had never quarreled. You know the quotation, "The course of true love never did run smooth." Well, I thought we should have at least *one* quarrel, and I was afraid we should never have the opportunity to do so. So, I invented an opportunity. I ranted and raved, charged him with infidelity, and swore I would see him no more.

JULIA: And you let him depart so and have not seen him since?

LYDIA: It was the next day my aunt found the matter out. I intended only to tease him three days at the most, and now I have lost him forever.

JULIA: If it is true love indeed, Lydia, your Beverly will return. But consider, my cousin, he is but an ensign, and you have thirty thousand a year.

LYDIA: I lose most of my fortune if I marry without my aunt's consent before I come of age, but I have determined to marry anyway. Nor could I love the man who would wish to wait a day for the sake of my fortune. (LUCY *enters, upset.*)

LUCY (*Excitedly*): Oh, ma'am, Sir Anthony Absolute has just come home with your aunt.

LYDIA (*Calmly*): They'll not come up here, Lucy. Keep a watch.

JULIA (*Rising*): I must go, dear cousin. I'll take another opportunity to pay my respects to Mrs. Malaprop, who may detain me as long as she likes with her sentences that go on and on forever, full of big words which she doesn't understand and which she uses in the wrong places. (LUCY *opens door a crack, looks out, and closes it quickly.*)

LUCY: Oh, ma'am! They are both coming upstairs!

LYDIA: I'll not detain you, Julia. Adieu, my dear cousin. You'll find another staircase through my room.

JULIA (*Going right*): Goodbye, dear Lydia. (*Exits right.*)

LYDIA: Now, Lucy, is the room in order? (*She straightens cushions, etc.*) Go and announce them at the door, as though we didn't know they were coming up.

LUCY: Yes, ma'am. (*She goes to the door, opens it and announces.*) Mrs. Malaprop. Sir Anthony Absolute. (MRS. MALAPROP, *an over-dressed, foolish matron, and* SIR ANTHONY, *a pompous but lively middle-aged man, enter from left.* LUCY *goes out.*)

MRS. MALAPROP (*Pointing imperiously to* LYDIA *while addressing* SIR ANTHONY): There, Sir Anthony, stands the deliberate simpleton who wants to disgrace her family by marrying a fellow not worth a shilling.

LYDIA (*Protesting*): Madam, I thought you . . .

MRS. MALAPROP (*Imperiously*): You thought, miss! I don't know any business you have to think at all. Thought does not become a young woman. But the point which Sir Anthony and I wish to request of you is that you promise to forget this Beverly fellow—to *illiterate* him, I say, from your memory.

LYDIA: Madam, our memories are independent of our wills.

SIR ANTHONY: Surely the young lady does not pretend to remember what she is ordered to forget!

LYDIA: What crime, madam, have I committed to be treated thus?

MRS. MALAPROP: Now don't attempt to *extirpate* yourself from the matter; you know I have proof *controvertible* of it. But tell me: will you take a husband of Sir Anthony's choosing? Will you give up this Ensign Beverly if we give you another choice?

LYDIA: Could I belie my thoughts so far as to give that promise, my actions would certainly as far belie my words.

MRS. MALAPROP: Well, then, take yourself out of my sight. You are fit company for nothing but your own ill humors.

LYDIA (*Curtsying*): Willingly, madam. Your servant, Sir Anthony. (*Majestically she sweeps out of the room.*)

MRS. MALAPROP (*Furiously*): There's an *intricate* hussy for you!

SIR ANTHONY: That's the natural consequence of her reading. I have seen her maid coming from the circulating library. Those vile places are like an evergreen tree of diabolical knowledge.

MRS. MALAPROP: Fie, Sir Anthony. You surely speak *laconically*.

SIR ANTHONY: Why, Mrs. Malaprop, what would you have a woman know?

MRS. MALAPROP: I would by no means wish that a girl were a *progeny* of learning. I would never let her meddle with Greek or algebra, or any of your astronomical, mathematical instruments. But, Sir Anthony, I would that she have a *supercilious* knowledge in *geometry*, that she might know something of the *contagious* countries. And above all, she should be a perfect mistress of *orthodoxy*, so that she should not mispronounce and misspell words as our young ladies of today do so often. That is the sum and substance of it, and I don't think there is a *superstitious* article in it.

SIR ANTHONY: I will dispute the question no further, Mrs. Malaprop, for I must confess that you are a truly polite arguer, every third word you say being on my side of the question. But to the more important subject of debate; you say you have no objection to what I propose?

MRS. MALAPROP: None, I assure you. I am under no positive engagement to anyone for Lydia's hand. Perhaps your son, Captain Jack, will have success in winning her away from this Ensign Beverly person.

SIR ANTHONY: I will go to him at once and tell him of our plan.

MRS. MALAPROP: You know we have never seen your son, Sir Anthony. I hope there is no objection on his side.

SIR ANTHONY: Objection! Let him object if he dare! No, no, ma'am. My son, Captain Jack, knows better than to oppose me.

MRS. MALAPROP: Well, then, Sir Anthony, I shall prepare Lydia to receive your son's advances. And I hope you will represent her to the Captain as an object not altogether *illegible*.

SIR ANTHONY (*Gaily*): I will, Mrs. Malaprop. I will. (*Curtain*)

*   *   *

SCENE 3

TIME: *A few hours later.*

SETTING: *A street.*

BEFORE RISE: JACK ABSOLUTE, *a handsome young man in dress uniform, enters with* LUCY.

JACK: And did your mistress, Miss Languish, give you no message for me today, Lucy?

LUCY: None, sir. How could she? Her aunt, Mrs. Malaprop, keeps a close watch on her. Ever since the old lady discovered Miss Languish's devotion to you, she has forbidden my mistress to write a word.

JACK (*Laughing slyly*): But surely, Lucy, you have something to *tell* me from your mistress?

LUCY (*Coyly*): As for that, sir— (*She stretches out her hand*) I might be persuaded to remember a word or two.

JACK (*Putting a coin into her hand*): Out with it then!

LUCY: Miss Languish bids me tell you that she loves you dearly—and that her aunt, Mrs. Malaprop, is making her ready to marry another.

JACK: Another? It cannot be—it must not be! Tell your mistress . . . (SIR ANTHONY *enters from the opposite side.* JACK *sees him and whispers hurriedly to* LUCY.) Never mind, Lucy. I've no time for messages now. Be off with you at once!

LUCY (*Curtsying*): Very good, sir. (*She goes out.*)

JACK (*Aside, to the audience, as* SIR ANTHONY *approaches*): Now for a parental lecture. I hope he has heard nothing of what has brought me to Bath. If he finds out about my courting Miss Languish under the name of Ensign Beverly, all is done. I wish with all my soul that the gout had held him fast in Devonshire! (*Turning to* SIR ANTHONY *and smiling*) Father!

SIR ANTHONY (*Pumping* JACK'S *hand*): Ah, Jack, my boy. How good it is to see you.

JACK: I am delighted to see you, sir, and looking so well!

SIR ANTHONY: Tush, let us not dwell on my health as a topic of conversation. No, no, Jack. I have important business with you. To be brief and to the point, I know that the income of your commission, along with the allowance I have been giving you, is not sufficient for a lad of your spirit.

JACK: You are very good, sir.

SIR ANTHONY: And as it is my wish to see you make some figure in the world, I desire to fix you at once in a noble independence.

JACK (*Delightedly, aside to the audience*): He's going to settle a fortune on me, I'll warrant! (*To* SIR ANTHONY) Sir, your kindness overpowers me. Yet, you would not have me quit the army?

SIR ANTHONY (*Blithely*): Oh, that shall be as your wife chooses.

JACK (*Astounded*): My wife, sir!

SIR ANTHONY: Yes, of course, Jack. The independence I was speaking of is by marriage. The fortune is saddled with a wife.

JACK: Pray, sir, who is the lady?

SIR ANTHONY: What's that to you? Come, promise to love and to marry her directly.

JACK: Why, sir! I cannot obey you.

SIR ANTHONY (*Dumfounded*): What? Why, curse me if I ever call you Jack again!

JACK: Nay, sir, but hear me.

SIR ANTHONY: I won't hear a word. So give me your promise by a nod, Jack—I mean, you dog . . .

JACK: What? Promise to link myself with some mass of ugliness?

SIR ANTHONY (*Beside himself with rage and frustration*): Zounds, sirrah! The lady shall be as ugly as I choose. She shall have a hump on each shoulder; she shall be as crooked as the moon. Her one eye shall roll, she shall have the skin of a mummy and the beard of a goat, yet I'll make you ogle her by day and sit up all night to write sonnets on her beauty.

JACK: This is reason and moderation indeed!

SIR ANTHONY (*Flaring*): So, you will fly out! Why can't

you be cool, like me? I shall give you six hours to consider all this, and if you persist in refusing, I'll strip you of your commission. I'll disown you. And curse me if I ever call you Jack again! (*Furiously, he storms out.*)

JACK (*To the audience*): Now this is a pretty mess. If I do not marry the lady my father has chosen for me, I lose my fortune. If I do marry her, I lose my Lydia. Was ever a man as perplexed as I? (FAG *enters from left side, in a great hurry.*)

FAG: Oh, sir, sir!

JACK (*Irritably*): What is it, Fag? Must you always interrupt me when I'm thinking?

FAG: Begging your pardon, sir—but I have just had news. Your father and Mrs. Malaprop have been together, and they are planning for you to marry Miss Lydia!

JACK: What's this? What's this? My father wants to force me to marry the very girl I am plotting to elope with?

FAG: The same, sir!

JACK (*Quickly*): Zounds, sirrah! Find my father, and bring him here at once. He just went down the street—that way. Fetch him at once! At once!

FAG (*Dashing off*): Yes, sir!

JACK (*Delightedly, to the audience*): Bless me if this isn't the luckiest thing! If what my man, Fag, has told me be true, my father shall find a penitent son, waiting only to do his every bidding. Of course, he must not know that I am the same as Ensign Beverly—at least, not yet. For the moment, it will suffice for me to repent of my bad behavior and willful stubbornness. So, so—here he comes. (SIR ANTHONY *enters, pretending not to see* JACK. JACK *goes to him and blocks his way.*)

JACK (*With exaggerated humility*): Oh, sir, sir.

SIR ANTHONY: Fellow, get out of my way.

JACK: Oh sir, you see a penitent before you.

SIR ANTHONY: I see an impudent scoundrel before me.

JACK: Sir, I have been reflecting and considering on your past goodness and kindness and condescension to me. I have likewise been thinking upon duty and obedience, sir, and so I am ready to acknowledge my error, submit to your will, and marry the lady.

SIR ANTHONY (*Shaking his hand enthusiastically*): Why, now you are talking sense. Confound you, you shall be Jack again. And now, I will tell you of the lady: prepare, Jack—prepare for rapture. What think you of Miss Lydia Languish?

JACK (*Pretending to try to place the name*): Languish? Languish? No, I don't believe I know the girl.

SIR ANTHONY: What? Did you never meet her? She lives here in Bath with her aunt, Mrs. Malaprop.

JACK: Malaprop? Languish? I don't remember ever to have heard the names before. Yet, stay; I think I do recollect a Languish. She's an ugly little girl, isn't she?

SIR ANTHONY (*Chuckling*): Ugly? Zounds, no! She is a blooming, love-breathing seventeen!

JACK: Why, sir, you had promised me a girl with a beard and one eye, if you will recollect.

SIR ANTHONY: Oh really, boy, did you take me seriously? No, no, the lady is a love, a veritable love. And except for a certain Ensign Beverly, whom she seems to prefer, there will be no objection at all.

JACK: I am pleased to hear that she is attractive. Yet, as a dutiful son, I own that were she ninety-plus-nine and hideous as a troll, I'd marry her if you wished it so.

SIR ANTHONY (*Putting his arm around* JACK's *shoulder*): Come, come, my dutiful boy. I'll write a note to Mrs. Malaprop, and you shall visit the young lady directly. And if you don't come back stark mad with rapture, if

you don't—I'll marry the girl myself! (*They go off together, laughing, as the lights fade.*)

*   *   *

SCENE 4

TIME: *An hour later.*
SETTING: *The drawing room of* MRS. MALAPROP'S *house.*
AT RISE: MRS. MALAPROP *is seated on a settee.* LUCY *stands
in the doorway, announcing the guests.*

LUCY: Sir Anthony and Captain Jack Absolute, ma'am.
(JACK *and* SIR ANTHONY *enter, and* MRS. MALAPROP
rises to greet them.)
MRS. MALAPROP: Ah, Sir Anthony. How *delicious* to see
you again. And Captain Jack Absolute. How glad I am
to meet you.
JACK (*Gallantly*): Permit me to say, madam, that as I have
never yet had the pleasure of seeing Miss Languish, my
principal inducement in this affair is the honor of being
allied with Mrs. Malaprop, whose intellectual accom-
plishments and unaffected learning are so well known.
MRS. MALAPROP (*Simpering*): La, sir, you do me too much
honor. (*Aside, behind her fan.*) Why, he's the very *pine-
apple* of politeness! (*To* JACK *and* SIR ANTHONY) You
know, I believe, Captain Absolute, that Lydia has at-
tached her affections on one Ensign Beverly, a useless,
penniless scoundrel, of whom none of us knows anything.
JACK (*Airily*): Oh, I have heard of the silly affair. I'm not
at all prejudiced against her on that account. But it
must be very distressing to you, ma'am.
MRS. MALAPROP: It gives me the *hydrostatics* to think of
him!
SIR ANTHONY: Well, you must calm yourself, madam. Soon

this Ensign Beverly will be out of the picture completely.

MRS. MALAPROP: How can I calm myself, Sir Anthony? Look. Here is a letter from him which I intercepted this very day.

JACK (*Aside, to the audience*): Oh, the devil. My last note!

MRS. MALAPROP: Wait, Sir Anthony. Wait until you have heard with your own ears what the *vermilion* has to say. Will you read it, Captain Absolute?

JACK (*Taking the letter and reading aloud*): "My soul's idol, my adored Lydia." Hmm, very tender indeed. "I am excessively alarmed at the intelligence you send me, the more so as my new rival . . ."

MRS. MALAPROP: That's you, sir.

JACK: "Has universally the character of an accomplished man of honor."

SIR ANTHONY: Well, that's handsome enough.

MRS. MALAPROP: But go on, sir.

JACK: "As for that weather-beaten old she-dragon who guards you"—why, whom can he mean by that?

MRS. MALAPROP (*Furiously*): Me, sir! Me, sir! I am the weather-beaten old she-dragon. The scoundrel! But go on a bit, sir.

JACK: "I am told that the same ridiculous vanity which makes her deck her dull chat with hard words she doesn't understand"—

MRS. MALAPROP: There, sir. An attack upon my language. Sure, if I *reprehend* anything in this world, it is the use of my *oracular* tongue, and a nice *derangement* of *epitaphs!*

SIR ANTHONY: Why, this Beverly ought to be hanged and horse-whipped!

MRS. MALAPROP: He ought indeed, sir.

JACK: But pray, could I not see the lady for a few minutes?

MRS. MALAPROP: I doubt if she'll come down, sir.

JACK: Then, tell her Ensign Beverly is below—she'll come right enough.

MRS. MALAPROP: 'Twould be a trick she well deserves. (*Calls offstage*) Lydia! Lydia! Nay, sir, she will not hear. I'll go up, and tell her it is Captain Absolute come to wait on her. (*Going toward the exit*) And she'll come down, or I shall know the reason why!

JACK: Thanks, good Mrs. Malaprop. (*As* MRS. MALAPROP *goes out,* JACK *turns to the audience.*) Oh, here will be the devil to pay. The fiction cannot continue for long.

SIR ANTHONY: Now, Jack, prepare yourself for love. Such a girl is Lydia Languish! Such charm! Such modesty! Such delicacy! (*From offstage comes* LYDIA's *voice raised in an indignant scream.*)

LYDIA (*Offstage*): I won't have anyone but my Ensign Beverly!

MRS. MALAPROP (*Offstage*): Come along, you impudent hussy! (MRS. MALAPROP *drags* LYDIA *onstage by the ear.* LYDIA *turns in the doorway, plants her feet firmly, crosses her arms and glares straight ahead, refusing to look at anyone.*)

LYDIA: This is an interview I shall have no appetite for, madam.

MRS. MALAPROP: Now, Lydia, behave yourself. Show your breeding, even if you have forgot your duty.

SIR ANTHONY (*Trying to win her over*): You look charming today, dear Miss Languish.

LYDIA: Humph!

MRS. MALAPROP: You have infinite trouble, Sir Anthony, in this affair. I am ashamed for the cause. Lydia, Lydia, turn around, I beseech you. Face the gentlemen, and pay your respects.

LYDIA (*With determined coldness*): Very well, madam.

(*She turns and sees* JACK.) Beverly! How can this be? 'Tis my Beverly!

JACK (*Looking heavenward*): Alas, the game is up!

SIR ANTHONY (*Confused*): Beverly? The devil it is! This is my son, Captain Jack Absolute!

MRS. MALAPROP (*Indignantly to* LYDIA): For shame, hussy, for shame. Beg Captain Absolute's pardon at once.

LYDIA (*Smiling sweetly at him*): I see not Captain Absolute, only my beloved Beverly.

SIR ANTHONY: The girl's mad!

MRS. MALAPROP: Indeed, Sir Anthony, I believe she is. What do you mean, Lydia, by Ensign Beverly? This is Captain Absolute—your husband that shall be.

SIR ANTHONY (*Throwing up his hands*): Oh, she's as mad as bedlam. The girl has lost her— (*Suddenly beginning to put two and two together.*) Or has this fellow been playing us a rogue's trick? (*He glares at* JACK.)

JACK (*Innocently*): Sir?

SIR ANTHONY (*Firmly*): Come here, sirrah. Who the devil *are* you?

JACK: Faith, sir, I'm not quite clear myself. But I'll endeavor to recollect. Mrs. Malaprop, I am your most respectful admirer and shall be proud to add most affectionate nephew. I need not tell my Lydia that she sees her faithful Beverly before her. Knowing the singular generosity of her temper, I assumed that name and station which would assure her of the sincerity of my love—a love which I now hope to enjoy in a more elevated character.

LYDIA (*With a trace of disappointment*): So there's to be no elopement after all.

SIR ANTHONY (*Laughing*): Upon my soul, Jack, thou art a very impudent fellow. (*Imitating* JACK'S *earlier behavior.*) Languish? Oh yes, an ugly girl with a beard!

MRS. MALAPROP (*Laughing uproariously*): Oh, sir, then you were both Ensign Beverly and Captain Jack Absolute. What a grand joke! Ha, ha, ha— (*She stops her laughter suddenly and abruptly.*) But wait. A new light breaks in upon me. How now—Captain. Did *you* write those letters, then?

JACK (*Uncomfortably*): Now, madam—

MRS. MALAPROP (*Advancing on him*): What? Am I to thank you for the elegant *compilation* of "an old weather-beaten she-dragon"—hey?

SIR ANTHONY: Now you're in for it, Jack!

MRS. MALAPROP: Mercy! Was it you that reflected on my parts of speech?

SIR ANTHONY (*Benignly coming to the rescue*): Come, come, Mrs. Malaprop, we must forget and forgive. Odds life! Just the thought of young love, and I could almost find it in my heart to be good-humored. Come, Mrs. Malaprop. They long to fly into each other's arms, I warrant. Come. We must leave them alone.

MRS. MALAPROP (*Moving toward the door with* SIR ANTHONY): You are right, Sir Anthony. We'll leave them alone. You go first, and I will *precede* you. (*Arm in arm, they go out.*)

LYDIA (*Happily*): At last, my love. But which "my love" shall you be: Captain Absolute or Ensign Beverly?

JACK: Whichever you desire, my dearest Lydia. I care not what I am called, so long as from this day forward, Absolute and Beverly are no longer rivals! (*They embrace tenderly as the curtain falls.*)

THE END

(NOTE: *If desired, the cast may recite the following epilogue, in the style of the period, at the curtain call.*)

THOMAS: As we have rivals been in Cupid's cause,

FAG: We'll rivals be, now, only for applause.

LUCY: And if you have enjoyed our gay effulgence,

JULIA: We humbly ask your generous indulgence.

MRS. MALAPROP: We've made our errors, and we've made amends.

SIR ANTHONY: We hope we've also made you for our friends.

LYDIA: So if you have enjoyed these foolish trifles,

JACK: We pray that you applaud us—and THE RIVALS.

Production Notes

THE RIVALS

Characters: 4 male; 4 female.

Playing Time: 25 minutes.

Costumes: 18th century dress. Lydia, Julia and Mrs. Malaprop wear long dresses and wigs and carry fans; Lucy wears a maid's uniform. Mrs. Malaprop is lavishly overdressed. Fag and Thomas wear servants' clothes—tunics, doublet and hose, and buckled shoes; Thomas carries a whip. Sir Anthony wears conservative costume of an 18th century gentleman. Jack wears a captain's uniform.

Properties: Books, coin, letter.

Setting: Scenes 1 and 3 take place before the curtain; the space represents a street. Lydia's boudoir (Scene 2) should be colorfully and elaborately furnished with soft chairs, tables, a mirror, in the style of the period. Mrs. Malaprop's drawing room (Scene 4) may use some of the same furniture as in Scene 2, but the room should be arranged more formally; there may be pictures hung, lamps, bric-a-brac, etc.

Lighting: Stage lights dim at end of scenes, as indicated.

The Flying Dutchman

by Heinrich Heine

Characters

KATHERINE MACLAREN
GRANDMOTHER
DAVID
MACLAREN
THE FLYING DUTCHMAN

SCENE 1

SETTING: *The main room of MacLaren's cottage. Down left, a wide window overlooking the cliffs and the sea. Up left, the door to the outside. Down right, a door to the rest of the house. At center, a large fireplace. Over the fireplace hangs the smoke-darkened painting of* THE FLYING DUTCHMAN.

AT RISE: KATHERINE, *a beautiful girl of nineteen, is arranging wildflowers in a vase. Her elderly* GRANDMOTHER *is setting a table for four.*

GRANDMOTHER: Aren't you finished with those flowers yet, Katherine?

KATHERINE (*Smiling*): Only a minute more, Granny. Look how pretty they are.

GRANDMOTHER: Your fussing with them won't make them prettier.

KATHERINE: I suppose not. But I do want everything to be perfect for Father's homecoming. You've no idea how far I had to walk before finding the heather I wanted.

GRANDMOTHER (*Lovingly*): After all these months at sea, your father won't have eyes for heather, my girl—not when he can keep his eyes glued to his only daughter.

KATHERINE (*With a final touch to the bouquet*): There, it's done! Where shall I put them, Granny?

GRANDMOTHER: In the center of the table, I suppose. After all the time you've spent arranging them, they may as well take the place of honor.

KATHERINE (*Going to the table*): Why, what's this? *Four* places, Granny?

GRANDMOTHER: Aye. One for David.

KATHERINE (*Angrily*): David! Now, you haven't gone and asked David to join us for dinner, have you?

GRANDMOTHER: That I have.

KATHERINE (*Protesting*): On Father's very first night home from his voyages? To invite a stranger?

GRANDMOTHER: A stranger you call him? David, that's to be your husband come next Michaelmas?

KATHERINE (*Angrily*): He's *not* to be my husband, and you're not to say he is.

GRANDMOTHER (*Surprised*): But, Katherine! I thought 'twas all arranged. He told me himself!

KATHERINE: I care naught for what he may have told you.

GRANDMOTHER: But your father has all but given David his word!

KATHERINE: It's *my* word that has not been given—and I'll not marry David, not ever; no, not if he should ask me every day for a year.

GRANDMOTHER: Whatever can you find to object to in him?

He's handsome enough, I'll warrant, and rich enough, too.

KATHERINE: Aye, rich and handsome he is. But a farmer! Oh, Granny, how could I ever marry a farmer—I, who was born with the sea in my blood? I am the daughter of a sailor, and the granddaughter of a sailor, and it's the bride of a sailor I must be.

GRANDMOTHER (*Angrily*): *I* was the bride of a sailor, and much good it did me! Killed in a storm at sea he was, when we'd been wed no more than five years; and I with three little ones. The sea took my husband, and both my sons. And then my daughter—your mother—the sea took her as well, for didn't she meet her death by falling into the sea— (*Points out window*)—from that very cliff? The sea has meant nothing but death. You're mad to want a sailor for a husband, when you could have David—a firm, steady lad, who'd never leave you to go wandering across the oceans, leave you to worry each day and cry each night, wondering if you'll ever see him alive again.

KATHERINE (*Fervently*): I'd neither worry nor cry about a husband at sea, for that's where a real man belongs. Out, out where the wind is free and the air is strong with salt. Oh, if *I* were a man—

GRANDMOTHER (*Interrupting sternly*): You're *not* a man. And you're not a child, either. I am ashamed to hear you speak such foolishness, Katherine. You don't know what it's like to be wedded to a seafaring man. David is the man you should wed.

KATHERINE (*Angrily*): David, David, David! Rather than marry that dull and stolid farmer, I'd say yes to the first sailor that should ask me—aye, even were it the Flying Dutchman himself! (*She looks up at the painting as she says this.* GRANDMOTHER *is horrified.*)

GRANDMOTHER: God protect you, Katherine! You know not what you say!

KATHERINE (*Staring at the portrait, almost mesmerized*): The Flying Dutchman. . . .

GRANDMOTHER (*Anxiously*): Come away from that portrait, child!

KATHERINE (*Turning to face her*): Who is he, Granny? Ever since I can remember, that portrait has hung there over the fireplace. But no one has ever told me who he is.

GRANDMOTHER: And reason enough for that! It's a dark story—a terrible story.

KATHERINE: Tell it to me!

GRANDMOTHER: No, no, child. I would to God I had never heard it myself.

KATHERINE (*Turning back to the painting*): The Flying Dutchman. I warrant *he* was a sailor, for he has a strong face, and the sturdy frame of one who has lived at sea. Those eyes have stared at a clouded sky, searching for the North Star! That hair has felt the salt wind pulling at it. That face has felt the sting of the briny spray.

GRANDMOTHER: Aye, he was a sailor—a sailor under a terrible curse.

KATHERINE (*Facing her again*): A curse! (*Runs to her and kneels at her feet.*) Tell me.

GRANDMOTHER: No, no. 'Tis too awful a tale for a young girl to hear.

KATHERINE: Did you not say yourself that I am no longer a child?

GRANDMOTHER: I—I am afraid. It is not wise to speak of such things.

KATHERINE: Then why hint at them? Everyone knows that portrait is the Flying Dutchman. But when I ask about it, I am pushed aside with fears and frights and fancies.

GRANDMOTHER (*After a short pause*): Perhaps you *should* be told. Then you will not be so quick to make jokes about things that wiser folk than you speak of in whispers.

KATHERINE (*Eagerly*): Tell me!

GRANDMOTHER (*Leaning back in her chair, closing her eyes*): It was years and years ago. I doubt me there's any alive today who knows exactly when 'twas that it happened.

KATHERINE: When what happened?

GRANDMOTHER: There was a sea captain—a Hollander— aye, he that is known as the Flying Dutchman. . . . (KATHERINE's *eyes go to the portrait*.) The legend tells that a fearful storm arose as he was headed home. For days his ship was tossed about by the winds and waves, but no more progress could it make than a piece of rotten driftwood riding the tide. It was a wonder it did not go down the first day.

KATHERINE: Did it go down at last, the Dutchman's ship?

GRANDMOTHER: Nay, though mayhap it had been better for the Dutchman if his ship *had* gone down.

KATHERINE: Why? What happened?

GRANDMOTHER: The sailors begged the captain to put into port for safety . . . to lay over until the storm subsided. But he was a fearful stubborn man, the Hollander, and he would not be thwarted. At last, he vowed a vow . . . a terrible vow . . . that same vow that was to become his curse.

KATHERINE (*After a pause, softly*): He vowed . . . ?

GRANDMOTHER: He vowed that he would get around the rockbound coast in spite of the storm though he should sail to the Day of Judgment. (*After a pause, solemnly*) And the Devil took him at his word. Aye, the Devil doomed that seafaring Dutchman to sail the seven seas forever, until he could be set free by a woman—a woman who would be faithful to him until death. The Devil in his stupidity believes that the woman has not been born who can be true to one man, and so he allows the captain to land once every seven years to find a wife—and so perhaps to break the curse. Poor Dutchman! He is often only too glad to be saved from those faithless wives, and to get back on board. (*As if coming out of a dream, briskly*) That is the curse of your Flying Dutchman. And you so foolish as to say you'd marry him!

KATHERINE (*Trying to laugh away her belief in the tale*): But Granny, 'tis only a legend, a fable. Such things cannot be true.

GRANDMOTHER: Aye, it's true enough. Whenever the ghostly ship meets another vessel, some of the unearthly sailors come in a boat and beg the others to take a packet of letters home for them. These letters must be nailed to the mast, else some misfortune will happen to the ship—above all if no Bible be on board, and no horseshoe nailed to the foremast. The letters are always addressed to people whom no one knows, and who have long been dead, so that some late descendant gets a letter addressed to a faraway great-great-grandmother, who has slept for centuries in her grave.

KATHERINE (*Going to the portrait*): And has there never been a woman who was true to this captain, to release him from his curse?

GRANDMOTHER (*Softly*): No. None.

KATHERINE: *I* should prove true to such a man. I should lift his curse and free him forever, were I given the chance!

GRANDMOTHER (*Rising angrily*): God forbid! The Flying Dutchman lies under the hand of the Devil. 'Tis only ruin that can come to those that mix with him! (*A *knock at the door startles the women. Then* DAVID *enters.*) David! (*Laughs*) Oh, but you startled me out of a year of my life, lad. We didn't hear you approach. Come in, and welcome.

DAVID: Good even to you. And to you, Katherine. I apologize if I am early. But MacLaren's ship has been sighted from the hills. 'Twill be in the harbor by now.

KATHERINE: Praise God, then, for his safe return. Let us go down to the foot of the cliff, Granny, and make him welcome.

DAVID: And me, Katherine? Have you no word to make *me* welcome?

KATHERINE (*Shortly*): It seems to me that a homecoming night should be for family alone. But as you are here, David, why then welcome.

DAVID: Are there no warmer words for one who is to be your husband?

KATHERINE: I do not know that you are to be my husband.

DAVID: Is it not agreed that we are to wed next Michaelmas?

KATHERINE: There has been talk of it, 'tis true. But it is not so settled as all that. Have you my father's pledge to it?

DAVID: 'Tis *your* pledge to it I seek. If you will have me, MacLaren will not say me nay. If you will not, your father's pledge alone were not enough to make me take you for my wife. I will not have you against your will, Katherine.

KATHERINE: And I will not have you against my father's. Until his word is given, look for no answer from me.

DAVID: But I do, Katherine. I ask you straight out: will you have me for your husband? I love you, well you know it. And there is none in the country can find a thing to say against me.

KATHERINE (*Softly*): *I* would say a thing against you.

DAVID (*Taken aback*): 'Tis the first I knew you had complaint against me. Name it.

KATHERINE (*Slowly*): You are a farmer. A stay-at-home. Oh David, would you have me go with you and live among your fields and hills and forests—I, who have the sea in my blood? Without the sea to look at every day, without the sound of the surf in my ears, I would go mad! Do not ask it of me!

GRANDMOTHER (*Shocked and upset*): Say not so, Katherine. You speak as a child. 'Tis only a fancy. 'Twill pass.

KATHERINE (*Coldly*): 'Tis no fancy, and 'twill *not* pass. You have asked for an answer, David, and I have given it. I will not be your wife.

DAVID (*Bowing his head*): So be it. Good even, Katherine.

GRANDMOTHER: You are not going, David? See, there is a place set for you at table.

DAVID: Katherine is right, old woman. Homecoming nights are sacred to family alone, and I am no longer of this family. Good night. (*He turns abruptly and goes to the door.*) If you should change your mind. . . .

KATHERINE: I will not change my mind.

DAVID: Still, I'll call again, if I may. So long as you are not pledged to another, Katherine, I claim the right to call upon you now and again.

KATHERINE (*Lightly*): As for that, you may waste your time as you will. You'll not find the door barred against you. And then (*Looking at her* GRANDMOTHER)—some in this house will always have a welcome for you.

DAVID (*Quietly*): I see how it is. (*Bowing slightly*) Good even, then. (*He exits.*)

GRANDMOTHER: Oh, Katherine, you are a foolish, willful girl. To have the taking of such a man as David, and to say him nay!

KATHERINE (*Petulantly*): Enough, Granny, enough!

GRANDMOTHER: What will your father say when he hears of this? You know he longs to see you wedded and settled.

KATHERINE: Then let my father find a sailor for my husband!

GRANDMOTHER (*Bitterly*): Aye, and let him, then, provide you with bolts of black silk, for 'tis a short-lived time between sailor's bride and sailor's widow!

KATHERINE (*Abruptly pulling a shawl from a peg by the door*): The ship has been sighted, and we stand chattering here like children. Will you come down the cliffs with me to greet my father? (*As she speaks, the door opens and* MACLAREN, *a middle-aged sea captain, enters, several packages in his arms.*)

MACLAREN: Too late, my girl, for here he is!

KATHERINE (*Joyfully*): Oh, Father, Father, you're home! (*Embracing him*) God be thanked, you're safely home.

MACLAREN: Aye, safely home. Granny, a kiss for you, too!

GRANDMOTHER (*As he kisses her cheek*): We should have been below to greet you as you set foot on land.

MACLAREN (*Laughing*): I wonder that you were not?

KATHERINE (*Shamefacedly*): The—the time slipped by so fast, Father. We—we didn't realize it was so late.

MACLAREN (*Teasingly chucking her under the chin*): Aye, aye. *I* know well enough what kept you here! Was it not your suitor, David, that I spied going away from here as I climbed the cliff? (*With mock self-pity*) What lass has time to think of her poor old father when there's a handsome lad come a-wooing?

GRANDMOTHER (*Sarcastically*): Aye, and a pretty welcome your daughter gave him!

KATHERINE: Hush, Granny!

MACLAREN: Frowns, Katherine?

KATHERINE: It is no matter.

GRANDMOTHER (*Angrily*): She has refused David! Do you hear? Refused the likeliest lad in all these parts.

MACLAREN: Katherine, is this true?

KATHERINE (*Sullenly*): It is. I know you will be angry, but I have refused him.

MACLAREN: Angry? Nay, not a whit of it, Katherine! Come, no frowns, either of you. 'Tis my homecoming. Let us have smiles!

GRANDMOTHER (*Still cross*): Well! If the father has no sense, I'm a fool to expect sense of the daughter!

MACLAREN (*Gently*): If the girl will not have him, I cannot force her. (*Boisterously*) Besides, I have had such fortune that I could not be cross tonight had Katherine refused a hundred likely husbands!

KATHERINE (*Eagerly*): Good fortune? Tell us!

MACLAREN (*Settling himself in a chair by the fire*): 'Tis only two days since I had the strangest adventure of all my sailing life. As we lay at anchor some hundred miles down the coast, another vessel moved into the bay alongside mine. A strange, dark, old-fashioned vessel it was, the like of which I have seen only in ancient books. It was too dark to see her flag. "Well," thought I, "tomorrow morning we shall have a better look at her." Within the hour, however, there came a halloo, and I was invited by her captain to board her. Look! (*He opens one of the packets, revealing many precious stones.*)

GRANDMOTHER (*Overwhelmed*): What's this? What's this?

MACLAREN (*Avidly*): Diamonds! Rubies! Emeralds!

KATHERINE (*Wonderingly*): How did you come by this treasure?

MACLAREN: It was amazing! The foreign captain—he of the ancient vessel—his ship was weighted down with precious stones such as these. He sold them to me.

GRANDMOTHER: But how could you have afforded them? These jewels are worth a king's ransom!

MACLAREN (*Delightedly*): That is the strangest part of all. The captain appears not to know their value! I paid no more for all these stones than you would pay in the marketplace for five pounds of tea.

KATHERINE (*Happily*): Good fortune indeed! This journey of yours has made you a rich man, Father.

MACLAREN: If that were all, it were enough. Yet there is more! Our fortune is but beginning!

GRANDMOTHER: More? Tell us quickly!

MACLAREN: When we had concluded our business, and I had bought all the gems for which I had enough ready money, that captain invited me to dine with him. And over dinner, he asked me the strangest question.

KATHERINE: That was . . . ?

MACLAREN (*Slowly*): Did I know of a young woman familiar with a seaman's ways who might look favorably upon him as a husband?

GRANDMOTHER (*Terrified*): Dear God!

MACLAREN (*Eagerly*): Katherine, Katherine! Do you know what this can mean? A wealthy man—rich beyond telling—comes here in search of a wife. I have invited him to take dinner with us tonight.

KATHERINE (*Strangely*): And I have given David his dismissal. It is almost as though I dismissed David because I knew the captain was coming.

MACLAREN (*Wonderingly*): And there is yet another omen! Look! (*He rips the wrappings off another parcel, and yards of white fabric come falling out*) I bought this cloth when I had been a-voyaging but three weeks. That's seven months ago. White cloth such as this, I thought, should deck my daughter Katherine as a bride. (*Laughing*) But little did I think I'd bring both bridal dress and bridegroom, too! (*There is a crash of thunder, followed immediately by three knocks on the door.* MACLAREN *rises excitedly*) 'Tis he, our guest, the captain! (*All three turn toward the door.* MACLAREN *takes a step forward as if to go to open it, when it flies open. Another crash of thunder. Standing in the doorway is the man of the portrait:* THE FLYING DUTCHMAN.)

KATHERINE (*In awe, as though hypnotized; very softly*): The Flying Dutchman!

CURTAIN

*   *   *

SCENE 2

TIME: *Several days later.*

SETTING: *The same as Scene 1.*

AT RISE: MACLAREN *stands at the window, looking out but not seeing; he is deep in thought.* GRANDMOTHER *is fussing at the fireplace with the teakettle. Every few minutes, she casts an angry glance at* MACLAREN *and purses her lips. When the tea is ready, she puts the teapot on the table almost angrily.*

GRANDMOTHER: Your tea.

MACLAREN (*With a start*): What's that, Granny?

GRANDMOTHER: Your tea is ready.

MACLAREN (*Moving to the table*): And yours?

GRANDMOTHER: I care for none.

MACLAREN (*Laughing*): Still in the sulks, Granny?

GRANDMOTHER (*Settling herself into a chair, pulling her shawl around her*): You know I never sulk.

MACLAREN: Oh no, not you! It's days and days that you've been angry now.

GRANDMOTHER: Well, then, what if I am? Haven't I the right?

MACLAREN: Oho, so I was right after all. Well, then, what is it?

GRANDMOTHER: You'd not listen to me were I to tell you.

MACLAREN (*Beginning to become angry*): Come, come, old woman. I've humored you enough. If you have aught to say, say it and be done with it.

GRANDMOTHER: Well then, I will, and much appetite I hope you'll have for it! It's about that man—the captain.

MACLAREN (*Staring ahead, blowing on his tea*): Aye, I thought as much. Well, and what about him?

GRANDMOTHER (*Going to him*): Come to your senses, MacLaren! Don't you know who he is?

MACLAREN (*Evenly*): Aye, I know who he is. A sea captain, master of a great vessel. An old bachelor, in search of a willing wife. A merchant, in possession of a fortune greater than any in Scotland.

GRANDMOTHER: That's not what I mean, and well you know it. You *do* know what I mean, and for all your fancy talk you can't hide from the truth. (*Fiercely*) Who is he?

MACLAREN (*Glances involuntarily at the portrait, then looks away*): I've told you all I know.

GRANDMOTHER (*Almost to herself*): A merchant . . . a captain . . . an old bachelor. All you know—and yet you let him woo your daughter?

MACLAREN: What else do I *need* to know? Is he not rich? Is he not kind? Does he not look with favor on Katherine? And she on him? That is what I know and what I want to know.

GRANDMOTHER (*Ironically*): I think that in spite of yourself, you know more. (*There is a knock at the door.* GRANDMOTHER *opens it, and* DAVID *enters.*)

DAVID: A good day to you in this house.

GRANDMOTHER: A good day to you, David, and welcome.

MACLAREN (*Shaking his hand*): David, lad! I expected to see you before this. It is not friendly to wait so long to come and bid me welcome.

DAVID (*Embarrassed*): I did not like to intrude myself.

GRANDMOTHER: Tea, David?

DAVID: Thanks.

MACLAREN: Glad I am of the company, lad! (*Smilingly, looking at* GRANDMOTHER) It is not pleasant to drink one's tea alone.

DAVID (*Trying to be casual*): Is—Is Katherine not at home, then?

MACLAREN: She is out just now—gone walking on the moors.

DAVID: Oh? Perhaps I'll go out, then, and look for her.

MACLAREN (*Uncomfortably*): She is not alone, I think.

DAVID (*Pretending he does not know*): She has another suitor, then. One of the lads from your ship, I suppose?

MACLAREN (*Evasively*): It is a seafaring man, yes.

DAVID (*Insistently*): From your ship?

MACLAREN: Why, that is—no. Not from my ship.

DAVID: Then it is true.

MACLAREN (*Hoping to change the subject*): Granny, where's the boy's tea?

GRANDMOTHER (*Bringing it to the table*): Why should she *not* have a new suitor, David? Did she not give you her refusal?

DAVID: It's the suitor himself I mind.

MACLAREN: If she has refused you, I don't see that it's any concern of yours who woos her in your stead. But if you must know: the man is a sea captain.

DAVID (*Staring at him*): But not just *any* sea captain, Mac-

Laren, *is* it? This man is none other than the Flying Dutchman!

MACLAREN (*Smiling*): Do not tell me, lad, that you believe such old wives' tales! From Granny they are one thing. But from you. . . .

DAVID (*Fiercely*): It *is* the Flying Dutchman, MacLaren. Admit it.

MACLAREN (*Angrily*): You've spent too much time with your sheep, David. Your wits have become those of a sheep. Flying Dutchman! Nonsense! The man is a sea captain from a foreign land. True, his dress is strange. True, he has greater wealth than any man I've ever known. True, he seldom speaks. But is this reason to turn him into—into some sort of fairy tale creature such as children believe in? I tell you, the man is made of flesh and blood, just as we are. He is my friend. And—if he should wish it—he will be my son.

DAVID: You would willingly see your daughter wed to a man who is under the curse of the Devil?

MACLAREN (*Hotly*): I would willingly see my daughter wed to *this* man were he the Devil himself! (*The door opens;* KATHERINE *and the* DUTCHMAN *enter.*)

KATHERINE (*With forced cheerfulness*): What's all this talk of devils? You'd think it were a Sunday, and the whole household discussing the morning's sermon. (*Easily*) Good day to you, David. Granny, here are some wild berries I picked. They will be good with dinner. (*The* DUTCHMAN *moves quietly toward the fireplace.*)

GRANDMOTHER (*Taking the basket of berries, as* KATH-ERINE *begins to pour out tea*): Thank you, Katherine.

KATHERINE (*Handing a cup of tea to the* DUTCHMAN): A cup of tea. David, will you have a cup of tea? (*He just stares at her.*) You have had your tea, then.

MACLAREN (*Trying to lighten the mood*): Aye, he had his tea with me.

KATHERINE: Then it was my father you came to visit.

DAVID: No, Katherine. It was you I came to see.

KATHERINE (*Lightly*): I thought I had made my feelings plain, David.

DAVID (*Firmly*): You told me I might call until you were pledged to another.

KATHERINE: Yes. (*Looking him full in the face for the first time*) But now, David, I *am* pledged to another.

GRANDMOTHER (*Dropping the basket of berries*): Katherine!

DAVID (*Taking a step back*): Pledged?

MACLAREN (*Rising, smiling*): Is this true?

KATHERINE (*Steadily*): The Captain has asked me to be his wife. And I have accepted him.

GRANDMOTHER (*Weeping*): Oh Lord, it is not true! It cannot be true!

MACLAREN (*To the* DUTCHMAN): Is it as the girl says? Are you betrothed?

DUTCHMAN: With your consent.

MACLAREN (*Warmly*): Consent? Aye, that you have, and glad I am to give it. Yes, say I!

KATHERINE (*Happily, linking her arm with the* DUTCHMAN'*s*): And yes, say I!

GRANDMOTHER (*Staring at him, slowly*): And what say *you*, Captain?

DUTCHMAN: If the girl will have me, it shall be so.

GRANDMOTHER: You love her?

DUTCHMAN: I do.

GRANDMOTHER: And you do not fear for her? (*He is silent.*) You do not answer, Captain.

DUTCHMAN: What would you have me say?

GRANDMOTHER: I would have you tell the truth! I would

have you say who you are, and what your past has been. If you love the girl, surely you fear for her—for has it not always been so? The women you love come to ruin!

DUTCHMAN (*Simply*): I do not fear for Katherine.

KATHERINE (*Defiantly*): Why should he fear? (*Tenderly, to the* DUTCHMAN) Oh, my love, if they but knew you as I know you, how glad they would be that we have found one another. They would know your pain, as I know it, and would welcome the chance to bring you ease. They would know your gentleness, as I know it, and be glad of the peace it brings me. They would know your strength, and envy me, that I have you to lean on. (*Bitterly*) But they are foolish, childish people. They fear you, because they do not know you, and because—

DUTCHMAN (*After a pause*): Because?

KATHERINE (*Lightly*): Because they have heard a fairy tale once, and believe it to be true. (*She moves away from him a step or two.*)

DUTCHMAN (*To* GRANDMOTHER): Are you afraid of me? (*To* DAVID) Is there a story? (*They are silent.*) Oh, Katherine, why have you not spoken of this before?

MACLAREN: Why should the girl speak of such foolishness? It is their fancy, their madness. Really, it is too laughable!

DUTCHMAN (*Simply*): Then we could have laughed at it together, she and I.

KATHERINE: No. It is not that. It is because I do not care if the story be false *or* true. I love you, and I have sworn to you that I will be true to you. And I would not violate that pledge if all they have heard be ten *times* true.

DUTCHMAN: What have they heard? (*There is silence. To* GRANDMOTHER) What have you heard? (*Silence. He seizes* DAVID) Speak! What have you heard?

DAVID (*In a voice choked with terror*): That you are the

Flying Dutchman! (*The* DUTCHMAN *reels back a step, as though he has been hit.*)

DUTCHMAN: The Flying Dutchman.

KATHERINE (*Running to him protectively*): Pay them no mind, my love! It is only their fancy!

DUTCHMAN (*Low*): No. It is no fancy.

GRANDMOTHER: Dear God in Heaven!

DUTCHMAN (*Looking at* KATHERINE'*s face, a look of pain in his own*): I am who they say I am. I am the Flying Dutchman.

KATHERINE: What if that be true? You are my betrothed! I love you!

DUTCHMAN: No. It cannot be. I cannot wed you, Katherine.

KATHERINE: Why not, if you love me?

DUTCHMAN: *Because* I love you! (*Almost to himself*) And because you know. If you did not, it would have been different. There would have been no fear, no wondering. But now, it cannot be. I had hoped. . . . I had thought that in you. . . . (*Laughing bitterly*) But once again, I have lost my wager! You would have been true, if you had not known, and I would have been free. But now I must wait another seven years, and then seven years more, and seven times seven times seven times seven years. . . .

KATHERINE (*Weeping*): Oh no, my love! I cannot let you go. I have sworn I will be true, and I *will* be true. You have been cursed, my love, but it is I that shall set you free.

MACLAREN (*Sternly*): Katherine! The man has confessed. I forbid you to marry him!

KATHERINE (*Wildly*): You turn against him too, Father?

DAVID: Listen to your father, Katherine. This man lies under the Devil's curse, and cannot be released until a woman prove true to him till death. For centuries there has been none to do it!

DUTCHMAN: What the lad says is true, Katherine. For centuries there has been none.

KATHERINE (*Wildly*): But I am she, I swear!

MACLAREN (*Loudly, strongly*): Katherine, you will not wed this man!

KATHERINE (*Weeping*): Not wed him! Not wed him! (*Suddenly a strange look comes into her face.*) And yet— there is another way! For I will free him! I must!

GRANDMOTHER (*Clutching her heart*): My God, my God! Ai-eee! (*She falls to her knees.* DAVID *and* MACLAREN *turn to her. At the same moment,* KATHERINE *darts from the room.*)

GRANDMOTHER (*Gasping*): Stop her! Stop her!

MACLAREN (*Turning around*): Where is she?

DAVID (*Running to the window*): She's running to the cliffs!

MACLAREN (*Holding the crumpled body of* GRAND-MOTHER): Stop her! Stop her!

DAVID: Too late! (*Turns away, buries his face in his hands*) Too late!

MACLAREN: What is too late? Is she . . . ? (*Moan comes from* GRANDMOTHER, *who begins weeping. The* DUTCH-MAN, *down center, clasps his hands before him and looks upward, a strange smile on his face.*)

DAVID (*Sobbing*): Dead. Dead! She has thrown herself into the sea!

DUTCHMAN: And I am free! She has been faithful unto death, and set me free! Katherine! My love! We shall be together, now, forever! Together, for all time, and at rest! We are free!

GRANDMOTHER (*Weeping, unrolling the bolt of white cloth*): White . . . cloth . . . for a bride . . . White

. . . cloth . . . for a shroud. . . . (*The* DUTCHMAN *stands transfixed, a beatific smile on his face.* MACLAREN *and* DAVID *stare at him brokenly, and the curtain falls.*)

THE END

Production Notes

THE FLYING DUTCHMAN

Characters: 3 male; 2 female.

Playing Time: 30 minutes.

Costumes: Appropriate common dress of the 18th century. Katherine wears a simple, ankle-length dress; Grandmother wears a dark dress and an apron. David wears overalls and a work shirt. MacLaren is dressed in a captain's uniform appropriate to the time; The Flying Dutchman wears a much older style uniform.

Properties: Vase, wildflowers, shawl, packages, gems, bolt of white cloth, teapot, teakettle, teacups, basket of berries.

Setting: Scene 1: The simple main room of MacLaren's cottage, with large fireplace at center and painting of The Flying Dutchman hanging above it. Left exit leads outside, right exit to rest of cottage. Scene 2: The same as Scene 1.

Lighting: No special effects.

Sound: Thunder, as indicated in the text.

The Bishop's Candlesticks

(from *Les Miserables*)

by Victor Hugo

Characters

JEAN VALJEAN
VOICE OF THE JUDGE
MADEMOISELLE FLEURY
MADAME MAGLOIRE
BISHOP
THREE GENDARMES

PROLOGUE

Before the curtains. The stage is dark, except for a spotlight on JEAN VALJEAN, *who stands abjectly to one side, his hands tied behind his back, his head bowed. He is a middle-aged man, very poorly dressed. The* VOICE OF THE JUDGE *is heard, loud and sonorous, over a loudspeaker system.* VALJEAN *does not react to what he hears, except, perhaps, that he seems to become more and more abject. (Note: If desired, the* JUDGE *may be played by an actor who appears at the other side of the stage.)*

VOICE OF THE JUDGE: Jean Valjean, for the attempted theft of a loaf of bread, you are sentenced to five years at hard labor. (*The sound of a gavel rapped three times is heard.*)

Jean Valjean, for escaping from the galleys after four years of serving your sentence, your time is hereby extended an additional three years. (*The gavel is rapped three times.*)

Jean Valjean, for attempted escape during your sixth year of imprisonment, and for resisting capture, your sentence is extended five years—two with the double chain. (*The gavel is rapped three times.*)

Jean Valjean, for attempted escape and for four hours of freedom, your time shall be extended three years. (*The gavel is rapped three times again. There is a pause.*)

Jean Valjean, you have spent nineteen years in prison. You have served your sentence. (*Pause*) Jean Valjean, you are free. (*For the first time,* VALJEAN *raises his head. His expression is blank.*)

VALJEAN (*Without emotion*): I have served nineteen years in prison, for stealing a loaf of bread. And now . . . I am free. (*The spotlight goes out, and the curtain opens immediately.*)

*   *   *

Scene 1

TIME: *About eight o'clock in the evening. Fall, 1815.*

SETTING: *The front room of the Bishop's home.*

AT RISE: MADAME MAGLOIRE, *a middle-aged portly housekeeper, and her friend,* MADEMOISELLE FLEURY, *a spinster of the same age, are sitting over their teacups, gossiping.*

MLLE. FLEURY (*Surprised*): You mean to say you haven't heard about him?

MME. MAGLOIRE: No, I must confess I have not.

MLLE. FLEURY: But, my dear, the whole town is talking about him. The ugliest man I have ever seen, I assure you.

MME. MAGLOIRE: I thought you said that nobody has seen him.

MLLE. FLEURY: Nobody has seen him for the last three days, my dear. But before that, he made application for a room at the inn, and they had a good look at him there. They turned him away, of course.

MME. MAGLOIRE: Of course. But then, you have not seen the man himself?

MLLE. FLEURY: Well, no, not personally. But the innkeeper's wife got a good look at him in the candlelight, and she told the laundress all about it. Now, you *know* how laundresses love to talk, so naturally my laundress got a complete description. Of course, I would never gossip with a common laundress, but fortunately she told the cook all about it. Well, when the cook came running to Mamma with the story—what could Mamma do but listen? And then, of course, Mamma told me. So I can tell you for a fact that this vagabond is the ugliest man in the world. Everyone is talking about him. They say he's probably a runaway convict, but *I* say he's more likely a murderer at the very least.

MME. MAGLOIRE: Lord in Heaven, it's a wonder we aren't all killed in our beds.

MLLE. FLEURY: It is, indeed, Madame Magloire, considering how useless the police are in this town.

MME. MAGLOIRE: But surely the constable has been alerted to the fact that there's a desperate criminal running about.

MLLE. FLEURY (*Airily*): Oh, I have no doubt he's been alerted, for all the good it will do. You know what ill will there is between the prefect and the mayor. They're more concerned with doing each other harm than they are with doing any of the rest of us good. So it's little protection we can expect from the police. No, no, we must all become our own police, and guard ourselves as best we can.

MME. MAGLOIRE: You're lucky, Mademoiselle Fleury, that at least you have your brother living with you. That must be some comfort, I'm sure.

MLLE. FLEURY: It is, of course. But then you have the Bishop.

MME. MAGLOIRE: It's little protection I'd get from him, I'm afraid. He's strong enough, Heaven knows, and not wanting in courage. But he's so intent on considering the goodness in man that he never will give a thought to man's wickedness. Not that I mean to speak against God's work, but it does seem to me that our good Bishop is much too trusting.

MLLE. FLEURY (*Rising and preparing to go*): If I were you, my dear, I'd just lock the bolts tight when I go to bed . . . and then be extra careful in my prayers.

MME. MAGLOIRE (*Laughing ironically*): Lock the bolts! That's a good one. I've been after the Bishop for years to put a decent lock on the doors, but he won't hear of it. (*An offstage clock begins to chime eight.*)

MLLE. FLEURY: Eight o'clock already. Really, I must be going. I don't want that murderer to attack me on my way through the square.

MME. MAGLOIRE: And I must begin setting the table for dinner. One thing I can say for the Bishop—he is always punctual.

MLLE. FLEURY: Well, I wish I could stay and wish him a good evening, but with all these murderers and vagabonds and scoundrels about, one can't be too careful.

(BISHOP *enters. He is a wise, strong-willed but gentle man in his mid-fifties.*)

MME. MAGLOIRE: Ah, Monseigneur, Mademoiselle Fleury was just regretting that she had to leave before you came. But you are just in time.

BISHOP: Good evening, Mademoiselle Fleury. I hope you are well.

MLLE. FLEURY: As well as can be expected, thank you, Monseigneur. I do apologize for dashing off like this, but with all that's going on in the town these days, I really don't like to be out too late. And it gets dark so early at this time of year; have you noticed that?

BISHOP (*Dryly*): I believe it happens regularly in that fashion every year at this season.

MLLE. FLEURY (*Vaguely*): Yes, I suppose it does. Well, good night to you.

BISHOP: Good night, Mademoiselle. I hope you may reach home safely.

MME. MAGLOIRE: It was so nice talking to you, my dear. Do come again.

MLLE. FLEURY: I will, thank you. Goodbye. (*She goes out. MME. MAGLOIRE begins to set the table. BISHOP sits down.*)

MME. MAGLOIRE (*As she works*): Poor Mademoiselle Fleury. I should not wish to be in her shoes right now, walking across the square unescorted. (*Not getting any response, she tries again.*) I suppose you've heard the talk in town, Monseigneur.

BISHOP (*Calmly*): I heard something of it indistinctly. Are we in any great danger, then?

MME. MAGLOIRE (*Happy to be able to continue her gossip*): I should say we are, Monseigneur. There's a mysterious vagabond hiding about.

BISHOP (*Without curiosity*): Oh?

MME. MAGLOIRE: A terribly ugly man, with a rope, they say, and a cloth sack. Nobody knows quite who he is, but everybody is agreed that something will happen to-night. The police are so badly organized. To live in this mountainous country, and not even have street lights—it is too barbaric. You know, Monseigneur, we really ought to get some bolts and other proper fastenings for the door.

BISHOP: A latch is quite sufficient, Madame Magloire. A bishop's door should be ever ready to open.

MME. MAGLOIRE: But with this runaway in town, this murderer! This house is not safe at all—even if you are the Bishop. And if you will permit me, I should like to go to the blacksmith shop tomorrow and get some bolts. For I say that a door which opens by a latch on the outside to the first comer, why, nothing could be more horrible. And then, you have the habit of saying "Come in" even at midnight, no matter who it is that may knock. As though there were even need to knock. One might just raise the latch . . . (*There is a knock at the door.*)

BISHOP (*Who has not been listening too closely*): Come in.

MME. MAGLOIRE: There, you see? You just say "Come in" as though there were no harm in the world . . . (JEAN VALJEAN *enters, carrying a cloth sack.* MME. MAGLOIRE *shrieks.*) Good heavens! It's he!

BISHOP (*Gently, to* VALJEAN): Good evening, my friend. What can I do for you?

VALJEAN (*Defiantly, almost angrily*): See here: I will tell you right off who I am. My name is Jean Valjean. I am a convict. I have been nineteen years in the galleys. A week ago I was set free and started for Pontarlier, which is my destination. For four days I walked from Toulon. When I reached this town three days ago, I went to an inn, and they sent me away because of my yellow passport. I went to another inn; they said "Get out." It was the same with one as with another. For two nights I went into the fields to sleep beneath the stars, but there were no stars. A good woman saw me and showed me your house. "Knock there," she said. I have knocked. What is this place? Is it an inn? I have money—my savings, one hundred and nine francs and fifteen sous which I have earned in the galleys by my work for nineteen years. I will pay. What do I care? I have money. I am very tired —and I am so hungry. May I stay?

BISHOP: Madame Magloire, put on another plate.

VALJEAN: Did you understand me? I am a galley-slave—a convict. There is my passport, yellow as you can see. That is enough to have me thrown out wherever I go. Will you read it?

BISHOP (*Waving aside the passport*): I do not wish to see it. You may stay here. Sit down and warm yourself, monsieur. We will take supper presently, and your bed will be made while you sup.

MME. MAGLOIRE: But don't you realize who—

BISHOP: Kindly put on an extra plate, as I asked before. (MME. MAGLOIRE *goes to cupboard.*)

VALJEAN (*Astonished*): True? True? You will keep me? You will allow me to stay? A convict? You call me "monsieur" and don't say "Get out, dog!" as everybody else does. I thought that you would send me away, so I told you straight off who I am. I shall have a supper and a bed, like other people, with a mattress, and sheets?

BISHOP: Of course you shall, my good man.

VALJEAN: It is nineteen years since I have slept in a bed . . .

MME. MAGLOIRE (*Peremptorily*): If I may offer my opinion . . .

BISHOP (*Interrupting her gently, but looking at her sternly*): Madame Magloire, as we have a guest for dinner, we must use the good silver. Will you fetch it? (*Upset and angry*, MME. MAGLOIRE *goes to cupboard and takes down the silver, muttering to herself.*)

VALJEAN: Tell me, monsieur, who are you who treats me so kindly? You are an innkeeper, aren't you? I will pay you well.

BISHOP: I am a priest who lives here, monsieur.

VALJEAN (*Happily*): Oh, Monsieur le Curé, every time you call me "monsieur," it is like water to a dying man.

BISHOP: After dinner is prepared, Mme. Magloire, you must make ready the room next to mine for our guest. You will feel much better after a good night's rest, eh, monsieur?

VALJEAN (*Curiously*): You are going to let me sleep in the room next to your own? Have you reflected upon it? Who tells you that I am not a murderer?

BISHOP (*Simply*): God will take care of that. Mme. Magloire, the light grows dim. Should we not have some candlelight?

MME. MAGLOIRE (*Sullenly*): Ah, I understand. You wish me to use the silver candlesticks as *well* as the silver plates (*Contemptuously*) for our guest.

VALJEAN: Monsieur le Curé, you are good. You don't despise me. (MME. MAGLOIRE *goes to the mantelpiece and takes down two heavy silver candlesticks. She puts them on the table.* VALJEAN *continues speaking.*) You take me into your house. You give me supper; you will light your candles for me. And I haven't hidden from you where I come from and how miserable I am.

BISHOP: You need not tell me who you are. This is not my house. It is the house of God. It does not ask any comer whether he has a name, but whether he has an affliction. You are suffering; you are hungry and thirsty; be welcome. And do not thank me. Do not tell me that I take you into my house. This is the home of no man, except him who needs asylum. I tell you, who are a traveler, that you are more at home here than I. Whatever is here is yours.

VALJEAN (*Overwhelmed, and on the point of tears*): Stop, stop, Monsieur le Curé. You are so kind that I don't know what I am. All that is gone.

BISHOP: Shall I tell you what you are? I had no need to ask your name. I knew you before you told me.

VALJEAN (*Astonished*): Really? You knew me?

BISHOP (*Simply*): Yes. Stranger, you are my brother. (BISHOP *quietly sits at the table.* VALJEAN *stares at him in wonder.* MME. MAGLOIRE *throws up her hands and sighs, as the curtain falls.*)

*   *   *

SCENE 2

TIME: *Early the next morning.*

SETTING: *The same.*

AT RISE: *The stage is lighted dimly through the window. A clock chimes five. After a moment,* JEAN VALJEAN *comes into the room. He moves stealthily and quietly. He pauses in the center for a moment, shakes his head and puts his hand to his forehead. He goes to the window, opens it, looks out. Then he goes to the cupboard, opens it softly and takes out silver basket. Occasionally looking about to make sure he is not being watched, he puts the silver, piece by piece, into the crude sack he carries. When he has loaded the sack, he tosses empty basket out of the window, gives one*

*last look around the room, and then stealthily climbs
out through the window. This pantomime is not rushed,
but there is a feeling of sustained suspense. The lights
black out to denote the passage of a few hours. After
a pause, the clock chimes seven. The lights come up
and fill the room. It is day.* MME. MAGLOIRE *is setting
the table for breakfast. After a moment, the* BISHOP
*enters, carrying the empty silver basket, which he
casually sets on a chair by the door.*

MME. MAGLOIRE: Back from your morning walk, Monseigneur?

BISHOP: It is a glorious morning, Madame Magloire. It
did me good to stroll around the garden. (*Laughing
slightly*) Our guest has not stirred himself yet?

MME. MAGLOIRE: I haven't heard a sound out of him this
morning.

BISHOP: Poor man, he must be exhausted. Well, it will
do him good to sleep late.

MME. MAGLOIRE: I'll set the table for three for breakfast.
I'll wager he'll be up fast enough when he smells the
bacon frying. (*She goes to the cupboard and begins
taking out plates, etc.*)

BISHOP: You're probably right. He had a hearty enough
appetite for his dinner last night, but it will be several
days before he feels he has had all the food he wants.

MME. MAGLOIRE (*At the cupboard; to herself*): That's
strange—I was sure I had put it back in here.

BISHOP: What's that, Madame Magloire?

MME. MAGLOIRE: The silver basket. I was certain I put
it back into the cupboard last night. And now it isn't
there.

BISHOP: If it is the silver basket you are looking for, it is
over there on the chair.

MME. MAGLOIRE (*Going to it, relieved*): Heaven be praised!

I didn't know what had become of—but—but there is nothing in it! Where is the silver?

BISHOP: Ah, it is the silver, then, that troubles you. I do not know where that is.

MME. MAGLOIRE (*Shrieks*): Good heavens, it is stolen! That man who came last night must have stolen it!

BISHOP (*Protesting*): Now, Madame Magloire . . .

MME. MAGLOIRE (*Angrily*): We'll see soon enough if I am right. (*She dashes off to investigate the bedrooms.*)

BISHOP (*Looking after her, a slight frown on his face*): Let us hope you are wrong. (*More softly*) But, of course, if you are right, it would explain how the silver basket came to be lying in the garden. And how the window came to be open. (MME. MAGLOIRE *returns.*)

MME. MAGLOIRE: It is just as I suspected, Monseigneur. The man has gone and the silver is stolen. (*She runs to the window.*) See, here is how he got out—through the window, so he would not be seen. I warned you to mend that hole in the garden wall where anyone might enter, but you would never listen. Now this is the price we have to pay for your foolishness. That abominable fellow has gone, and stolen our silver!

BISHOP (*Mildly*): You must calm yourself, Madame Magloire. In the first place, did this silver belong to us? Consider. I have for a long time wrongfully withheld this silver. It belonged to the poor. Who was this man? A poor man, evidently.

MME. MAGLOIRE: Alas, it is not for my sake that I am so upset. It's all the same to me. But it is on your account, Monseigneur. What are you going to eat from now?

BISHOP (*Surprised*): How so? Have we not tin plates?

MME. MAGLOIRE: But tin smells.

BISHOP: Well, then, we can eat from iron plates, I suppose.

MME. MAGLOIRE: Iron tastes bad.

BISHOP: Wooden plates, then. It is all one to me.

MME. MAGLOIRE (*Horrified*): Was there ever such an idea? The Bishop decides to eat from wooden plates! Monseigneur, it is not proper. Oh, when I think of it! To take a man in like that, and to give him food and a bed. And then to have the silver stolen from us in the night. But, I must say it's a mercy he did nothing but steal. We might have been murdered in our beds. Oh, I tried to warn you, Monseigneur. Mademoiselle Fleury and I, we both tried to warn you.

BISHOP (*Beginning to lose his temper*): Really, Madame Magloire, you begin to put me out of patience. The next thing I know you will have yourself convinced that the poor man did indeed kill us, and that masses ought to be sung for the repose of our souls.

MME. MAGLOIRE (*Offended*): You may treat the matter lightly if you like, Monseigneur. But as for me—the very thought of it makes chills run all over me. We could have been killed!

BISHOP: For the last time, may I remind you that we were *not* killed? (*There is a knock at the door.*) Come in, come in. (3 GENDARMES *enter, dragging* VALJEAN *along with them. The* 1ST GENDARME *carries the sack of silver. The* 2ND GENDARME *holds a rope tied around* VALJEAN'S *wrists behind his back.* VALJEAN *hangs his head; he has become, once again, abject as earlier.*)

MME. MAGLOIRE (*In amazement*): It's he! They've taken him prisoner!

1ST GENDARME: Excuse us for bothering you, Monseigneur . . .

VALJEAN (*Looking up, surprised*): Monseigneur? Then you are not the curé?

2ND GENDARME (*Roughly, to* VALJEAN): Silence! It is Monseigneur, the Bishop.

BISHOP (*To* VALJEAN, *jovially*): Good morning, Monsieur Valjean. I am glad to see you again. Forgive me for not having been awake when you left this morning.

MME. MAGLOIRE: Monseigneur, what do you—?

3RD GENDARME: Then you know this man, Monseigneur?

BISHOP (*Smoothly*): Of course I know him.

MME. MAGLOIRE (*Angrily*): Monseigneur . . .

BISHOP (*Interrupting*): But tell me, Monsieur Valjean, why did you not take the candlesticks as well?

VALJEAN (*Confused*): The—the candlesticks?

BISHOP: Don't you remember?

VALJEAN (*In a daze*): Remember? No, nothing.

BISHOP: When I gave you the silver, I also gave you the candlesticks. They are silver, too. They would bring a good price—at least two hundred francs, if not more. Why did you not take them along with your plates? Fetch the candlesticks, Madame Magloire.

MME. MAGLOIRE (*Angrily doing as he tells her*): Don't tell me there is any silver left in the house!

BISHOP (*Calmly*): They are on the mantelpiece, Madame Magloire, where they are always kept.

1ST GENDARME: Then what this man said was true, Monseigneur? We met him in the square. He seemed to be running away, so we arrested him to ask him a few questions. We found this—his sack full of silver.

BISHOP (*Interrupting with a smile*): And he told you that it had been given to him by a good old priest with whom he had passed the night. I see it all.

2ND GENDARME: That is *exactly* what he told us.

BISHOP: So you brought him back here to see if he was telling the truth . . . or, more precisely, because you were sure he was *not* telling the truth. It is all a mistake.

1ST GENDARME: Our apologies. If that is so, we can let him go.

MME. MAGLOIRE (*Furious*): You're going to let them—?

BISHOP (*Ignoring her*): By all means, let him go. The poor man is innocent of any wrongdoing.

1ST GENDARME (*Abruptly to the other* GENDARMES): Untie him. We have made a mistake.

VALJEAN: Is it . . . is it true that they are letting me go?

2ND GENDARME (*Rudely*): Did you not hear the Bishop? You are free.

VALJEAN (*Muttering to himself, as he is being untied*): Free . . . free.

BISHOP (*To the* GENDARMES): Gentlemen, I thank you for your trouble.

3RD GENDARME: Our apologies, Monseigneur. We did not know this man was your friend. We were only doing our duty.

BISHOP: Of course, of course. I understand. Good morning to you.

2ND GENDARME: Thank you, Monseigneur. Sorry to have made a mistake. Good morning. (*The* GENDARMES *exit, looking puzzled. When the door is closed, the* BISHOP *turns to* MME. MAGLOIRE *with a slightly ironic smile.*)

BISHOP: And you were complaining, Madame Magloire, about the inadequacy of the police in this town.

VALJEAN (*Unable to believe what has happened*): And I —I am really free to go?

BISHOP: Of course, my friend. But before you go, here are your candlesticks. Take them.

VALJEAN (*Trembling as he takes them*): Why? Why do you do this for me?

BISHOP: I have told you. You are my brother. By the way, my friend, when you come again, you need not come through the garden. You can always come in and go out by the front door. It is closed only with a latch, day and night.

VALJEAN (*Confused*): You—you would let me return? After all that has happened? I must be dreaming. Everything is spinning around in my head. I am so confused.

BISHOP: Go in peace, my friend. But never forget that you have promised me to use this silver to become an honest man.

VALJEAN: But I—I do not remember. I do not recollect your giving me the silver, or my giving you a promise. I remember . . .

BISHOP (*Urgently*): Forget what you remember! Your memories of the past are all a dream now. I give you the silver freely. And I want your solemn promise that you will use it to become an honest man. Promise me that you will start a new way of life. A new life!

VALJEAN (*Considering*): An honest man. (*Happily*) Yes, yes. I *will* start a new life. I promise!

BISHOP: Jean Valjean . . . my brother. You no longer belong to evil, but to good. It is your soul that I am buying for you. I withdraw it from dark thoughts and from the spirit of perdition forever, and I give it to God. (VALJEAN *kneels at the* BISHOP'S *feet. The* BISHOP *places his hand on* VALJEAN'S *head and looks upwards.* MME. MAGLOIRE *looks on, touched and thoughtful, as the curtain falls.*)

THE END

Production Notes

The Bishop's Candlesticks

Characters: 6 male; 2 female.

Playing Time: 25 minutes.

Costumes: The Bishop wears dark-colored clerical garments. The Gendarmes wear uniforms. Madame Magloire and Mademoiselle Fleury wear full, long nineteenth-century peasant costumes. Jean Valjean wears ragged, worn clothing.

Properties: Gavel, teacups, basket, silverware, plates, yellow passport, silver candlesticks, cloth sack, rope.

Setting: The front room of the Bishop's home. A door at one side leads outside; a door at the other side leads to the other parts of the house. There is a window upstage center. A large dining table and chairs are at center; there are also a mantelpiece and a cupboard in which silver and plates are kept.

Lighting: Spotlight on Jean Valjean during prologue; the lights are dim at the opening of Scene 2, then black out and rise again.

Sound: Knock at the door, clock chiming.

Wuthering Heights

by Emily Brontë

Characters

CATHERINE EARNSHAW
HINDLEY EARNSHAW, *her brother*
ELLEN DEAN, *the housekeeper*
HEATHCLIFF
EDGAR LINTON

SCENE 1

BEFORE RISE: *The sound of wind over a loudspeaker rises to an intense pitch, then subsides somewhat. Over the wind is heard the wailing, plaintive voice of* CATHY *calling eerily,* "Heathcliff! Heathcliff!"

*   *   *

TIME: *Late eighteenth century.*

SETTING: *The great kitchen at Wuthering Heights, a large manor on the English moors.*

AT RISE: *The sound of thunder and rain is heard off right, at opening and throughout the scene.* ELLEN DEAN, *the elderly housekeeper, moves busily about the room, preparing things on a great tea tray.* CATHY, *about eighteen, beautiful and finely dressed, tries to remain out of the way but is too nervous.*

CATHY (*Anxiously*): You won't forget the jam will you, Nelly? You must be sure not to forget the jam.

ELLEN: How is it likely that I'd forget it, Miss Catherine, with you reminding me of it every five minutes?

CATHY: It's just that Edgar—Mr. Linton, that is—is so very fond of your blackberry jam. I'm sure he wouldn't think it was a proper tea if you didn't serve it.

ELLEN: It seems to me that you're taking a particular interest in pleasing Mr. Linton.

CATHY (*Flustered*): I—nonsense, Nelly. Whatever are you hinting at?

ELLEN (*Blandly*): I wasn't hinting at anything, miss.

CATHY (*Petulantly*): Yes, you were so hinting, Ellen Dean. Just because I ask you to be sure to serve blackberry jam . . .

ELLEN (*Pointedly*): Just because you ask me to be sure to serve blackberry jam *seven times.*

CATHY (*Sharply*): Don't be impertinent, Nelly. I *am* mistress in this house, am I not?

ELLEN (*Coldly*): I beg your pardon, miss, I am sure.

CATHY (*Flying to her, remorsefully*): Oh, Nelly, Nelly, I'm sorry I spoke so. I didn't mean it, Nelly darling. Say you forgive me. Oh, you *do* forgive me, don't you? Look, Nelly, it's your Cathy asking you to forgive her.

ELLEN: Well. . . .

CATHY: Oh, *please,* Nelly darling. You must forgive me! My tongue ran away with me. I'm *so* nervous today.

ELLEN (*Smiling*): Very well, Miss Cathy. I forgive you.

CATHY: Oh, bless you. And I promise I won't say another word of criticism, but just sit here as quiet as a mouse while you get the tea things ready.

ELLEN (*Plunking jam down on the tray*): Very well. Now *there's* your blessed jam.

CATHY: Oh, you *are* an angel, Nelly.

ELLEN: But see that your precious Mr. Edgar Linton doesn't eat it all. I want to give some to Heathcliff with his supper. *Heathcliff* likes my jam *too,* you know.

CATHY (*Anxiously*): Heathcliff won't be here, will he? Oh, what if he *is* here? Nelly, you must be sure not to let Heathcliff into the drawing room while Mr. Linton is here—not for anything in the world.

ELLEN (*Reprovingly*): Miss Cathy! How can you say such things? Why, Heathcliff is the dearest friend you have in the world.

CATHY (*Impatiently*): Oh, I know that. But surely you can understand. Heathcliff's so—so wild—so untamed. And Mr. Linton is such a gentleman. They don't get on together, you know they don't. And I want everything this afternoon to be perfect—just as Edgar likes it to be. (*Wheedling*) Promise you won't let Heathcliff into the drawing room this afternoon, Nelly.

ELLEN (*Shocked*): But this is Heathcliff's home!

CATHY (*Angrily*): It's *not* his home, Ellen Dean, and you're not to say it is.

ELLEN: Cathy!

CATHY: Wuthering Heights is *not* Heathcliff's home. He was not born here and he does not belong here. If he lives here, that's quite a different matter. But he's a gypsy, a foundling—no better than a servant.

ELLEN: Miss Catherine, your father loved Heathcliff as though he were his own son—ever since he found the boy as a very young child and brought him here to Wuthering Heights.

CATHY: My father may have found Heathcliff, as you say, and brought him here, and loved him. But my father is dead. My brother Hindley is master here now. Hindley hates Heathcliff; he's always hated him. And I—

ELLEN (*Interrupting hotly*): You wouldn't dare to say it,

Miss Catherine. You wouldn't dare to say that *you* hate Heathcliff, too.

CATHY (*Weakening*): Perhaps I don't *hate* him. But we belong to different worlds now, Heathcliff and I. Surely you see that, Nelly. Oh, it was different before, I know. We were *children*. Naturally we clung to each other— particularly when Hindley was so brutal, and hated us both. But we are not children any more, Nelly.

ELLEN (*Softly*): I know.

CATHY: Heathcliff is a servant, and I am a lady. We can no longer be—what we once were to one another. You must see that, Nelly. (*Almost to herself*) And Heathcliff must be made to see it, too.

ELLEN (*Seriously*): But Heathcliff loves you, Miss Catherine.

CATHY (*Impertinently*): He has no business to do so. I have never invited him to love me.

ELLEN (*Sadly*): Perhaps you know best, miss. But when I think of all those happy times, with the two of you running along the moors, laughing with each other as the wind streamed through your hair, or sharing your secrets with each other . . .

CATHY (*Pained*): Stop it, Nelly. You've no right to remind me of those times.

ELLEN: But they are part of the truth about Heathcliff, too, miss.

CATHY (*Softly*): Yes. His tenderness with me—his affection. They are part of the truth.

ELLEN (*Gently*): And your affection for him—?

CATHY (*Slowly*): That is part of the truth, too. My affection for him.

ELLEN: You are so close to each other, you and Heathcliff.

CATHY (*Becoming hard again*): We *were* close—once. We are so no longer.

ELLEN (*Shaking her head*): It's hard to think that that closeness between you is gone.

CATHY (*Proudly*): It's not hard to think of at all. That was silly childishness. We have grown apart, Heathcliff and I. And now he means no more to me than that! (*Snaps her fingers.* HINDLEY *enters from left, a crude, loutish young man of about twenty.*)

HINDLEY: Have you nothing better to do, Ellen Dean, than stand and gossip with your mistress? There's work to be done.

ELLEN (*Subdued, curtsying*): I'm sorry, Mr. Hindley. It will not happen again. (*She busies herself with the tea things.*)

HINDLEY: See that it doesn't. I've no appetite for providing you with a home unless you earn your keep. And, Catherine, mind that you don't give her an excuse for not working. There's no need for you to be in the kitchen.

CATHY (*Obviously afraid of him*): I—I'm sorry, Hindley. I just wanted to remind Nelly—to remind Mrs. Dean that she was to serve jam with the tea.

HINDLEY: Does she need reminding, then, after all these years as housekeeper at Wuthering Heights? No, I suspect that I know the real reason you're here, my girl. Looking for that precious Heathcliff of yours, I'll warrant.

CATHY (*Flushed, but with dignity*): I have no concern with Heathcliff, brother. You have ordered me to have nothing to do with him, and I have obeyed your wishes.

HINDLEY: I'm glad to hear it. Not that I'll have much longer to worry about the two of you.

CATHY (*Involuntarily*): Hindley! What do you mean?

HINDLEY: I've just been talking with that (*Sneering*)

sweet young gentleman of yours—Mr. Linton of Thrushcross Grange.

CATHY (*Excitedly*): Edgar? Is he already here?

HINDLEY: He is. The young man's taken with you, Catherine, there's no doubt of it. You play your cards right, and the Linton fortune will leap into your lap, just see if it doesn't. (*Thunder sounds far off right.*)

CATHY: And have you left him alone in the drawing room? Oh, I must go to him. We must entertain him!

HINDLEY (*Laughing*): Look at her, Ellen Dean. How the blood comes to my sister's pretty young cheeks, just at the thought of Edgar Linton's fortune.

CATHY: Hindley!

ELLEN (*Quietly*): I am sure you do your sister an injustice, sir.

HINDLEY (*Laughing, to* CATHY): You'd best compose yourself, my girl. You wouldn't want that poor fool to see you in this state. I'll go and amuse him for a few minutes. But see that you're along quickly.

CATHY: Thank you, Hindley, I will. (*Just as he is leaving*) And, Hindley . . .

HINDLEY (*Turning in the doorway*): Eh?

CATHY: Don't—don't say anything to Edgar that would —that would—

HINDLEY: That would upset your chances of capturing him? Never fear, sweet sister. I'm much too anxious to see you married to the man for that. (*He goes out left.*)

CATHY (*Running to the mirror, anxiously*): Oh Nelly, do I look all right? Is my hair neat? I wonder—should I have a sprig of heather?

ELLEN: You look beautiful, Miss Catherine. You'll capture the man, sure enough, as your brother suggests.

CATHY (*Horrified*): But surely you don't think as Hindley does—that it's the *money*, Nelly!

ELLEN (*In an odd tone*): I? I think nothing, Miss Catherine. (HEATHCLIFF *enters from right, carrying a large armload of wood. About nineteen, he is vigorous and darkly handsome—and there is a touch of mystery about him. He does not see* CATHY, *but goes to* ELLEN.)

HEATHCLIFF: I've fetched you enough wood for a winter, Nelly. And just in time, too. Ten minutes more and the storm would have caught me.

ELLEN: Thank you, Heathcliff.

HEATHCLIFF: It's a bad rain that's headed this way. (*Seeing* CATHY) Cathy, I didn't see you.

CATHY (*Coolly, turning to the door*): I am just leaving, Heathcliff.

HEATHCLIFF (*Putting the wood on the settle*): You can't run off like that, Cathy, without a word. It's been so long since I've seen you.

CATHY (*Evasively*): I know. Hindley . . .

HEATHCLIFF (*Laughing*): Come, come, Cathy. When were we ever frightened of Hindley before?

CATHY: Please, Heathcliff, I must go.

HEATHCLIFF: But you can't be busy this afternoon—can she, Nelly? You're not going out, are you? You didn't order a carriage.

CATHY (*Evasively*): No, I—of course I'm not going out. It's raining.

HEATHCLIFF: Then why have you that silk frock on? Nobody coming here, I hope.

CATHY (*Changing the subject*): You must put the firewood away, Heathcliff. Nelly, tell him he must. (*Thunder sounds far off right.*)

HEATHCLIFF: Don't ask me to do it, Nelly. Hindley doesn't often free us from his accursed presence. I'll not work any more today, Cathy, but stay with you.

CATHY (*Helplessly*): Nelly . . .

ELLEN (*Gently, to* HEATHCLIFF): Guests are expected, Heathcliff. Mr. Linton is calling on Catherine.

HEATHCLIFF (*Scornfully*): So you'd turn me out for that pitiful, silly friend of yours, eh, Cathy? I suppose he's a fine gentleman, and I'm no longer good enough for you.

CATHY (*Indignantly*): Edgar Linton is not silly—though you are right about his being a gentleman.

HEATHCLIFF (*Desperately*): But it's raining, Cathy. Surely he won't come in this storm.

CATHY: He—he's already here. And that's quite enough about it, Heathcliff. Leave me alone!

HEATHCLIFF (*Angrily*): So he's here, is he? Then go to him! Go at once! Fly! I shouldn't dream of holding you from your pleasure, my lady.

CATHY (*Hotly*): I am going. And you needn't think it does not give me great satisfaction to do so. (*Turns in the doorway*) Mrs. Dean, you will bring the tea when I ring for you.

ELLEN (*Taken aback, coldly*): Indeed, miss. (*Curtsies*) When did I ever not do so? (CATHY *goes out left and slams the door. Both stare after her. There is a pause.* HEATHCLIFF *goes silently to the settle and begins to move the wood.*) You say nothing, Heathcliff?

HEATHCLIFF (*Tensely*): What would you have me say, Nelly? You see how she treats me. What has *happened* to her? Why has she changed? She was never this way before.

ELLEN (*Shaking her head*): But time passes, Heathcliff, and you have both changed.

HEATHCLIFF: It is she who has changed. Not I! She cares nothing for me—while I care everything for her.

ELLEN: I would not say that she cares nothing. Do you remember the other day when Hindley struck you with his riding crop?

HEATHCLIFF: It is not likely I could forget it.

ELLEN: She cried for you, Heathcliff. She tried not to let me see, but I did see. She cried for you.

HEATHCLIFF: *I* have cried for *her,* Nelly, if it comes to that. And I have had more reason to cry than she. (*The storm grows louder for a moment, then subsides.*)

ELLEN (*Sighing*): Yes, you had the reason of pride.

HEATHCLIFF (*After a pause*): Hark to the wind. How it whistles! And the drumming of the rain.

ELLEN: It will be the worst storm of the season, if I know the signs.

HEATHCLIFF (*Contemptuously*): I do wonder that our little Mr. Linton dared to brave the weather and come to the Heights.

ELLEN: You dislike him so much, Heathcliff?

HEATHCLIFF: I do—and yet, to tell the truth, I envy him.

ELLEN (*Laughing*): What? Envy Edgar Linton—you? I *am* surprised. Why, you're taller than he, and younger —and twice as broad across the shoulders. You could knock him down in a twinkling if you liked.

HEATHCLIFF: But if I knocked him down twenty times, that wouldn't make him less handsome or me more so.

ELLEN: A good heart will help you to a bonny face, my lad. Indeed, *I* think you very handsome, in a certain way. Who knows but your father was Emperor of China, and able to buy up, with one week's income, Wuthering Heights and Thrushcross Grange together! Were I in your place, I would frame high notions of my birth, and the thoughts of what I was should give me courage and dignity to support the oppressions of our little gentleman.

HEATHCLIFF: I wonder that they have not rung for tea to be served to "our little gentleman."

ELLEN: Perhaps they are so engrossed in their talk they don't notice.

HEATHCLIFF (*Contemptuously*): Talk! It's *thoughts* that engross one—thoughts. (*Storm sounds swell and subside.*)

ELLEN (*Idly*): And what thoughts engross you?

HEATHCLIFF: I daresay you will be shocked to know. I'm always trying to settle how I shall pay them back—Hindley and Edgar—for robbing me of Cathy's love. I don't care how long I wait, if I can only do it at last.

ELLEN: For shame, Heathcliff. It is for God to punish wicked people.

HEATHCLIFF: No, God won't have the satisfaction that I shall. I only wish I knew the best way! But I shall plan it out. And it's a strange thing, but while I'm thinking of that, I feel no pain from anything. (HINDLEY *enters from left.*)

HINDLEY: Mrs. Dean.

ELLEN: Shall I bring in the tea now?

HINDLEY: We shall need no tea. The young man's flown.

ELLEN: I do not take your meaning, sir. How—flown?

HINDLEY (*Laughing*): Just left in his carriage. I saw from the upstairs window. Thought he'd be drowned if he waited another moment, I'll wager. No doubt my good sister will be down to tell you all about it, foolish child!

HEATHCLIFF (*Sternly*): Do you speak of Miss Catherine in that tone, sir?

HINDLEY (*Aggressively*): And if I do? Do not forget for a moment, Heathcliff, that I am master here.

HEATHCLIFF (*Firmly*): I forget nothing.

HINDLEY (*Backing down a bit*): You have forgotten your

chores, at least. You were told to fill the woodbox. It is yet half empty.

ELLEN (*Protesting*): But Mr. Hindley, in such rain—

HEATHCLIFF (*Calmly staring at* HINDLEY): Never mind, Nelly. I am not afraid of a bit of water, as some are. And the air is fresher in the stables than here. (*He stares at* HINDLEY *a moment longer, then casually turns and strides out right.*)

HINDLEY (*Raging*): Insolent puppy! Mrs. Dean!

ELLEN: Sir?

HINDLEY: I shall have my dinner in my room tonight. Alone.

ELLEN (*Curtsying, as he goes out left*): Very good, sir. (*Left alone, she shakes her head and begins putting cups away. To herself*) I know not which is worse—the storm outside or the one beneath the roof of Wuthering Heights! (*Seeing the jar of jam on the tray*) And there —after all the talk, the blackberry jam never tasted! (CATHY *enters from left, almost timidly.*)

CATHY: Nelly? Are you alone?

ELLEN: Yes, miss.

CATHY: Where's Heathcliff?

ELLEN: About his work in the stable, I suppose.

CATHY: Oh Nelly, I am very unhappy.

ELLEN (*Dryly*): A pity. You're hard to please; so many friends, and so few cares, and yet you can't make yourself content.

CATHY: Will you keep a secret for me?

ELLEN: Is it worth keeping?

CATHY: Yes, and it worries me. I want to know what I should do. Edgar Linton has just asked me to marry him, and I've given him an answer.

ELLEN (*Taken aback*): You haven't, Miss Catherine!

CATHY: Before I tell you whether it was a consent or a refusal, you tell me which it ought to have been.

ELLEN: Really, miss, how can I know?

CATHY: I accepted him, Nelly. Be quick, and say whether I was wrong.

ELLEN: You have accepted him. What good is it discussing the matter? You have pledged your word, and cannot retract it. (*The door, right, opens, and* HEATHCLIFF *enters, thoroughly drenched, and carrying another arm-load of wood. The others do not see him, and when he sees* CATHY *he tiptoes behind the settle, out of sight of* CATHY *and* ELLEN.)

CATHY: But say whether I should have done so, do!

ELLEN: There are many things to be considered. First and foremost, do you love Mr. Edgar?

CATHY: Of course I do.

ELLEN: Why do you love him?

CATHY: Well—because he is handsome, and pleasant, and rich.

ELLEN: Poor enough reasons. Do you love Mr. Heathcliff?

CATHY (*Starting*): Heathcliff?

ELLEN: Be honest, Miss Catherine. Do you love Mr. Heathcliff?

CATHY: I—I'm not sure. Sometimes I think I do. Sometimes I think I love him more than life itself. I have only to look into Heathcliff's eyes, and I know his every thought. Such black eyes! They burn into the very core of my being. Sometimes I think he'll end by driving me mad.

ELLEN: I should say you loved Heathcliff more than you will ever love Mr. Linton.

CATHY: Perhaps you're right. In my deepest heart, I feel I have no more business to marry Edgar Linton than

I have to be in heaven. But don't you see, Nelly? It would degrade me to marry Heathcliff; so I mean never to let him know how much I love him. Oh, Nelly, he's more myself than I am. Whatever our souls are made of, his and mine, they are the same; and Edgar's is as different as a moonbeam from lightning, or frost from fire. But Edgar Linton is the man I will marry, because Heathcliff is so low. He's a gypsy—a stranger. I—I'm almost afraid of him. And what we fear, they say we come to hate. Deeply as I love Heathcliff, I think that with a part of me, I shall always hate him, too. Yes, yes, I'm sure of it, Nelly. I love Heathcliff—but even more, I hate him. (*Behind the settle,* HEATHCLIFF *drops the pile of wood and darts swiftly out right.* CATHY *jumps up, terrified*) What was that?

ELLEN (*Looking about*): Perhaps a shutter banging in the wind.

CATHY (*Runs to the window*): The shutters are fast. Oh—Nelly!

ELLEN (*Frightened*): What is it?

CATHY: Someone is running down the road. Someone was listening!

ELLEN: Who is it, miss? Not—not Heathcliff?

CATHY (*In agony*): Oh, Nelly, it is! It *is* Heathcliff! He must have been listening all the while. I must stop him!

ELLEN (*Holding her fast*): You are mad, Miss Catherine! Think of the storm!

CATHY (*Trying to pull free*): But he heard, Nelly, he heard. I must stop him. I must explain. Heathcliff! (*She breaks free and runs to the door, and struggles to open it.*) Heathcliff! Stop! (*She pulls the door open, tenses a moment against the wind, then darts out.*) Heathcliff!

ELLEN (*Standing in the doorway, calling out, horrified*): Miss Catherine! Come back! The storm!

CATHY (*From off right, her voice growing fainter as the wind and rain become stronger*): Heathcliff! Heathcliff! (*Curtain*)

*   *   *

SCENE 2

BEFORE RISE: *The same sounds are heard over the loudspeaker as before: the raging wind and rain, and* CATHY's *plaintive cry: "Heathcliff!"*
TIME: *Three years later.*
SETTING: *The same.*
AT RISE: *The room is much more brightly lighted than before.* EDGAR LINTON, *an aristocratic, slight man in his mid-twenties, finely dressed, is pacing up and down before the fire in an agitated manner.* ELLEN, *little changed, is trying to comfort him.*

EDGAR: It is madness, Mrs. Dean, sheer madness.
ELLEN (*Consolingly*): Come, come, Mr. Linton, surely you exaggerate. Can it be such a terrible thing for Miss Catherine—I mean to say, Mrs. Linton—to wish to come back here to visit Wuthering Heights, after so long an absence? After all, she has been away for three years. Surely it is a natural wish.
EDGAR: The doctors have ordered that she have complete rest—that nothing be allowed to upset or excite her. It is only a month since Catherine has been allowed to leave her bed. Undertaking the journey from Thrushcross Grange to the Heights has been too much of a strain on her.
ELLEN: But it's such a little distance, sir. And she seemed so well when she walked in the door—her cheeks were so rosy . . .

EDGAR: That is what alarms me. Ever since her illness, Catherine has been pale. The heightened color you observed in her cheeks is from excitement, not from health.

ELLEN: Perhaps it would have agitated her even more to be denied this visit.

EDGAR: Yes, yes, I know. That alone is the reason I consented.

ELLEN: And she seemed so happy to see the house once more. Why, she has not been here since the day you and she were married.

EDGAR (*In a changed tone*): But does it not seem odd to you, Mrs. Dean, that Catherine should wish to come back to a home where she had been so unhappy as a girl?

ELLEN (*Thoughtfully*): It is true that Catherine endured many unhappy hours here. But there were happy times, too, Mr. Linton. Do not forget that it was in this house that you proposed to her.

EDGAR (*Smiling*): It is good of you to mention that, Mrs. Dean. How well I remember that night. Such an awful storm as there was that night.

ELLEN: It was the worst in several years. Storms blow up often in these parts, but that was the worst of them.

EDGAR: That was the night the gypsy boy disappeared, was it not? What was his name—Heathcliff?

ELLEN (*Softly*): Yes. Heathcliff.

EDGAR: He was never heard of again, I believe. Odd—his disappearing like that, I mean, with no reason.

ELLEN: I would not say there was no reason.

EDGAR: But it *was* a mystery of sorts, wasn't it? I remember, Catherine used to speak of him quite often during the first few months of our marriage. Always in a strange, wistful way. But when our little girl was born, she never mentioned him again. (*Shrugging*) She must have forgotten all about him. (*Far off right, a roll of thunder is heard.*)

ELLEN (*Pointedly*): There is little that Miss Catherine forgets, Mr. Linton.

EDGAR: She seems to have forgotten her old hatred for her brother Hindley. When I left them together in the drawing room just now, Catherine was behaving as though there had never been so much as a cross word between them.

ELLEN: Miss Catherine always had strange ways of showing her feelings.

EDGAR: Whatever do you mean by that remark, Mrs. Dean?

ELLEN: No offense, I'm sure, sir.

EDGAR: And I take none. But explain yourself.

ELLEN: I should say that if Miss Cathy is civil with her brother, it is because she no longer fears him. But if I know her, she hates him still—more, perhaps, than ever. It is those of whom she does not speak at all that she esteems most highly.

EDGAR: Catherine does indeed behave in a contrary manner at times. One never can be sure what she is thinking. It is as though her mind were miles and miles away. Sometimes I fear for her sanity. It is not her bodily health alone that has been shattered, I fear.

ELLEN (*With genuine concern*): I hope that you exaggerate, sir.

EDGAR (*Thoughtfully*): I am not sure. (*He sighs, shakes his head, then looks suddenly left.*) But, hush—I think she is coming.

CATHY (*Off left*): And now, Hindley, I must visit the kitchen. (*CATHY enters from left, followed by HINDLEY. He is little changed, but she has altered greatly; she is paler, more fragile.*)

HINDLEY: I tried to make her rest, Linton, but she will have none of it. (*Thunder, off right.*)

EDGAR (*Going to her*): You must not overexcite yourself, my dear.

CATHY: Nonsense, Edgar, there is nothing wrong with me. And I want to see every room in the house—every room. (*Running to* ELLEN) Oh, Nelly, darling Nelly!

ELLEN (*Embracing her*): Welcome back to Wuthering Heights, Miss Catherine.

CATHY: It's hard for me to realize that I'm really here once again—here in our own snug kitchen. It all seems so long ago. (*Moving about, touching the furniture and objects*) The funny old looking glass—was it always so cracked and discolored, Nelly? And the mantel. How high it used to seem, when I was little. Now I can reach it without standing on my toes. It's all just as I remembered it.

ELLEN: Nothing has changed here, miss, in the past few years.

CATHY: But the settle—the settle has changed! Surely the one we had was not so large, Nelly—no, not by half.

HINDLEY: What's wrong with the girl, I wonder? Of course it's the same settle, Cathy.

CATHY (*With an odd look at* ELLEN, *as she runs her hand along the settle*): But this one is so tall—so broad. Someone might hide behind it, even, and we not know he was there. Someone might be standing behind it now, listening to every word we say.

EDGAR (*A trifle worried*): Come, Cathy, my love, you must sit down. You are becoming feverish, I think. You promised me that you would rest.

HINDLEY: Linton is right, Catherine. You have had enough excitement for one day. Let your husband take you home.

CATHY: But I haven't had a proper visit with Nelly, Edgar. Oh, darling, *do* let me stay a little longer—just to talk to Nelly.

EDGAR: Will you promise to be good, and sit quietly by the fire? I don't want you to tire yourself, my darling. Remember what the doctors have said.

CATHY: Yes, yes, I promise. You and Hindley must go and fetch the carriage. I want to be alone with Nelly for a few minutes.

HINDLEY: Come along, Linton. Ten minutes more will do no harm, I'm sure.

EDGAR (*Moving toward the door*): Very well. But no more than ten minutes, mind. And see that she doesn't exert herself, Mrs. Dean.

ELLEN: I will indeed, sir. (*The men go out at left.*)

CATHY (*After a slight pause, in a low voice*): Oh, Nelly, Nelly, can you guess what it means to me to be here again—here at the Heights?

ELLEN: Of course, Miss Catherine. This was your home.

CATHY (*Sharply*): It's not for that I came. My home! The misery I endured here, the pain, the suffering. For that I would never have set foot in this house again. No, no. I had to come—because he is here.

ELLEN (*Looking at her sharply*): What do you mean, Miss Catherine?

CATHY: He is here. In every corner, on every stair, at every window, I see Heathcliff.

ELLEN: Heathcliff!

CATHY: Oh, Nelly, you cannot guess what torture these past three years have been. There has never been an hour, never a moment, when his face was not before me. The torment of it, the agony! To know he is gone, but not to know where. To know that he ran away, and that he was driven by me. And to know I love him—that I always have, and that I always will.

ELLEN: Don't think such thoughts, miss. The doctors say you must be calm.

CATHY: The doctors! And that is part of it, too. This health of mine that concerns my husband so. I wonder if he would be so solicitous if he knew that what destroyed me was that night on the moors in the storm—that night when I ran wild in the wind and rain, trying to find Heathcliff, trying to bring him back.

ELLEN (*Alarmed at her intensity*): Come and sit down, my dear. You are feverish.

CATHY: The window, Nelly. Open the window. I want to hear the wind again. Such a wind as blows across the moors!

ELLEN: I dare not open it, Miss Catherine. You'd catch your death!

CATHY (*Laughing suddenly*): Hindley thought I did not remember the settle! He believed me, Nelly. But you knew better, didn't you? (*Thunder, off right. At the same moment, there is a loud knocking at the door, right.* CATHY *jumps up.*) There is someone at the door, Nelly.

ELLEN: Yes, Miss Catherine. I'll just see who it is.

CATHY (*Frightened*): No, no. I'm afraid. I don't wish to see anyone.

ELLEN: But, miss, I must open the door.

CATHY: Let me go away first. Wait just a moment, till I go away.

ELLEN: Very well, miss. As you prefer.

CATHY (*Imploringly*): But send him away quickly—whoever it is. I must leave soon, and I want to come back to kiss you goodbye. I may kiss you goodbye, mayn't I, Nelly?

ELLEN (*Gently*): Of course, Miss Catherine. (*There is pounding on the door.*) I'll send whoever it is away just as soon as I can.

CATHY (*Whimpering*): I'm frightened—I'm frightened! (*She runs out at left, casting a fearful look behind her. ELLEN shakes her head, and turns to open the door, right, when it bursts open, and HEATHCLIFF enters. He is finely dressed in a dark suit and riding cloak. ELLEN does not recognize him.*)

ELLEN: What, sir, do you walk into a house without being invited?

HEATHCLIFF (*Smiling*): Is it my old nurse, Nelly Dean?

ELLEN (*Taken aback*): No! Can it be Heathcliff?

HEATHCLIFF: Have I altered so much that you know me not?

ELLEN: Why, sir! You are a gentleman. Your clothes—your manner—I should not have known you.

HEATHCLIFF: Oh, yes, I have come up in the world since I left Wuthering Heights. I left this house a gypsy beggar, and I come back a wealthy gentleman. Who would have dreamed that night . . .

ELLEN (*Interrupting quickly*): Oh, let us not speak of that night!

HEATHCLIFF (*Ironically*): To think that I owe all this to her. (*He indicates his finery.*) She led me to wealth, did Cathy—but she led me to misery, too.

ELLEN: I must pinch myself to believe that you are not a ghost. Is it really you come back, Heathcliff?

HEATHCLIFF: It is really I. You are not glad to see me, Nelly?

ELLEN (*Anxiously*): Oh, for myself, gladder than I can say. I have missed you, Heathcliff, and worried for you. But Miss Catherine . . .

HEATHCLIFF (*Eagerly*): Miss Catherine—yes, yes, go on.

ELLEN (*Intensely*): No, you must not see her. It would be too cruel.

HEATHCLIFF: She has been cruel enough to me in my time, has she not, Nelly? And it is to see her that I have come. They told me at Thrushcross Grange that she is here. Will you go and fetch her?

ELLEN: Do not ask it of me. I dare not. I could not answer for the consequences.

HEATHCLIFF (*Determinedly*): If you will not bring her to me, then I must find her for myself. (*He starts toward the door, left, when it opens, and* CATHY *enters.*)

CATHY: Has the person gone, Nelly? May I come— (*She stops when she sees* HEATHCLIFF. *They stand quite still, staring at each other.*)

ELLEN (*Crying*): What madness this is! Mr. Linton! Mr. Hindley! (*She runs off left in alarm.*)

CATHY (*Quietly*): Is it really you, Heathcliff? (*Thunder off right.*)

HEATHCLIFF (*Rushing to her and embracing her*): Oh, Cathy! Oh, my life! How can I bear it?

CATHY (*Pushing him away gently*): Are these tears on your cheek, Heathcliff? What now? You have broken my heart. And yet you bewail the deed, as if you were to be pitied. I shall not pity you—not I!

HEATHCLIFF (*Holding her by the arms*): You were never one to pity, Catherine.

CATHY: How strong you are! How many years do you mean to live after I am gone?

HEATHCLIFF: Do not speak, Cathy. Only let me hold you.

CATHY: I wish I could hold *you*—hold you till we were both dead. I shouldn't care for your suffering. I care nothing for your suffering. (*Pushes him firmly away, and paces*) Why shouldn't you suffer? I do. Will you forget me, Heathcliff? Will you say, twenty years hence,

"That's the grave of Catherine Earnshaw Linton. I loved her, long ago, and was wretched to lose her; but it is past." Will you say so?

HEATHCLIFF: Don't torture me till I'm as mad as yourself.

CATHY: No, no—*you* could never suffer as *I* do.

HEATHCLIFF (*Dryly*): You speak of suffering, after what you did to me? Cathy, you drove me away—!

CATHY (*Simply*): Yes. I drove you away.

HEATHCLIFF: You admit, then, that you caused me this grief, this pain, this aching loneliness? Did you love me so little, Cathy?

CATHY (*Proudly*): I loved you so much.

HEATHCLIFF: You loved me! I fear you are mad indeed.

CATHY: You doubt it? That I loved you? That I love you still? Heathcliff, Heathcliff, don't you understand that we would have destroyed each other, you and I? Torn each other to bits? Yes, I loved you then. Why else would I have torn the very heart from my bosom, if not to save you? Look at what you have become for leaving me—a gentleman! And *this* is your thanks, your understanding? I am dying, Heathcliff—and you have broken my heart!

HEATHCLIFF: No, I have not broken your heart. You have broken it. And in so doing, you have broken mine. So much the worse for me, that I am strong. Do you think I want to live? What kind of living will it be when you are in the grave?

CATHY (*Sobbing*): Let me alone! If I've done wrong, I'm dying for it. It is enough. Forgive me!

HEATHCLIFF: It is hard to look at those eyes and not forgive. I forgive what you have done to me.

CATHY (*In anguish*): Oh, why on earth did you ever return?

HEATHCLIFF: I had to come back. I had to see you once more. But now I must go.

CATHY: Don't go, Heathcliff, don't go. I shall die!

HEATHCLIFF: I must go, Cathy. But from this hour, I know that our souls are forever intertwined. From this day, we are never apart. Do what you will with me. Torture me, torment me. I will stand agony forever, but I will be alone no more!

CATHY (*Stretching out a hand to him*): Heathcliff! (*He turns swiftly and goes out right.* CATHY *stands transfixed, her hand outstretched. After a pause, in an altered voice*) Heathcliff? Heathcliff? (*Pause*) Let us go out on the moors. (*She walks slowly to the door and opens it, then opens the window.*) Is my hair neat, Nelly? Do I look all right? (ELLEN *and* EDGAR *rush in from left.*)

EDGAR: Cathy!

CATHY (*She does not hear him*): I wonder, Nelly—should I have a sprig of heather? (*Thunder off right.*)

ELLEN (*Putting her arm around her, gently*): There, there, miss. Everything is all right now.

CATHY (*Without hearing her or looking at her*): Heathcliff? Heathcliff? (*Pause*) Open the window, Nelly. I want to hear the wind. (*The lights dim quickly; in the darkness are heard, over the loudspeaker, the wind and rain, and* CATHY's *voice calling, "Heathcliff! Heathcliff!" Curtain.*)

THE END

Production Notes

WUTHERING HEIGHTS

Characters: 3 male; 2 female.

Playing Time: 30 minutes.

Costumes: Appropriate dress of the period. Cathy's gown in
Scene 1 is pretty and elaborate. In Scene 2, she wears a coat
and hat. Ellen wears a simple, dark dress and an apron.
Edgar is dressed in an elegant suit of the period, and
Hindley wears riding clothes. Heathcliff wears rough work
clothes in Scene 1, changes to suit and riding cloak for
Scene 2.

Properties: Two armloads of firewood, tea tray with cups,
saucers, etc., pot of jam.

Setting: The great kitchen at Wuthering Heights, a large
manor on the English moors. There is a door, down right,
to the outside, another door left, to the rest of the house,
and a window, right center. A fireplace is up center. The
room is furnished with a high-backed settle, which stands
by fireplace, and a table, chairs, cupboards, etc. A mirror
hangs on the wall to the left of the fireplace.

Lighting: The room is dimly lit for Scene 1, brighter for
Scene 2.

Sound: Thunder, rain, and wind, as indicated in text.

PART TWO

Plays for Reading

Around the World in Eighty Days

by Jules Verne

Characters

THOMAS FLANAGAN	TWO TRAIN CONDUCTORS
ANDREW STUART	PARSEE
GAUTIER RALPH	BRAHMIN
PHILEAS FOGG	PRINCESS AOUDA
PASSEPARTOUT	PILOT
FOUR MEN	BUTLER
DETECTIVE FIX	NARRATOR
CONSUL	

NARRATOR: In 1872, the man who has come to be known as the Father of Science Fiction wrote what many critics consider his best novel. Certainly, it has proved to be his most popular. Oddly enough, this book was not concerned with foreseeing technological achievements of the future, as were his other books, but with proving the possibility of achieving the fantastic at once. The author was, of course, Jules Verne, and the story you are about to hear is taken from his well-loved book, *Around the World in Eighty Days*.

MUSIC: *Gay theme.*

NARRATOR: The story begins with a bank robbery. Fifty-five thousand pounds have been stolen from the Bank of England. The news is on everyone's lips, and in everyone's thoughts. In the drawing room of the Reform Club, four of the members are discussing the outrageous theft over a game of whist.

FLANAGAN: Well, gentlemen, what about that robbery?

STUART: I say the bank will lose the money.

RALPH: Oh, I don't know about that, Stuart. I think we may yet capture the thief. Skillful detectives have been sent to all the principal ports of America and the Continent, and he'll be a clever fellow if he slips through their fingers.

STUART: According to the *Daily Telegraph,* it wasn't a thief at all!

FLANAGAN: What? A fellow who makes off with all that money not a thief?

FOGG (*A cold, but sure voice*): The *Daily Telegraph* says he is a gentleman.

STUART: Right, Fogg! And I maintain that the chances are in favor of his getting away, for he must be a shrewd fellow.

RALPH: But where can he go? No country is safe for him!

FLANAGAN: Oh, I don't know. The world is big enough.

FOGG: It was once. Cut the cards, please.

FLANAGAN: What do you mean by that remark, Fogg? Has the world grown smaller?

FOGG: Certainly it has. A man can now go round it ten times more quickly than he could have a hundred years ago.

STUART: Precisely, Fogg. That is why the search for this thief will be more likely to succeed.

FLANAGAN: And also why the thief can get away more easily!

FOGG: Please be so good as to play your card, Mr. Stuart.

STUART: Just because you can go around the world in three months—

FOGG (*Interrupting calmly*): I beg your pardon. In eighty days.

FLANAGAN: Quite right, Fogg. Quite right! According to this chart here in the newspaper, the trip can be made in exactly eighty days. You see?

STUART: That chart may be all very good. But what may work on paper doesn't always work in actuality. That doesn't take into account bad weather, contrary winds, shipwrecks, railway accidents, and so on.

FOGG: Oh, yes. All are included. Two trumps.

STUART: You are right theoretically, Mr. Fogg. But practically—

FOGG: Practically also, Mr. Stuart.

STUART (*Laughing*): Ha! I'd like to see you do it in eighty days!

FOGG: Gladly.

STUART: No, man, I'm serious! I'll wager four thousand pounds that such a journey, made under this condition, is impossible.

FOGG: Quite possible, on the contrary.

STUART: Well, make it, then!

FOGG: I should like nothing better.

STUART: When, Mr. Phileas Fogg, when?

FOGG: At once. Only I warn you, you shall lose your four thousand!

FLANAGAN: Come, come, you two must be joking! Back to the game!

STUART: When I say I'll wager, I'll wager.

FOGG: All right. I have a deposit of twenty thousand pounds at Baring's, which I will willingly risk upon it.

RALPH: Twenty thousand pounds!

FLANAGAN: Which you might lose, Fogg, by a single accidental delay?

FOGG: The unforeseen does not exist.

RALPH: But Mr. Fogg, eighty days are only the estimate of the least possible time in which the journey can be made.

FOGG: A well-used minimum suffices for everything.

FLANAGAN: You are joking!

FOGG: A true Englishman doesn't joke when he is talking about so serious a thing as a wager. I will bet twenty thousand pounds, against anyone who wishes, that I will make a tour of the world in eighty days or less; in nineteen hundred and twenty hours, or a hundred and fifteen thousand two hundred minutes. Do you accept?

ALL (*In unison, amazed*): Yes, Mr. Fogg, we accept.

FOGG: Good. The train leaves for Dover at a quarter before nine. I will take it.

RALPH (*Incredulously*): This very evening?

FOGG (*Calmly*): This very evening. As today is Wednesday, the second of October, I shall be due in London, in this very room of the Reform Club, on Saturday, the twenty-first of December, at a quarter before nine P.M., or else the twenty thousand pounds will belong to you gentlemen. Here is my check for that amount. I am quite ready now. Diamonds are trump. Be so good as to play, gentlemen.

MUSIC: *Lively theme.*

NARRATOR: With that, Mr. Phileas Fogg, calmly, coolly and precisely closes the wager of twenty thousand pounds, one half his fortune, and resolves to go around the world in eighty days. Having won twenty guineas at whist, and taken leave of his friends, Fogg leaves the Reform Club at twenty-five minutes past seven, goes directly home, and summons his serving man, Jean Passepartout.

FOGG: Passepartout! Passepartout!

PASSEPARTOUT (*A jovial Frenchman*): Yes, Monsieur Fogg?

FOGG: We start for Dover and Calais in ten minutes.

PASSEPARTOUT (*Curiously*): Monsieur is going to leave home?

FOGG: Yes. We are going around the world.

PASSEPARTOUT (*Taken aback*): *Sacre bleu!* A—around the —world?

FOGG (*Calmly, as always*): Yes. In eighty days. But we haven't a moment to lose.

PASSEPARTOUT: But the trunks?

FOGG: We'll have no trunks; only a carpetbag, with two shirts and three pairs of stockings for myself, and the same for you. We'll buy our clothes on the way. Bring down my traveling cloak and some stout shoes. Make haste!

NARRATOR: Within ten minutes Passepartout, still amazed at what his master has said, presents himself once again to Mr. Fogg.

FOGG: You have forgotten nothing?

PASSEPARTOUT: Nothing, monsieur.

FOGG: Good. Take this carpetbag, and take good care of it, for there are twenty thousand pounds in it.

PASSEPARTOUT: Twenty—twenty thou—

FOGG: Twenty thousand pounds, Passepartout. Come along!

MUSIC: *Jaunty theme.*

NARRATOR: Within an hour of their strange departure, the news of Fogg's outlandish wager is splashed all over the London papers. Immediately, thought of the bank robbery drops from people's interest, and everyone is taken up with this strange Phileas Fogg.

FIRST MAN (*High British accent*): Around the world in eighty days! Impossible!

SECOND MAN (*High British accent*): Ridiculous!

THIRD MAN (*High British accent*): Absurd!

FOURTH MAN (*Drawling Cockney accent*): Just plain balmy!

NARRATOR: Wagers are placed. Will Fogg make it? Is it possible? While his name is on all the lips of London, Fogg himself is settled in a railroad car, calmly and unexcitedly reading his newspaper, seeming to be less concerned with his own voyage than is anyone else. The only interest he seems to show in the trip is in keeping a complete daily record of arrivals, departures, times and schedules in a small diary, which is as compact, complete and well-organized as Fogg himself. Suddenly, the confused Passepartout lets out a yelp.

PASSEPARTOUT: *Sacre bleu!*

FOGG: What is the matter, my good man?

PASSEPARTOUT: Alas! In my hurry—I—I—forgot—

FOGG: What?

PASSEPARTOUT: Monsieur—to turn off the gas in my room!

FOGG: Very well, young man. It will burn—at *your* expense! You may reimburse me when we return.

MUSIC: *Delightful theme.*

FOGG: Arrived at Dover—on time. (*Short pause*) Arrived at Calais—on time. (*Pause*) Board the steamer, *Mongolia*—on time. Bound for Suez.

SOUND: *Long blast of a boat whistle.*

NARRATOR: Unknown to Fogg, however, at the very moment he is setting sail for Suez, the London papers are once again filled with his name. A telegram from Detective Fix in Suez has been received by the Commissioner of Police. The message of the dispatch reads:

FIX (*A sly, evil man*): Rowan, Commissioner of Police, Scotland Yard: I've found the bank robber. Phileas Fogg.

Send without delay a warrant of arrest to Suez. Signed, Detective Fix.

NARRATOR: So that's it! Phileas Fogg fits the description of the bank robber, and preparations are under way to arrest him when he reaches Suez.

FIX: I tell you, Consul, this Phileas Fogg is the robber! We must arrest him the moment he lands.

CONSUL: Now, now, Mr. Fix. You are the detective; I am only the Consul. You may think Fogg is the bank robber, but if his papers are in order, and I have no warrant for his arrest, he may go on.

FIX: What? You're going to let this thief slip through your fingers?

CONSUL: I am not convinced that he *is* a thief. From his description in the newspaper, he sounds like an honest man.

FIX: Consul, great robbers *always* resemble honest folks. Take my word for it; Fogg is the thief.

CONSUL: We shall see, Detective Fix. We shall see.

MUSIC: *Light theme.*

NARRATOR: After arriving in Suez, Fogg goes to the Consul's office to have his passport examined. There, Detective Fix hopes to arrest him.

CONSUL: All seems to be in order here, Mr. Fogg. You may go.

FOGG: Thank you for your trouble, Consul. Goodbye.

FIX (*Furiously*): What, Consul? You're going to let him escape?

CONSUL: I have no legal grounds for keeping him.

FIX: You're letting a fortune in reward money escape you! But I'm not so foolish as you!

CONSUL: What are you going to do?

FIX: Send a dispatch to London for a warrant of arrest to

be sent instantly to Bombay, take passage on board the *Mongolia,* follow that rogue to India, and there, on English soil, arrest him politely, with my warrant in my hand, and my hand on his shoulder.

MUSIC: *Suspenseful theme.*

FOGG: October 20th, the *Mongolia* arrives at Bombay. Since we are not scheduled to arrive until the 22nd, we have gained two days on our program.

NARRATOR: Thus, as is his custom, Phileas Fogg makes another entry in his notebook concerning his journey's progress. At the same time that Mr. Fogg is enjoying the gain of time, Detective Fix is cursing it.

FIX: Two days gained, worse luck! No wonder the warrant for arrest hasn't arrived in Bombay yet. And no doubt Fogg will be gone before it has a chance to get here. I suppose the only thing to do is send another dispatch requesting a warrant, this one to be sent to Calcutta. I'm determined to catch this thief who calls himself Phileas Fogg!

SOUND: *Whir of railroad-train wheels.*

FOGG: Half-past twelve. Burhampoor. Everything on schedule.

SOUND: *Train wheels become louder for a moment, then subside.*

FOGG: Evening in the Sutpour Mountains. Everything on schedule.

SOUND: *Train wheels.*

CONDUCTOR (*Calling out*): Passengers will get out here! All passengers will get out here!

FOGG: What does this mean? We haven't reached the destination, Allahabad.

PASSEPARTOUT (*Excitedly*): Monsieur, no more railway!

FOGG: What do you mean?

PASSEPARTOUT: I mean to say the train is not going on.

FOGG: Conductor, what is the meaning of this?

CONDUCTOR: This is the end of the line. All passengers out!

FOGG: But where are we?

CONDUCTOR: At the hamlet of Kholby.

FOGG: Do we stop here?

CONDUCTOR: Certainly. The railway isn't finished.

PASSEPARTOUT: What? Not finished! *Sacre bleu!*

CONDUCTOR: No, there's still a matter of fifty miles to be laid from here to Allahabad, where the line begins again.

FOGG: But the papers announced the opening of the railway throughout!

CONDUCTOR: Can't help that, sir. The papers were mistaken!

PASSEPARTOUT: Oh, Monsieur Fogg, what are we to do? We are in the middle of a jungle!

FOGG (*Calmly*): We shall find some means of conveyance to Allahabad.

PASSEPARTOUT: But what will this do to your schedule, to your timing?

FOGG: I have gained two days so far, so that I have them to sacrifice. A steamer leaves Calcutta for Hong Kong at noon on the 25th. This is the 22nd, and we shall reach Calcutta in time. Come, Passepartout!

MUSIC: *Light-hearted theme.*

NARRATOR: Undaunted by this sudden interruption in his plans, Phileas Fogg looks about for a means of conveyance to Calcutta, and, after much difficulty and expense, manages to buy an elephant and to hire a driver who will take them to Allahabad. The driver is a Parsee, who knows the forest quite well, and with Fogg and Passepartout seated in howdahs, the Parsee guides the elephant into the forest. After traveling for twenty hours with little difficulty, though considerable discomfort, the three are surprised when, all of a sudden, with no warning, the elephant stops cold in his tracks.

Fogg: What's the trouble, driver?

Parsee: I don't know, Officer. The elephant seems to fear something.

Passepartout: What's that noise a way off? Sounds like people!

Fogg: Stand on the elephant's head, driver, and tell us what you see.

Parsee: A procession of Brahmins is coming this way. We must prevent them from seeing us, if possible. Quick, let us hide in that thicket. We shall be able to see them pass from there.

Passepartout (*After a short pause, in a whisper*): What are they doing?

Parsee (*Whispering*): It is a suttee.

Fogg (*Whispering*): What is a suttee?

Parsee: Do you see that woman, between the Brahmins, bound hand and foot, and moving along as though in a dream? She is the widow of that man, whose body you see being carried. Tomorrow at dawn the woman will be burned with the corpse of her husband.

Fogg: Is it possible that these barbarous customs still exist in India and that the English have been unable to put a stop to them?

Parsee: The English have little power over these savages of the jungle territories.

Passepartout: The poor wretch, to be burned alive!

Fogg: Suppose we save this woman. I have yet twelve hours to spare; we can devote them to that.

Passepartout: Why, you are a man of heart, Monsieur Fogg!

Fogg: Sometimes, when I have the time. But how are we to accomplish it? See how heavily she is guarded.

PARSEE: You must wait till night falls; then perhaps the guards will be asleep. They would kill you with slow tortures if you were caught!

FOGG: Very well, then. We shall wait here until nightfall, and then—well, then we shall see.

MUSIC: *Mysterious theme.*

NARRATOR: From their hiding place in the thicket, Phileas Fogg, Passepartout and their guide, the Parsee, watch the Brahmin priests perform their savage rites of prayer. At last night falls, but alas! Four guards, who have abstained from the drink which has made the others drowsy, remain awake to keep careful watch on their drugged victim, although the other Brahmins sleep on the ground.

PARSEE: See! All but the four guards are asleep beneath the full moon!

FOGG (*Bitterly*): Yes, but with those four brutes, how are we to accomplish anything?

PARSEE: I do not know, Officer. The situation looks grave.

FOGG: To let that young woman die is heartless. To try to save her would be foolhardy!

BRAHMIN (*At a distance, a cry of surprise*): Ahhhh!

FOGG: Something is happening! The guards are shouting!

PARSEE: Look, Officer. The corpse of the dead man. He is rising from the bier. He is not dead!

FOGG: How can that be?

PARSEE: The Brahmin priests are awake and bowing down. A miracle!

FOGG: Miracles are impossible. They don't occur!

PARSEE: What else can it be? The corpse is lifting the woman in his arms! He is carrying her this way! Oh, I am frightened!

FOGG (*Joyfully*): Look! It's Passepartout! He has taken the

place of the dead man under cover of darkness! Passepartout!

PASSEPARTOUT (*Breathing heavily*): Quick, gentlemen! Let
us be off! Help me lift the young lady into the howdah.
She is still drowsy. Quick! We must be off! As soon as
they find the naked corpse of the *real* dead man, all will
be over with us. Hurry!

MUSIC: *Excited theme.*

NARRATOR: Quickly, the travelers mount their elephant
and are on their way through the dense forest. By the
time the Brahmins discover the trickery that has made
them believe in a false miracle, Fogg and his friends are
far out of their reach. It is the cleverness and daring of
Passepartout that saves the life of the young Indian
woman, who turns out to be the fairest of India's fair—
Princess Aouda. As Fogg had predicted, the Parsee guide
succeeds in reaching Allahabad in time for him to make
his next connection. In gratitude Fogg says to the guide:

FOGG: Parsee, you have been serviceable and devoted. I
have paid you for your service, but not for your devotion.
Would you like to have this elephant? He is yours.

PARSEE: Your honor is giving me a fortune!

FOGG: Take him, guide, and I shall still be your debtor.

MUSIC: *Happy theme.*

FOGG: Allahabad reached—on schedule. (*Short pause*)
Benares reached—on schedule. (*Short pause*) October
25th. Due to arrive at Calcutta, and have arrived at Calcutta, on schedule, neither behindhand nor ahead of
time. (*Musing*) I gained two days between London and
Bombay, and I lost them in the journey across India and
the rescuing of Princess Aouda. But I don't mind admit-
ting to myself that I don't regret having her with us—
not for a moment!

MUSIC: *Happy theme.*

NARRATOR: Fix had not been able to reach Calcutta, and so once again Phileas Fogg sets out, this time accompanied by the lovely Indian girl, Aouda, as well as Passepartout. He is unaware that he is suspected of being the notorious bank robber.

FIX: Dear Scotland Yard: I am pursuing Phileas Fogg to Hong Kong, and hope that a warrant for his arrest will be there when we arrive. Hong Kong is the last English ground on which I may arrest him, and if I lose him there, he is lost to us forever. Detective Fix.

MUSIC: *Exciting theme.*

AOUDA (*A sweet-voiced young woman*): Mr. Fogg, I—I wish to acknowledge my debt of gratitude to you for saving my life.

FOGG: As I explained to you, Princess Aouda, it was chiefly Passepartout that was responsible for that happy event.

AOUDA: Do you look upon it, then, as a "happy" event?

FOGG: Yes, madam, I do indeed. I shall be sorry to see you leave us once we reach Hong Kong and you have access to your relations.

AOUDA (*Wistfully*): I, too, shall be sorry, Mr. Fogg.

MUSIC: *Romantic theme.*

FOGG: October 30th. We reach the Strait of Malacca. On time. (*Short pause*) October 31st. 4 A.M. We reach Singapore. On time (*Short pause*). Five o'clock A.M., November 6th, we reach Hong Kong. Due to mechanical difficulties, twenty-four hours behind schedule.

AOUDA: Do you make a record of every stop in your strange journey around the world, Mr. Fogg?

FOGG: Yes, and alas, I fear we shall not be able to make up the time lost. The *Carnatic,* on which we were to have sailed for Yokohama, has already gone, according to my timetable.

PASSEPARTOUT: A whole day lost! Is there no hope, Monsieur?

FOGG: We shall see. (*Calling out*) Pilot! Pilot!

PILOT: Yes, sir?

FOGG: Do you know when the next steamer will leave for Yokohama?

PILOT: At high tide tomorrow morning, sir.

FOGG: Ah! And what is the steamer's name?

PILOT: The *Carnatic*.

FOGG: But was she not to have gone yesterday?

PILOT: Yes, sir, but they had to repair one of her boilers, and so her departure was postponed till tomorrow.

PASSEPARTOUT (*Happily*): Oh, pilot, you are the best of good fellows!

MUSIC: *Triumphant theme.*

NARRATOR: The arrest warrant has not arrived, and seeing Phileas Fogg get away from him infuriates Detective Fix, who makes the following resolve.

FIX: I'll get him yet, if it's the last thing I do. Once he leaves Hong Kong, I've no power over him. But he seems to be serious about returning to England. I'll just follow him; and the moment he sets foot on British soil, I'll arrest that notorious bank robber. I'll get you yet, Mr. Phileas Fogg!

NARRATOR: In addition to Fix's plan going awry in Hong Kong, another plan concerning the journey of Mr. Fogg changes. It is Fogg himself who breaks the news to the Indian woman, Princess Aouda.

FOGG: Miss Aouda, I have unhappy news for you.

AOUDA (*Afraid*): What is it, Mr. Fogg?

FOGG: The wealthy uncle with whom you hoped to find shelter in Hong Kong resides here no longer. From all I have been able to learn, he has been gone from this place for two years, and now resides in Holland.

AOUDA: What ought I to do, Mr. Fogg?

FOGG (*Firmly*): It is very simple. Go on to Europe with us.

AOUDA: Oh, but I cannot intrude—

FOGG: You do not intrude, nor do you in the least embarrass my project. Passepartout!

PASSEPARTOUT: Yes, monsieur?

FOGG: Go to the *Carnatic* and engage three cabins. Princess Aouda is coming with us!

MUSIC: *Happy theme.*

FOGG: December 3rd. We arrive at San Francisco, on schedule.

SOUND: *Railroad-train wheels.*

FOGG: December 5th. We pass the Great Salt Lake, on schedule.

SOUND: *Train wheels.*

FOGG: December 7th. Green River, Wyoming. An unscheduled delay here, reason as yet unknown.

PASSEPARTOUT: Monsieur, it seems we are to be dogged with bad luck.

FOGG: What is the matter, Passepartout?

PASSEPARTOUT: A bridge up ahead has been weakened by the snow. They are afraid to run the train over it.

AOUDA (*Sympathetically*): Oh, Mr. Fogg, to be so near and yet so far!

FOGG: All is not lost. Conductor! Conductor!

SECOND CONDUCTOR: Yes, sir?

FOGG: What is the cause of this delay?

CONDUCTOR: The bridge up ahead is weakened. We daren't take the train over it. If the bridge should snap under the weight, it would mean instant death for us all.

FOGG: I must continue this journey without delay. Here is a reward of five hundred dollars. Put on the very highest speed you have, and we'll make it across.

CONDUCTOR (*Tentatively*): Well, sir—

FOGG: I'll make that reward a thousand dollars!

CONDUCTOR: Did you say a thousand? All aboard! All aboar—oard!

SOUND: *Train wheels.*

NARRATOR: Following the advice of Mr. Fogg, the train moves forward with all the speed it can muster. Faster and faster and faster still it goes, till it hardly rests upon the rails at all. Like a flash they pass over the bridge! The train leaps, so to speak, from bank to bank. Scarcely has the train passed the river, when the bridge, completely ruined, falls with a crash down into the rapids of Medicine Bow.

SOUND: *Train wheels.*

FOGG: December 11th. New York City, on time!

SOUND: *Steamboat whistle.*

FOGG: December 21st, twenty minutes before twelve noon. Liverpool, England. The eightieth day, and only six hours away from London.

FIX: How does it feel to have English soil beneath your feet once again, Mr. Fogg?

FOGG (*Coldly*): I beg your pardon, sir. How do you know my name?

FIX: Then you are really Phileas Fogg?

FOGG: I am.

FIX: Ah, good. Mr. Phileas Fogg, I arrest you in the Queen's name!

MUSIC: *Dramatic theme.*

NARRATOR: Six hours away from winning twenty thousand pounds, Phileas Fogg is placed under arrest by Detective Fix, who has traveled around the world with him to place him there. Phileas Fogg is now in prison. Placing his watch on the table, he sees the seconds turn into minutes, the minutes into hours, and his dreams vanish with the possibilities of reaching London by the specified time. If he is honest, he is ruined. If he is a knave, he is caught. At thirty-three minutes past two, he hears the key turn in the lock of his cell and the door is thrown open, revealing Detective Fix.

Fix (*Breathlessly*): Sir—sir—forgive me—a—a most unfortunate resemblance—the robber was arrested three days ago.

Fogg (*Calmly*): Am I then free?

Fix: Yes, yes. You are free.

Fogg: As you have observed me closely for many days, Detective Fix, you have noted that I am a man not given to physical violence. Allow me to make today an exception.

Sound: *Firm blow. Body falling.*

Fogg: Out cold! Which is, considering the time, how my chances of yet winning the wager are.

Music: *Anxious theme.*

Narrator: Having missed the regular train to London, Fogg, with Aouda and Passepartout, hires a special train to take him there. When they finally reach the London terminus, the clocks in the station all show the time to be ten minutes before nine. Having made the tour of the world, he is behind in reaching his goal by five minutes. He has lost the wager!

Music: *Unhappy theme.*

Passepartout: Poor Monsieur Fogg! Poor Monsieur Fogg!

Aouda: It is so hard to realize that he has lost his fortune. How is he taking it, Passepartout?

Passepartout: I have no idea, madam. Ever since we arrived here in his house last evening, he has confined himself to his room. I have not seen him!

Aouda: If only we could cheer him. If only—

Fogg: Passepartout.

Aouda (*Whispering*): Here he is.

FOGG: Will you be good enough to leave me alone with this lady for a few minutes?

PASSEPARTOUT: Certainly, monsieur.

FOGG: Will you pardon me, madam, for bringing you to England?

AOUDA: I—Mr. Fogg!

FOGG: When I decided to bring you far away from the country which was so unsafe for you, I was rich, and counted on putting a portion of my wealth at your disposal. Now I am ruined!

AOUDA: I know it, Mr. Fogg, and I ask you, in turn, to forgive me for having delayed you, and thus having contributed to your ruin. I am not concerned for myself, but what will become of you?

FOGG: As for me, madam, I have need of nothing.

AOUDA: But your friends? Your relatives?

FOGG: I have none, madam.

AOUDA: I pity you, then, for solitude is a sad thing, Mr. Fogg, with no heart in which to confide your griefs. They say, though, that misery itself, shared by two sympathetic souls, may be borne with patience.

FOGG: They say so, madam.

AOUDA: Mr. Fogg, do you wish at once a kinswoman and a friend? Will you have me for your wife?

FOGG (*After a pause*): I love you! Yes, by all that is holiest, I love you, and am entirely yours.

PASSEPARTOUT (*Very excited*): Monsieur! Monsieur!

FOGG: Ah, Passepartout. You are just in time to see me betrothed to this gracious lady.

PASSEPARTOUT: *Sacre bleu!* How wonderful! It seems that joy comes in pairs!

AOUDA: In pairs? What do you mean, Passepartout?

PASSEPARTOUT: Monsieur, today is not Sunday as you suppose! It is Saturday!

FOGG: Saturday? Impossible! Yesterday was Saturday!

PASSEPARTOUT: No, no, monsieur. Today is Saturday! By traveling always East, we gained a day's time. You have won the wager! You have won! But you must hurry! It is twenty-five minutes before nine. You have but ten minutes to reach the Reform Club. Hurry, Monsieur Fogg, hurry!

MUSIC: *Exciting theme.*

NARRATOR: Phileas Fogg dashes into street, hops into a cab, and is on his way. And at the Reform Club—

STUART: He has lost, gentlemen, he has lost.

FLANAGAN: One minute more, gentlemen. Fogg has one minute to make good his claim.

RALPH: There's no point in waiting. He can't possibly have won.

FLANAGAN: Fifteen more seconds, gentlemen.

STUART: Oh, give it up, Flanagan. The money is ours.

FLANAGAN: Five seconds more.

SOUND: *Door opening.*

BUTLER: (*Announcing stiffly*): Mr. Phileas Fogg!

STUART (*Amazed*): No!

FLANAGAN: Impossible!

RALPH: It can't be!

FOGG: But it is! Here I am, gentlemen. The twenty thousand pounds are mine. Admit it! I have won the money fairly and squarely, by doing what all of you considered impossible. I have gone around the world in eighty days!

MUSIC: *Triumphant theme.*

THE END

The Count of Monte Cristo

by Alexandre Dumas

Characters

EDMOND DANTES
ABBE FARIA
GENDARME
MERCEDES
FERNAND MONDEGO
DANGLARS
CADEROUSSE
VILLEFORT
TWO GUARDS
SHIP'S CAPTAIN
JACOPO
NARRATOR

SOUND: *Footsteps pacing slowly, steadily, on stone. After eight steps, pause, then begin again.*

NARRATOR: In solitary confinement, in the dungeons of that grim, forbidding prison known as the Chateau d'If, high on a rocky island above the sea, walks Edmond Dantes, ignored by justice, bereft of friends, forgotten by loved ones; Edmond Dantes, a poor French fisherman who is destined to become the richest man in the world, and the hero of Alexandre Dumas' classic novel, "The Count of Monte Cristo."

MUSIC: *Dramatic theme.*

NARRATOR: As our story begins, we find young Edmond Dantes pacing the floor of his horrible cell, pacing it as he has paced it every hour of every day for six long years, years that have been filled with grief, with frustration, and worst of all, with loneliness.

SOUND: *Footsteps pacing.*

EDMOND: Alone! Alone! How that word haunts my every thought! Alone! Alone with my four stone walls, whose every crack and chip is as well known to me as these fingers on my hands. Alone with my conscience, which is clear of any crime. Alone with my thoughts, which will not let me rest. My thoughts that never tire of wondering why and how I came to be here. My thoughts that return ever to my hope of vengeance against those who accused me falsely. And alone with the silence! My God, that is worst of all. The silence! Endless and echoing silence!

SOUND: *Scraping noise.*

EDMOND (*Quickly*): What was that? (*Short pause*) No. There is nothing there. I thought I heard a noise—but there is only silence. My mind is beginning to play tricks on me. (*Laughing bitterly*) Yes, I am beginning to go mad. They say that's what happens after years of solitary confinement! Mad!

SOUND: *Scraping noise again, this time louder.*

EDMOND: There it is again! Do I imagine it? No! I hear it! A sound! It's coming from this wall. There must be a prisoner on the other side, trying to make contact with me. A prisoner! Another person!

SOUND: *Loud tapping on a stone wall.*

EDMOND: Hello! Hello! Is there someone there? It's all right. Answer me! There are no guards about. Hello!

FARIA (*Far away throughout the scene*): Hello! Can you hear me?

EDMOND (*Joyfully*): A human voice! Yes, yes, I hear you! I am Edmond Dantes, a prisoner in the next cell!

FARIA: The next cell! My God, I am wrong then!

EDMOND: What is it, friend? What is it?

FARIA: I must have made a mistake in my calculations. For years I have been digging this tunnel. I thought it led to the island outside the prison. But at least I have found a companion; that is something. Listen, can you hear me?

EDMOND: Yes, I hear you!

FARIA: I am going to tap on one of the stones. Make a note of which stone it is. Tonight, after your guard has left, chip away the plaster and remove the stone. I have loosened it; it will come out easily. Tomorrow, slip through the hole, crawl through the tunnel I have dug, and come to me in my cell. Will you remember?

EDMOND: Yes, I shall remember and I shall come. Now, tap the stone!

SOUND: *Three taps on stone.*

EDMOND: I have it now. Till tomorrow then, friend.

FARIA: Till tomorrow, then, Edmond Dantes.

MUSIC: *Dramatic theme.*

NARRATOR: That night, after the guards make their rounds, Edmond eagerly sets to work, and in a short time, succeeds in dislodging the large stone, setting it loosely back into place so that it will not be discovered. The next morning, Edmond moves it aside, crawls through a long, narrow tunnel he finds, and soon emerges through a hole into another cell. There he faces an old, ragged priest, and though they are perfect strangers, the men embrace—so glad are they for human contact. Then, the priest speaks.

FARIA: You are Edmond Dantes. Welcome. Welcome.

EDMOND: Will you not tell me who you are?

FARIA: I am the Abbe Faria, a prisoner here since 1811.

EDMOND: Since 1811! That is even longer than I have been here.

FARIA: And yet, until last night, I did not give up hope of escape. Now, I see it is impossible.

EDMOND: Impossible? Why?

FARIA: I am an old man—old and sick. It took me years to accumulate enough implements to set to work. I made a rope ladder from threads taken from my mattress. I fashioned a knife from an old candlestick, matches from sulphur given me when I was ill. I made a needle from a fishbone. It took years! And then more years to dislodge the stone in my cell, years to dig the tunnel—only to discover that my calculations were wrong! Instead of ending outside the prison as I had hoped, I ended in your cell. No, I cannot go on with my dream. I am too old, too feeble. I shall die here.

EDMOND: Abbe Faria, I am young and strong. With your tools, I can find a way for us to escape. I shall begin your work again; and in the meantime, we shall have each other's company to sustain our hopes.

FARIA: Perhaps. Perhaps. But you must go now. You have been here long enough. The guards will come soon.

EDMOND: When may I come again?

FARIA: Tonight. Come tonight, Edmond Dantes. Edmond Dantes—my friend.

MUSIC: *Tense theme.*

NARRATOR: So the young prisoner finds in the old priest in the next cell a companion, a teacher, and a friend. Several hours out of every day the men are together, and soon they feel as though they have known each other always.

FARIA: How did it happen, Edmond, that you were imprisoned here?

EDMOND: I am not sure myself. My life was before me. I was about to be made captain of a ship, and I was preparing to marry my beloved, Mercedes. I can remember it all so clearly. It was at the banquet celebrating the signing of our marriage document. Everyone was happy, when suddenly the door flew open—

GENDARME: Which of you here is Edmond Dantes?

EDMOND: I am he.

GENDARME: Edmond Dantes, I arrest you in the name of the law.

MERCEDES: Heaven help us! No!

GENDARME: Come with us, Edmond Dantes.

EDMOND (*After a short pause*): I was bewildered. Who could have accused me of a crime? I tried to think of what enemies I might have, what people might have benefited from my imprisonment. First, there was Fernand Mondego. He loved Mercedes, but she would not have him. But if I were out of the way—

FERNAND: Mercedes, Edmond is in prison. He will be there for the rest of his life as a traitor to our country. Marry me, Mercedes. Marry me!

EDMOND: Then there was Danglars. He would have been made captain of the ship once I was out of the way.

DANGLARS: The only thing standing between me and my fortune is a young man named Edmond Dantes. I will not allow him to be captain; I will prevent his getting the captaincy at any cost.

EDMOND: There was a tailor, too, a man named Caderousse. My old father was in his debt, but as long as I was present, Caderousse feared to take advantage of my father. But without me there—

CADEROUSSE: Monsieur Dantes, your son is in prison and no longer can he pay your debts. Therefore I demand from you full payment immediately. Sleep in the streets! Go naked! Starve to death! What do I care? All I want is the money you owe me.

EDMOND: Last, there was the man who examined me after my arrest. He knew I was innocent of the crime charged against me, but to prove my innocence he would have had to condemn his father. Therefore, he preferred to condemn me. His name was Villefort.

VILLEFORT: What if this Edmond Dantes *is* innocent? Dare I risk my own father's neck in the case? No! Let Dantes be imprisoned. No one will ever know the difference.

EDMOND: And there, Abbe Faria, by a combination of the efforts of those four villains, you see how I have been condemned. But I have sworn vengeance; and if it is the last deed I ever do, I shall avenge myself on Villefort, Fernand, Danglars and Caderousse!

MUSIC: *Evil theme.*

NARRATOR: Thus, Edmond tells the old Abbe how he came to be imprisoned. The Abbe is a very intelligent man, and with his help, Edmond begins to educate himself, while planning an eventual escape from the horrible Chateau d'If.

FARIA: I can teach you much, Edmond, much that will be of value to you when and if you make good your escape from here.

EDMOND: Anything you care to tell me, Abbe, will find a ready memory. I regret that as a child I did not have the opportunity to learn more; but I think you will find me an apt pupil.

FARIA: Fine, Edmond. I will teach you all I know—English, Italian, Spanish, medicine, history and science. Within two years, if you are a ready student, you shall have learned all that I can offer.

EDMOND: Within two years' time! As short as that?

FARIA: Yes, and while you are learning, we shall be planning and preparing for our escape.

EDMOND: Excellent, Abbe! Let us begin at once!

MUSIC: *Active theme.*

NARRATOR: With the companionship of his new-found friend, and the excitement of the knowledge he is acquiring, Edmond's days fly faster than he would have believed possible. In addition to paying attention to his studies, Edmond and the Abbe Faria are busily working on a plan for escape, and within three years—years that seem to Edmond more like days, so full are they with the excitement of his knowledge and his plans—the two men are ready to try their escape. The night before they are to make their desperate attempt, Edmond pays a visit to his friend's cell, and is horrified to find the old priest writhing in agony.

FARIA (*With difficulty*): Edmond, is it you?

EDMOND: Yes. What is wrong, Abbe?

FARIA: My son, I fear I am dying!

EDMOND: Dying! Oh, do not say such things!

FARIA: Alas, Edmond, it is true. I am taken with a terrible illness, and I fear I cannot last the night. Go ahead with our plan for flight, my boy, and God speed you.

EDMOND: Do you think I would consider leaving this dungeon without you?

FARIA: My good Edmond, my health will not come back. I have had such attacks before. I know that this one will be fatal.

EDMOND: No, no! Your strength will return!

FARIA: It is not so. Even now my whole left side is para-
lyzed. You must go on without me, and let me die. It
will be enough for me to know that you have escaped,
my son.

EDMOND: As for your paralysis, what difference will that
make? I shall take you on my shoulders, and swim for
both of us.

FARIA: What progress would you make with such a load?
No, do not delay on my account, but go!

EDMOND: Never! I swear I will not leave you while you
live!

FARIA: Thanks, good Edmond. You will not have long to
wait. But first, while there is time, draw near to me. I
have something to give you.

EDMOND: What is it?

FARIA: Do you see this paper? It will be the making of
you!

EDMOND: What? That little scrap of frayed, yellowed writing?

FARIA: Yellowed though it is, it is the key to your fortune.
Listen! How I came to know of this, there is not time to
tell you. I give you my word, though, that it was honestly
come by. This paper is a map which will lead you to
the great Spada fortune, a fortune which should have
fallen into thieves' hands long ago, but that its where-
abouts were never known. Read the paper, Edmond.

EDMOND (*Reading*): "This 25th day of April, 1498, being
invited to dine by His Holiness Alexander VI, and fear-
ing that he may desire to become my heir by poisoning
me, I declare to the inheritor of this paper that I have
buried in the caves of the small island Monte Cristo all
I possess of gold, money, and jewels. I alone know of
the existence of this treasure, which I leave entirely to
the inheritor of this paper as my sole heir. Caesar Spada."

FARIA: Now, Edmond, you see how valuable that scrap of paper is!

EDMOND: A buried treasure. I can't believe it!

FARIA: You must believe it, for I can swear to the truth of it! Edmond, as soon as you have escaped from this prison, go to Monte Cristo and claim your treasure. It was mine; I bequeath it now to you.

EDMOND: Is there no one else with more right to this treasure?

FARIA: No one is left of the family. When Cardinal Spada, the last of the line, died, he left me his breviary; this paper was in it, and so the treasure is rightfully mine. I give it to you.

EDMOND: But I have no right to it. I am no relative of yours.

FARIA: You are my son, Dantes. You are the child of my captivity. God has—sent—you—to me. (*Gasps*)

EDMOND: Abbe! Abbe Faria! (*Softly*) Oh, no, no! The one friend I had in all the world—is dead.

MUSIC: *Dramatic theme.*

NARRATOR: With that, Edmond bids his dear comrade goodbye, and slips into his secret tunnel, pulling the stone back into place as he goes. Back in his own cell, he realizes once more the solitude and horror of the prison, and once again—as in the years before—he is surrounded by horrible, deathly silence, and tortured by his own thoughts.

EDMOND: Dead! I cannot believe it! Just as everything was going so well. Just as we had planned our escape, our road to freedom! It isn't fair! Oh, God, what in this world of ours is fair? Where is there justice? There is none, it seems, unless men find it for themselves. What have I done to deserve this fate? (*Sobbing brokenly*) Oh, Mercedes, Mercedes, my love. Have you been true to me? Where are you, Mercedes? Where are you? (*After a pause, the voices from the past come back to haunt* EDMOND *in his dreams. The actors reading these lines, therefore, should use a distant, dream-like tone.*)

MERCEDES: Edmond, I love you. I will marry you!

GENDARME: Edmond Dantes, I arrest you in the name of the law!

MERCEDES: Heaven help us!

FERNAND: Mercedes, Edmond is in prison. He cannot marry you!

MERCEDES: Edmond, my love!

FERNAND: Edmond is in prison! Marry me, Mercedes!

VILLEFORT: My father's life, or Edmond Dantes'? Imprison Dantes!

CADEROUSSE: Pay me my money, old Dantes!

FERNAND: Marry me, Mercedes!

MERCEDES: Edmond, my love! My love!

MUSIC: *Tragic theme.*

NARRATOR: That night, Edmond hides in the tunnel just next to the Abbe's cell, and overhears the following conversation.

1ST GUARD: So the old priest finally died, eh?

2ND GUARD: Yes, we've got another customer for the prison graveyard. Come on and hurry! I want to get the corpse into the sack and get out of here!

1ST GUARD: I don't blame you. This cell sends shivers down my spine. The sooner we've got the body into its burial sack, the better I'll like it!

EDMOND: Of course! This will be a much more certain way of managing my escape from prison. Once the guards are gone, I'll take the Abbe's body from the burial sack, carry him to my cell and cover him with my blanket. Then I'll take his place and be carried off to the cemetery—and freedom! Freedom! How sweet the word sounds, eh, Edmond Dantes?

MUSIC: *Tense theme.*

NARRATOR: As soon as the guards leave the Abbe's cell, Edmond sets his plan into operation. He brings the old priest's body to his own bed and covers him, so that the guards will suppose it is Edmond himself, asleep. He then quickly strips off his clothing, climbs into the burial sack, and sews it up from the inside with the old priest's needle. He also keeps the priest's knife ready in his hand, should there be any trouble. Barely is he in the sack when the guards return.

1ST GUARD: Well, there's the old priest—or what's left of him—right where we left him.

2ND GUARD: You didn't expect him to move, did you?

1ST GUARD: Come on, come on, Jacques. Let's not waste any time in getting him to the cemetery.

MUSIC: *Dramatic theme.*

NARRATOR: Edmond, inside the sack, feels himself hoisted to the shoulders of the guards and carried away. In a few minutes he feels a chill, and light seeps through the holes in the sacking. With joy Edmond realizes that he is outside the prison! On and on the guards carry him, and finally they set him down within sound of the ocean. Edmond feels motion, and with a chill of terror, realizes his fate.

SOUND: *Water lapping a shore, in background.*

EDMOND: The sea! Of course! Why didn't I realize that before? *That* is the prison cemetery! I am to be cast into the water!

SOUND: *Water swells, then subsides.*

1ST GUARD: There! I think we've rowed out far enough. We can dump the body here.

2ND GUARD: That's fine with me! I can't get away from it too quickly!

1ST GUARD: Well, just give me a hand in tying this cannon ball onto the bottom of the sack. That'll make it sink to the bottom.

2ND GUARD: I'll help you—though I don't think *this* corpse will need it. Who'd ever have thought the frail old priest would be so heavy?

1ST GUARD: I've heard it said that every year of age adds half a pound to the weight of the bones.

2ND GUARD: If that's true, *this* old prisoner must have been a hundred!

1ST GUARD: There! The weight is secure now. Ready to lift him?

2ND GUARD: Ready.

1ST *and* 2ND GUARDS (*In unison*): One—two—three—ugh!

SOUND: *Great splash.*

1ST GUARD: Over he goes! Look at the sack sink! I guess that's the last anyone will ever see of *that* corpse!

MUSIC: *Dramatic theme.*

NARRATOR: Fortunately, Edmond has carried off the old priest's knife in his hand, and as soon as the sack hits the water, he rips open the case which might have proved his coffin. With great effort, he manages to cut the cords which tie the weight to his body, and once free of them, he strikes out with all his strength, and swims in the direction of land. After hours of swimming, Edmond reaches a rocky cove, and crawls exhaustedly onto the beach, where he sinks into a deep slumber.

MUSIC: *Tense theme.*

NARRATOR: Next morning, Edmond wakes, and though for the first time in many years he smells the sweet air of freedom, it is still the smell of fear and terror that takes precedence for him.

EDMOND: Dear God, help me, your humble servant, Edmond Dantes. By now the jailer will have entered my cell, found the body of my poor friend, looked for me in vain, and given the alarm. Probably the tunnel has already been found. Boats of armed soldiers will be pursuing me. People will be warned to refuse shelter to a man found wandering about, naked and starving. The police of Marseille will be on the alert! Oh God, I have suffered, suffered more than enough, surely. Dear God, have pity on me!

MUSIC: *Dramatic theme.*

NARRATOR: As if in answer to his prayers, Edmond finds the wreckage from a small ship that has evidently been lost within the past few days. And wonder of wonders! Skimming along the water he sees another small ship, coming out of Marseille harbor and moving rapidly out to sea. Snatching a sailor's cap from among the wreckage, Edmond strikes bravely out to sea, and within a short time he is swimming alongside the one-masted vessel. As soon as his red cap is seen, Edmond is pulled onto the deck, and with an exhausted sigh, leans back.

EDMOND: Thank heavens! I am saved!

CAPTAIN: Who are you, stranger?

EDMOND: I am a Maltese sailor. Our boat was wrecked not far from here in last night's storm. I alone, of all the crew, live to tell of it.

JACOPO: If it hadn't been for us spotting you, even *you* might not have been left.

EDMOND: True enough; and I'm indeed grateful to you.

CAPTAIN: You're strange-looking for a sailor. You haven't shaved or had your hair cut in years!

EDMOND: I—I made a vow to our Lady of the Grotto not

to cut my hair or beard for ten years if I were saved in a moment of danger.

JACOPO: Looks as if you'll have to renew your vow, now, sailor!

EDMOND: I shall, and gladly!

CAPTAIN: What am I to do with you now, sailor?

EDMOND: I am an accomplished seaman, Captain. If you'll allow me to help on board, I shan't ask any wages, except for my food and a suit of clothes to cover my back.

CAPTAIN: Take the helm and let us see what you know. I'll think it over.

MUSIC: *Dramatic theme.*

NARRATOR: Edmond readily proves that he is an expert sailor, and soon he becomes a welcome addition to the small vessel's crew. At the end of his first day aboard, Edmond asks one of the sailors a question which seems singularly odd.

EDMOND: Tell me, Jacopo, what day is it?

JACOPO: The 28th of February.

EDMOND: In what year?

JACOPO: In what year! Have you forgotten it, then?

EDMOND: I—I was so frightened by the shipwreck—I—I have almost lost my memory. Tell me, I pray, what year is this?

JACOPO: Why, it's the year 1829.

EDMOND (*As a soliloquy*): February 28, 1829. Fourteen years to the very day since I was first arrested. I was nineteen when I first entered that horrible prison, Chateau d'If; now I am thirty-three. What has happened in these last years? Is my father yet alive? Does Mercedes still hope for my return? (*Bitterly*) What of my foes: Danglars, Fernand, Caderousse and Villefort? Where are they now? Well, wherever they are, I swear I will have my vengeance!

MUSIC: *Tense theme.*

NARRATOR: When the little ship arrives at its port, the Captain, who has become quite fond of Edmond, says to him:

CAPTAIN: When I took you aboard, my friend, I agreed to accept your services in exchange for bringing you to shore. But you proved invaluable to me in our journey, and so I must give you more. Here is some money— you'll need it—and you've certainly earned it fairly. Good luck to you, my friend.

NARRATOR: With his money, Edmond immediately buys a small craft, and sets out for the mysterious isle of Monte Cristo. On his way, grave doubts assail his mind.

EDMOND: Is this folly of me, to spend every cent I have in the world for a trip to an island I have never seen? What proof have I that the Abbe spoke the truth? He had been in prison for years; perhaps madness had seized his brain. Even if he were telling the truth, how can I be sure that no one has ever found the treasure? It was left there over three hundred years ago. In three hundred years, much may happen. Who knows what I shall find when I get to Monte Cristo?

MUSIC: *Tense theme.*

NARRATOR: Upon reaching the island, Edmond makes a careful search of every rock and tree, without success. He is on the point of giving up his search when he notices a small cave, almost hidden by an overgrowth of weeds. Quickly he enters the cave, and finds there a stone set into the floor, with a brass ring in it.

EDMOND: Now, God, if you will ever be with me, I pray that you be with me now. Open sesame!

NARRATOR: Edmond pulls the stone from the floor, and finds a flight of steps, cut into the stone, leading down beneath the earth's surface. Down and down and down he goes, his heart racing faster than his feet. When he reaches the bottom step, he lights a candle, looks about him, and knows that his dream has come true.

EDMOND (*Wonderingly*): Gold! Jewels! Coins of every kind! Diamonds, pearls, rubies, emeralds, sapphires and moonstones! The Abbe Faria was right! The fortune of the Spada family is all here. Millions' worth! And it is mine! What can I not do now? I am the richest man in the world! I can make all my dreams come true. And of those, the sweetest, most important dream is my dream of revenge. Beware, now, Fernand! Take care, Caderousse and Villefort! On guard, Danglars! Your days of success are numbered! Edmond Dantes, once a poor, ignorant fisherman, imprisoned on your accounts, shall have his vengeance. Beware, you villains, the wrath of the richest man in the world, the Count of Monte Cristo!

MUSIC: *Evil, triumphant theme.*

NARRATOR: That prophecy of vengeance which Edmond Dantes proclaims is to come true. How he experiences further adventures, achieves his ends, and finally discovers wisdom and happiness has been set down for all men to read in Alexandre Dumas' immortal classic, "The Count of Monte Cristo."

MUSIC: *Dramatic theme.*

THE END

A Christmas Carol

by Charles Dickens

Characters

FRED
EBENEZER SCROOGE
BOB CRATCHIT
A GENTLEMAN
GHOST OF JACOB MARLEY
GHOST OF CHRISTMAS PAST
LITTLE FAN
OLD FEZZIWIG
BELLE
GHOST OF CHRISTMAS PRESENT
MRS. CRATCHIT
CRATCHIT BOY
CRATCHIT GIRL
MARTHA CRATCHIT
TINY TIM
A YOUNG COCKNEY

MUSIC: *A gay Christmas carol.*
SOUND: *Slam of door.*
FRED (*Robust and happy*): A merry Christmas, Uncle!
   God save you!

SCROOGE (*A mean old man*): Bah! Humbug!

FRED (*Gaily*): Christmas a humbug, Uncle Scrooge? You don't mean that, I'm sure.

SCROOGE: I do. Merry Christmas! What right have you to be merry? What reason? You're poor enough!

FRED: Come then, what right have you to be dismal, what reason to be morose? You're rich enough!

SCROOGE: Bah! Humbug! What's Christmas time to you but a time for paying bills without money? A time for finding yourself a year older, but not an hour richer?

FRED: Though it has never put a scrap of gold or silver in my pocket, I believe that Christmas *has* done me good, and *will* do me good; and I say, God bless it!

CRATCHIT (*Applauding, from a slight distance*): Very well said, Mr. Fred!

SCROOGE: And *you*, Bob Cratchit, my fine young clerk. One more sound out of you, and you'll keep Christmas by losing your situation.

CRATCHIT (*Subdued*): Beg pardon, Mr. Scrooge.

SCROOGE: If I could work my will, nephew, every idiot who goes about with "Merry Christmas" on his lips would be boiled with his own pudding, and buried with a stake of holly through his heart.

FRED: Uncle!

SCROOGE: Nephew! Keep Christmas in your own way, and let me keep it in mine!

FRED: *Keep* it? But you *don't* keep it!

SCROOGE: Let me leave it alone, then. Good afternoon.

FRED: Don't be angry, Uncle. Come! Dine with us tomorrow!

SCROOGE: Good afternoon!

FRED: I am sorry with all my heart to find you so resolute, Uncle. Merry Christmas!

SCROOGE: Good afternoon!

FRED: And to you, too, Cratchit!

CRATCHIT: Thank you, sir.

FRED: And a happy New Year!

SOUND: *Door slamming shut.*

SCROOGE (*Muttering*): Christmas, indeed! Humbug! Bah!

SOUND: *Doorbell ringing.*

SCROOGE: Well, Cratchit. See who's at the door!

CRATCHIT: Very good, sir.

SOUND: *Door being opened.*

SCROOGE: And who are you?

GENTLEMAN: Scrooge and Marley's, I believe. Have I the pleasure of addressing Mr. Scrooge or Mr. Marley?

SCROOGE: Mr. Marley has been dead these seven years. He died seven years ago this very night.

GENTLEMAN: I have no doubt his liberality is well represented by his surviving partner.

SCROOGE (*Suspiciously*): Liberality?

GENTLEMAN: At this festive season of the year, Mr. Scrooge, it is more than usually desirable that we should make some slight provision for the poor and destitute, who suffer greatly at the present time.

SCROOGE: Are there no prisons?

GENTLEMAN: Oh, plenty of prisons.

SCROOGE: And the Union workhouses? Are they still in operation?

GENTLEMAN: They are. Still, I wish I could say they were not.

SCROOGE: Oh! I was afraid from what you said at first that something had occurred to stop them in their useful course. Let those who are badly off go to the institutions I have just mentioned.

GENTLEMAN: Many can't go there; and many would rather die.

SCROOGE: Let them do it, then, and decrease the surplus population.

GENTLEMAN: Oh, I'm sure you don't mean that, Mr. Scrooge. What shall I put you down for?

SCROOGE: Nothing!

GENTLEMAN: You wish to be anonymous?

SCROOGE: I wish to be left alone. Good day!

GENTLEMAN: I see. Good afternoon, Mr. Scrooge.

SOUND: *Door being shut.*

SCROOGE: Christmas, Christmas, Christmas! A poor excuse for picking a man's pocket every twenty-fifth of December. And you, Cratchit!

CRATCHIT: Yes, Mr. Scrooge?

SCROOGE: I suppose you'll want all day tomorrow.

CRATCHIT (*Timidly*): If quite convenient, sir.

SCROOGE: It's not convenient and it's not fair! If I were to dock you half a crown for it, you'd think yourself ill-used; and yet you don't think me ill-used for paying a day's wages for no work.

CRATCHIT: It's only once a year, sir . . .

SCROOGE: Bah! But I suppose you must have the whole day off. See that you're here all the earlier next morning. Good night, Cratchit.

CRATCHIT (*Fading*): Oh, I will, Mr. Scrooge. Good night, Mr. Scrooge! (*Slight pause*) And . . . Mr. Scrooge . . .

SCROOGE: Eh?

CRATCHIT: A merry Christmas, sir!

SCROOGE: Humbug! That's what it is—humbug!

MUSIC: *Lively theme, then into eerie music.*

SCROOGE (*Tossing in his sleep*): Mm-m . . . can't sleep . . . so tired . . . must get some rest . . .

SOUND: *Clock tolling twelve.*

SCROOGE (*After third peal*): Twelve midnight already? What's wrong with me? I can't sleep. Something must have upset me. Ah yes! That door knocker downstairs. Strange, that knocker. It looked like Marley's face . . . my old business partner, Jacob Marley. But that's impossible! What are you thinking of, Ebenezer Scrooge? It was the knocker, nothing else! Now get to sleep.

SOUND: *Chains dragging, far away, getting louder.*

SCROOGE: Eh? What sound is that? Someone's on the stair. Someone dragging a chain. Humbug! There's no one there. There's that noise again. Chains! It's humbug still! I won't believe it! He can't get in here; I locked the door before getting into bed. He can't get in here! But . . . wait! He's coming . . . *through* the door! It's Marley, that's who it is. Marley! I know him; it's Marley's Ghost! (*Louder*) What do you want with me?

MARLEY (*An unearthly voice*): Much.

SCROOGE: Who . . . who are you?

MARLEY: Ask me who I was.

SCROOGE: Who were you, then? You're a might particular!

MARLEY: In life I was your partner, Jacob Marley.

SCROOGE: Dreadful apparition, why do you trouble me?

MARLEY: It is required of every man that the spirit within him should walk abroad among his fellow men, and travel far and wide. And if that spirit go not forth in life, it is condemned to do so after death.

SCROOGE: You are fettered with chains, Marley. Tell me why.

MARLEY: I wear the chain I forged in life. I made it link by link, and yard by yard. I girded it on of my own free will, and of my own free will I wore it. Do you know the weight and length of your own chain?

SCROOGE: Jacob, old Jacob Marley, speak comfort to me, Jacob!

MARLEY: I have none to give, Ebenezer Scrooge. Hear me; my time is nearly gone.

SCROOGE: I will. But don't be hard upon me, Jacob, pray.

MARLEY: I am here tonight to warn you that you have yet a chance and hope of escaping my fate. You will be haunted by three spirits.

SCROOGE: Is . . . is that the chance and hope you mentioned, Jacob?

MARLEY: It is.

SCROOGE: I—I think I'd rather not.

MARLEY: Without their visits you cannot hope to shun the path I tread. Expect the first tomorrow, when the bell tolls one.

SCROOGE: Couldn't I take 'em all at once?

MARLEY: Expect the second on the next night at the same hour. The third will come the next night, when the last stroke of twelve has ceased to vibrate. Goodbye, Ebenezer Scrooge. Look to see me no more. Goodbye.

SCROOGE (*Amazed*): Why—he's vanished! Br-r! I'm cold. Humbug, I don't believe it! Ghosts! Ha! Humbug!

SOUND: *Clock tolls one.*

SCROOGE: One! Oh, dear! It's time for him to come, the first spirit. Nonsense, Ebenezer, there's no one coming. It's all humbug! (*Gasps*) Who . . . who are you? Are you the spirit whose coming was foretold to me?

CHRISTMAS PAST (*A kindly but ghostlike voice*): I am.

SCROOGE: Who . . . what are you?

C. PAST: I am the Ghost of Christmas Past.

SCROOGE: Long past?

C. PAST: No, your past. Rise, and walk with me. Come!

SCROOGE: Out the window? But I am a mortal, and liable to fall!

C. PAST: Bear but a touch of my hand upon your heart, and you shall be upheld in more than this.

SOUND: *Slight wind.*

SCROOGE: Good Heavens, I know this place. I went to school here when I was a boy!

C. PAST: The school is not quite deserted. A solitary child, neglected by his friends, is left there still.

SCROOGE: Poor boy . . . why . . . it's me! And who is that little girl running into the schoolroom?

C. PAST: Do you not recognize her?

SCROOGE: Why, it's my little sister, Fan!

FAN (*A young, girlish voice*): Ebenezer, dear brother!

SCROOGE: Poor Fan! How I miss her, now that she's dead.

FAN: I have come to bring you home, dear brother. Home, home! Father is so much kinder than he used to be, that home's like heaven. We're to be together all the Christmas long, and we'll be happy!

SCROOGE: Pretty little Fan! Fred's mother . . . and I turned Fred from my door.

C. PAST: Come, Ebenezer Scrooge. Another vision spreads before us!

SCROOGE: Why, where is this?

C. PAST: Another Christmas from your past, Ebenezer Scrooge.

SCROOGE: It's the Fezziwigs! Dear old Fezziwig—the best-hearted man there ever was. I worked for him when I was a lad. Old Fezziwig!

FEZZIWIG (*A jocular man*): Ho there, Ebenezer! It's Christmas Eve! No more work for the day. It's holiday time! Put up the shutters, my boy. And clear the floor! It's time for the Christmas dance. Come, come, Ebenezer. Hurry! 'Tis Christmas!

SCROOGE (*Laughing*): Bless his heart, old Fezziwig.

C. PAST: Come, Ebenezer Scrooge.

SCROOGE: Oh, let me stay a while longer.

C. PAST: No, another vision appears. You are older still . . . a young man, engaged to be married, I think.

SCROOGE: Yes. And that young lady, there—that was Belle, my intended. Lovely Belle . . .

C. PAST: Listen . . . and remember.

BELLE (*A sweet woman's voice*): It matters little, Ebenezer. To you, very little. Another idol has displaced me in your heart; and if it can cheer and comfort you in time to come, as I would have tried to do, I have no just cause to grieve. Our engagement is an old one, made when we were both poor. You are changed, Ebenezer. Gold and gain are all that matter to you now. I have no dowry, no fortune. And so I release you from your promise to marry me, with a full heart, for the love of him you once were. May you be happy in the life you have chosen.

SCROOGE: No more, Spirit! Show me no more! Take me home! No more!

C. PAST: So be it . . . Ebenezer Scrooge.

SCROOGE (*In wonder*): Why . . . why, I'm in my room. I'm home . . . and alone! Did I dream it all? No . . . I couldn't have. Belle . . . Fan . . . Fezziwig. Such a lot of memories. But I must sleep, I'm tired. So tired.

SOUND: *Clock tolls one.*

SCROOGE: What? One o'clock? Could I have slept through a whole day?

SOUND: *Bells jingling gaily.*

SCROOGE: But what sound is that? Bells jingling?

CHRISTMAS PRESENT (*Laughs heartily*): Ha, ha, ha!

SCROOGE: Laughter! Someone's in my sitting room! I'll see who . . .

C. PRESENT (*In a jovial, vigorous voice*): Come in! Come in, and know me better, man!

SCROOGE: Who—who are you, fellow?

C. PRESENT: I am the Ghost of Christmas Present. Look upon me!

SCROOGE: What's all this mess you've got in my room? Holly, mistletoe, ivy—turkeys, geese, poultry!

C. PRESENT: And see here! A roaring fire in the chimney, sausages, mince pies, plum puddings, oranges, pears, bowls of punch! A Christmas feast!

SCROOGE: All to teach me a lesson, no doubt. Well, if you have aught to teach me, let me profit by it. Spirit, conduct me where you will.

C. PRESENT: Touch my robe!

SOUND: *Wind.*

SCROOGE: What house is that, the one with the peeled paint, there?

C. PRESENT: Go to the window, and see. Watch the people who live there; listen to their words.

SCROOGE: It's a poor woman, with several young'uns by her side. She's talking to them.

C. PRESENT: Listen!

MRS. CRATCHIT: What has got your precious father, then? And your brother, Tiny Tim? And Martha wasn't as late last Christmas Day by half an hour!

CRATCHIT BOY: Here comes Martha now, Mother!

MARTHA: Merry Christmas, Mother, children!

ALL: Merry Christmas, Martha!

CRATCHIT GIRL: Wait till you see the goose, Martha!

MARTHA: I'm sorry I'm late, but there was so much work to be done.

MRS. CRATCHIT: Well, never mind, so long as ye are come. Sit ye down by the fire and have a warm, Lord bless ye!

GIRL: No, no! There's Father coming!

BOY: Hide, Martha, hide! We'll pretend you aren't coming!

MARTHA (*Gaily*): All right!

CRATCHIT (*Entering*): Merry Christmas, Mother, children!

ALL: Merry Christmas, Father! Merry Christmas, Tiny Tim!

TINY TIM: Merry Christmas! Mmm, the goose smells so good!

CRATCHIT: And how is . . . why, where's our Martha?

MRS. CRATCHIT (*Seriously*): Not coming.

CRATCHIT: Not coming upon Christmas Day?

MARTHA (*Laughing*): We're only teasing, Father. Here I am. And a merry Christmas to you!

GIRL: Come on, Tiny Tim. Come with us!

BOY: Come listen to the Christmas pudding sing in the copper!

TINY TIM: Oh, yes! Show me!

MRS. CRATCHIT (*Softly*): And how did little Tim behave?

CRATCHIT: As good as gold, and better. Somehow he gets thoughtful, poor little cripple, sitting by himself so much, and thinks the strangest things you ever heard. He told me that he hoped the people in church saw him, because he was a cripple, and it might be pleasant for them to remember upon Christmas Day, who made lame beggars walk and blind men see.

MRS. CRATCHIT: If only we could do something for him . . . but hush! Here come the children back again!

TINY TIM: I saw the goose!

BOY: And we smelled the pudding!

GIRL: It looks delicious!

MARTHA: And it will be delicious, too!

CRATCHIT (*Lustily*): And now—a toast!

ALL (*Ad lib*): A toast! Hurrah! Serve out the punch! (*Etc.*)

CRATCHIT: Mr. Scrooge! I'll give you Mr. Scrooge, the Founder of the Feast!

MRS. CRATCHIT: The Founder of the Feast, indeed! I wish I had him here. I'd give him a piece of my mind to feast upon, and I hope he'd have a good appetite for it.

CRATCHIT: My dear, the children. Christmas Day!

MRS. CRATCHIT: It should be Christmas Day, I'm sure, on which one drinks the health of such an odious, stingy, hard, unfeeling man as Mr. Scrooge. You know he is, Robert. Nobody knows it better than you do, poor fellow.

CRATCHIT: My dear, Christmas Day!

MRS. CRATCHIT: Very well. I'll drink his health for your sake and the day's, but not for his. Long life to him! A merry Christmas and a happy New Year. He'll be very merry and very happy, I'm sure.

ALL (*Listlessly*): To Mr. Scrooge.

CRATCHIT: And now, a merry Christmas to us all, my dears. God bless us!

ALL: God bless us!

TINY TIM: God bless us, every one.

SCROOGE (*In anguish*): Spirit, tell me if Tiny Tim will live.

C. PRESENT: I see a vacant seat in the poor chimney corner, and a crutch without an owner, carefully preserved. If these shadows remain unaltered by the Future, the child will die.

SCROOGE: Oh, no, kind Spirit. Say he will be spared!

C. PRESENT: Why worry about crippled Tiny Tim? If he be like to die, he had better do it, and decrease the surplus population. Man—if man you be in heart— remember and repent your words.

SCROOGE (*Miserably*): I do, I do. Oh, take me home, Spirit. Show me no more. Take me home!

C. PRESENT (*Mysteriously*): As you wish, Ebenezer Scrooge!

SOUND: *Wind wailing.*

SCROOGE: Take me home, home! Why—why I'm in my bed again. In my bed! Was it a dream? No, impossible. And yet—there's no holly, no mistletoe! But it wasn't a dream, I'm sure of it!

SOUND: *Clock tolling twelve.*

SCROOGE (*After the third toll*): Oh, dear, oh, dear, it's midnight! It's time for him to be coming, the Ghost I fear most of all—the third. The Ghost of Christmas Future. The Ghost of Christmas Yet to Come.

MUSIC: *Eerie theme.*

SCROOGE (*Gasps*): It's he—there in the shadows, I see him. A phantom, draped and hooded, coming like the mist! (*More loudly*) I am in the presence of the Ghost of Christmas Yet to Come? You nod. You are about to show me shadows of the things that have not happened, but will happen in the time before us. Is that so, Spirit? Ghost of the Future, I fear you more than any spectre I have seen. But as I know your purpose is to do me good, I am prepared to bear your company. Lead on! Lead on! The night is waning fast, and it is precious time to me, I know. Lead on, Spirit!

SOUND: *Wind.*

SCROOGE: What, Spirit? Do you, too, bring me to the home of my clerk, Bob Cratchit? You motion me toward the window. There is Mrs. Cratchit by the fire, with her sewing. And the children—they're so quiet! Still as statues, they are.

MARTHA: Are you crying, Mother?

MRS. CRATCHIT: No, dear, it's—it's the light, it hurts my eyes. They're weak by candlelight, and I wouldn't show weak eyes to your father when he comes, for the whole world. It must be near time for him to come.

MARTHA: Past it, rather.

BOY: He walks a little slower than he used to, these past few evenings, Mother.

MRS. CRATCHIT: I've known him to walk with—I've known him to walk with Tiny Tim upon his shoulder, very fast indeed.

GIRL: So have I, Mother.

MARTHA: And so have we all.

MRS. CRATCHIT: But he was very light to carry, and his father loved him so, that it was no trouble. Now, there's your father at the door!

MARTHA: Come here, Father. Sit by the fire.

CRATCHIT (*Slowly, sadly*): Thank you, Martha, my dear.

GIRL: Your tea is ready, Father.

MRS. CRATCHIT: You—you went today, Robert?

CRATCHIT: Yes, my dear. I wish you could have gone. It would have done you good to see how green a place it is. But you'll see it often. I promised him that we would. (*With a break in his voice*) My . . . little child. My . . . Tiny Tim.

SCROOGE: Poor Tiny Tim . . . oh, why did he have to die? You draw me with you, Spirit. This court through which we hurry now—I know this place. This is where my place of occupation is. I see my office. Let me look in. Why . . . why, it's not my office! The furniture has been changed. That man at my desk, who is it? Why, it's my nephew, Fred! What is the meaning of this? Will you answer my questions, Phantom? But no; you draw me on. A churchyard, overrun with weeds and grass, the growth of vegetation's death, not life. What miserable place is this, unkept, uncared for? What wretched souls find their ends beneath this neglected soil? You single out a grave, Spectre. Before I draw nearer to that stone to which you point, answer me one question. Are these the shadows of the things that will be, or are they the shadows of the things that may be? You answer not, but point to a headstone. The stone is decayed—I can't make out the name. I can only feel out the letters. They spell Eb . . . Ebe . . . Ebenezer

Scrooge! Then this wretched grave, this dismal end, is mine! No, Spirit, oh, no! Spirit, hear me. I am not the man I was. Why show me this, Spirit? I will change! I will honor Christmas in my heart, and try to keep it all the year. I will live in the Past, the Present, and the Future. The Spirits of all three shall strive within me. Oh, tell me I may sponge away the writing on this stone. Tell me so! Tell me! Tell me!

SOUND: *Clock tolling one.*

SCROOGE (*Whimpering*): Tell me, Spirit! Tell me! Why— why, I'm in my room. I'm home—I'm alive! Oh, Jacob Marley, I will change! Heaven and Christmastime be praised! I say it on my knees, Jacob, on my knees! Oh, I don't know what to do. I'm as light as a feather, as happy as an angel. I'm as merry as a schoolboy! Merry Christmas, old room, old bed curtains! Merry Christmas, old saucepan! But what am I standing here for? I must find out what day it is!

SOUND: *Window being opened.*

SCROOGE: Hallo! Hallo there, what's today, boy?

A YOUNG COCKNEY (*At a slight distance*): Today? Why, it's Christmas Day!

SCROOGE: Thank heavens! Christmas! Then I haven't missed it. Hallo, my fine fellow!

COCKNEY: Yes, sir?

SCROOGE: Do you know the poulterers in the next street but one, at the corner? Do you know whether they've sold the prize turkey that was hanging up there—not the little one, but the great big one?

COCKNEY: It's hanging there now, sir.

SCROOGE: Is it? What an intelligent boy you are! Go and buy it—here's the money, and a half-crown extra for you.

COCKNEY (*Impressed*): Yes, *sir!*

SCROOGE: And have them send it to this address. Merry Christmas!

COCKNEY: Merry Christmas to you, too, sir!

SCROOGE: Ha, ha! I'll send it to Bob Cratchit's! He shan't know who sent it. What a surprise it will be—twice the size of Tiny Tim! But what am I standing here in my nightshirt for? I've things to do, people to see. I must be off. Whee!

MUSIC: *Gay theme.*

SOUND: *Knock at door; door opens.*

SCROOGE: Fred!

FRED (*Amazed*): Why, who is this I see?

SCROOGE: It's I, your Uncle Scrooge. I've come to dinner, for Christmas, you know. Will you let me in, Fred?

FRED: Let you in! You'll be lucky if I don't shake your hand off! Merry Christmas, Uncle Ebenezer! (*Calling off*) Nancy! Look who's here! Set another place at table. It's Uncle Scrooge, for Christmas!

MUSIC: *Delightful theme.*

SCROOGE: Ah, what a wonderful time that was at Fred's yesterday. What a charming girl his wife is. I really must do something for them! (*In secret glee*) Oho, but here comes Bob Cratchit. I hoped I'd get here to the office ahead of him to surprise him!

SOUND: *Door opening.*

SCROOGE (*Sourly*): Hallo! What do you mean by coming here at this time of day, Cratchit?

CRACHIT (*Timidly*): I'm very sorry, Mr. Scrooge, sir. It won't happen again, sir, I promise. I was making a bit merry yesterday, and . . .

SCROOGE (*Growling*): Now, I'll tell you what. I'm not going to stand for this sort of thing any more, and therefore I am about to—raise your salary!

CRATCHIT (*Aghast*): Mr. Scrooge!

SCROOGE (*Laughing genially*): A merry Christmas, Bob. A merrier Christmas, my good fellow, than I've given you for many a year. I'll raise your salary—and we must find the best doctor in all of London for that young son of yours.

CRATCHIT: I—I don't know what to say, Mr. Scrooge.

SCROOGE: Don't say anything, Bob, old fellow. This is the happiest Christmas of my life.

CRATCHIT: And of mine. As Tiny Tim observed, God bless us, every one!

MUSIC: *Christmas finale.*

THE END

Through the Looking-Glass

by Lewis Carroll

Characters

ALICE
THE RED QUEEN
TWEEDLEDUM
TWEEDLEDEE
THE WHITE QUEEN
HUMPTY DUMPTY
THE WHITE KNIGHT
NARRATOR

NARRATOR: Alice was sitting in the big easy chair, playing with Dinah, her cat, and wondering what the best thing to do might be. If Dinah had been a person, instead of a cat, they might have had a game of chess. Alice was very fond of chess. Or perhaps they could play make-believe, for Alice was very fond of make-believe, too. She was trying to decide which would be better—chess or make-believe; and not coming up with a satisfactory answer, she thought she might consult Dinah herself on the matter.

ALICE: Kitty, can you play chess? Now don't smile, my dear. I'm asking it seriously. Whenever I play, you

watch me so closely that I almost think you understand
the game. And when I say "Check," you always purr
with pleasure. Kitty dear, let's pretend that you're the
Red Queen. Do you know, I think if you sat up and
folded your arms, you'd look exactly like her. *Do* try
to look like the Red Queen, Kitty. Oh, you bad cat,
why don't you cooperate? If you're not good directly,
I'll put you right into Looking-Glass House. What's
that, Kitty? Don't you know what Looking-Glass House
is? Come here and I'll show you. You see, it's the house
just on the other side of our looking-glass. The room
on the other side, of course, is just like our drawing-
room on this side, only with everything reversed. But
that's just to fool us. Just beyond that doorway—the
part you can't see in the looking-glass—I'm sure there
are the most wonderful things anyone could ever imagine. Oh, how I wish I could get into Looking-Glass
House. Let's pretend that there *is* a way. Let's pretend
that the glass has become as soft as gauze, so that we
can get through. Why—why, Kitty. The glass *is* getting
soft. It's turning into a sort of mist, I declare. Kitty,
I'm going through the glass. What fun! I'm going
through the looking-glass!

MUSIC: *Gay theme.*

NARRATOR: Sure enough, Alice found herself able to step
through the looking-glass over the mantel and right
into Looking-Glass House. She looked around. Everything in the room was just the same as in her own
drawing-room at home, but it was all reversed. Was it
really the same, she wondered, or did it just appear
to be? She spied a book on the table and turned over
a few pages.

ALICE: What curious writing! It's not like proper writing
at all. I wish I could read it—but I don't know the

language. Why, it's a looking-glass book, of course. I'll have to hold it up to the glass to see what it says. Oh, I see. It's a poem. "Jabberwocky."

> " 'Twas brillig, and the slithy toves
> Did gyre and gimble in the wabe:
> All mimsy were the borogoves,
> And the mome raths outgrabe."

How funny. It *seems* to be English, and yet somehow it doesn't quite make sense. Somehow it seems to fill my head with ideas—only I don't know exactly what they are. Oh, it's all as new and different as I imagined! What a wonderful, curious place is Looking-Glass House!

MUSIC: *Delightful theme.*

NARRATOR: Anxious to see what lay behind the door she had always thought so much about, Alice threw the book aside and dashed out of the room. Without thinking twice she ran down the stairs and out into the garden. Imagine her surprise when she collided with—of all people—the Red Queen herself. She looked just like the Red Queen in Alice's chess set, crown and all; but by some miracle, she had grown, so that she was now as tall as Alice herself.

RED QUEEN: Well, young lady, where do you come from? And where are you going?

ALICE: I—I'm not quite sure, ma'am. I seem to have lost my way. ▪

RED QUEEN: I don't know what you mean by *your* way. All the ways around here belong to me. Curtsy while you're thinking what to say. It saves time. And always say "Your Majesty."

ALICE: I only wanted to see what your garden was like,

Your Majesty. I declare, it's marked out just like a large chessboard.

RED QUEEN: Of course it is, my dear.

ALICE: Oh, I see! It's a great huge game of chess that's being played. Oh, what fun it is. I wish I could play. I wouldn't mind being a Pawn, if only I might join—though of course I should like to be a Queen best.

RED QUEEN: That's easily managed. You can be the White Queen's Pawn, if you like. And you're in the Second Square to begin with. When you get to the Eighth Square, you'll be a Queen. Now, take my hand, my dear, for we must begin to run.

ALICE (*Beginning to pant for breath*): Where are we—running to?

RED QUEEN: Faster, faster! Don't try to talk!

ALICE: My—goodness. I've never—run so fast—in my life. Are we almost there?

RED QUEEN: Almost there? Why, we passed it ten minutes ago. Faster! (*Sighing*) There now. You may rest a little.

ALICE: Oh, I'm so glad. But—but we're under the same tree we were under when we started. Everything's just as it was.

RED QUEEN: Of course it is. What did you expect?

ALICE: Well, in *our* country, you generally get to someplace else if you run very fast for a long time as we've been doing.

RED QUEEN: A slow sort of country! *Here,* you see, it takes all the running you can do just to keep in the same place. If you want to get somewhere else, you must run twice as fast. Now then: at the end of two yards, I shall give you your directions. (*Pause*) You have nothing to say?

ALICE: I didn't know I was supposed to say anything.

RED QUEEN: You *should* have said "It's extremely kind of

you to tell me all this." But we'll pretend you have said it. Your instructions are to get to the Eighth Square as fast as you can. Then you'll be a regular Queen. Now, a few words of advice. Speak in French when you can't think of the English for a thing; turn out your toes as you walk; and remember who you are. That's all you need to know. Goodbye!

ALICE: Goodbye, Red Queen. And thank you ever so much for starting me off.

RED QUEEN: Think nothing of it, my dear. I shall see you again in the Eighth Square, when we are Queens together. And won't that be feasting and fun! Goodbye.

ALICE (*In amazement*): I declare! She's running faster now than she did before. How complicated it is to play chess when you're one of the pieces yourself. I can hardly believe that I'm actually a Pawn. Oh, I *do* hope that sometime soon I shall reach the Eighth Square and become a Queen! I wonder, how am I supposed to begin?

NARRATOR: It was not a very difficult question for Alice to answer, as there was only one road. After walking along for a little way, Alice came to two signs. One of them said "To Tweedledum's House"; the other said "To the House of Tweedledee". And both signs pointed in the same direction.

ALICE: I do believe that they live in the same house. I wonder I never thought of that before. I'll go and visit them—but I won't stay long. Only long enough to be polite, and to ask them if they know the way to the Eighth Square. Why, there they are! And they look just as though they were statues, with their arms about each other's necks. Oh dear, I wonder if I should speak first, or if I should wait for one of them to begin? Perhaps if I wait a moment, they'll begin.

TWEEDLEDUM: If you think we're waxworks, you ought to pay, you know. Waxworks weren't made to be looked at for nothing. Nohow!

TWEEDLEDEE: Contrariwise, if you think we're alive, you ought to speak.

ALICE: I'm sure I'm very sorry. I didn't mean to be rude —but seeing you standing here reminded me of the poem. You know "Tweedledum and Tweedledee agreed to have a battle, for Tweedledum said Tweedledee had spoiled his nice new rattle."

TWEEDLEDUM: It isn't so. Nohow.

TWEEDLEDEE: Contrariwise. If it was so, it might be; and if it were so, it would be. That's logic.

ALICE: Could either of you gentlemen please tell me the best way to the Eighth Square?

TWEEDLEDUM: You've begun wrong. The first thing in a visit is to say "How do you do?" and shake hands.

ALICE: It would never do to say "How do you do?" now, though. We seem to have gone beyond that somehow, haven't we?

TWEEDLEDUM: Nohow. And thank you *very* much for asking.

TWEEDLEDEE: So *much* obliged. Will you help me put up my umbrella? Thank you very much. There, that's it.

ALICE: Do you think it's going to rain?

TWEEDLEDUM: No, I don't think it is. At least not under this umbrella. Nohow.

ALICE: But it may rain outside the umbrella, mayn't it? On me, I mean.

TWEEDLEDEE: It may if it chooses. We've no objection. Contrariwise.

ALICE (*Hurt*): You don't seem very polite.

TWEEDLEDUM (*Gasping*): Do you see *that?*

ALICE: It's only a rattle. Not a rattle*snake,* you know. Just an old rattle—quite old and broken.

TWEEDLEDUM (*Angrily*): Exactly. It's spoilt now, spoilt, spoilt!

ALICE: You needn't be so angry about an old rattle.

TWEEDLEDUM: But it *isn't* old, I tell you. I bought it only yesterday. My nice new rattle! And it's all Tweedledee's fault. You agree to have a battle about it, don't you, Tweedledee?

TWEEDLEDEE (*Bored*): I suppose so. Only Alice must help us dress up.

ALICE: I will do no such thing. It's foolish to have a battle over such a silly thing. If you want to fight, you may go ahead. But you needn't count on my help.

TWEEDLEDUM: If you won't help, then you won't. Besides, you haven't time. You must be off to the next square.

TWEEDLEDEE: It's just over the hill. You can't miss it. And thank you very much for calling.

ALICE: Thank *you* for your directions. And I hope you don't hurt yourselves.

TWEEDLEDUM: Oh, we never do. Nohow.

TWEEDLEDEE: Contrariwise. Ready, Tweedledum?

TWEEDLEDUM: Ready. One, two, three—go!

MUSIC: *Happy theme.*

NARRATOR: There seemed to be nothing she could do to stop the battle, so Alice left the two brothers and went in the direction they had indicated. As she walked along, the wind blew somebody's shawl in her direction, and Alice caught it. Farther along the road she saw a funny little old lady running toward her. It was, without doubt, the owner of the shawl—and Alice noticed that she looked very much like the chess piece of the White Queen.

ALICE: I'm very glad I happened to be in the way, ma'am,

when your shawl came floating along. Here, let me help you adjust it. Tell me, am I addressing the White Queen?

WHITE QUEEN: Well, yes, if you call that a dressing. It isn't *my* notion of the thing at all, for you're doing it all wrong.

ALICE: If Your Majesty will only tell me the right way to begin, I'll do it as well as I can.

WHITE QUEEN: I don't know what's the matter with that shawl. It's out of temper, I think. I've pinned it here, and I've pinned it there, but there's no pleasing it. And look at the mess my hair is in.

ALICE: Perhaps what you need is a lady's maid.

WHITE QUEEN: I'm sure I'll take *you* with pleasure. Two pence a week is what the position pays—and, of course, jam every other day.

ALICE: I don't want you to hire *me*—and I don't care for jam.

WHITE QUEEN: It's very *good* jam.

ALICE: Well, I don't want any jam. Not today, at any rate.

WHITE QUEEN: You couldn't have it even if you *did* want it. The rule is, jam tomorrow and jam yesterday—but never jam today. It's jam every *other* day. Today isn't any other day, you know.

ALICE: I don't understand you. It's all so dreadfully confusing.

WHITE QUEEN: That's the effect of living backwards. But there is one great advantage in it: my memory works both ways, and it's nice to remember things before they happen.

ALICE: I'm sure *mine* works only one way.

WHITE QUEEN: How sad for you. (*Shrieking*) Oh, oh, oh. My finger's bleeding! Oh, oh, oh, oh, oh.

ALICE: What is the matter? Have you pricked your finger?

WHITE QUEEN: I haven't pricked it yet—but I soon shall. Oh, oh, oh. There, you see? The pin of my brooch has come undone, and I must fasten it up again.

ALICE: Take care, you're holding it all crooked. Oh, you've stabbed yourself with it.

WHITE QUEEN (*Calmly*): That accounts for the bleeding, you see. Now you understand the way things happen here.

ALICE: But why don't you scream *now?*

WHITE QUEEN: I've done all the screaming already. What would be the good of having it all over again? Now then: how old are you?

ALICE: I'm seven and a half.

WHITE QUEEN: I believe you. Now I'll give *you* something to believe. I'm just one hundred and one, five months, and a day.

ALICE: I can't believe that.

WHITE QUEEN: Can't you? Try again. Draw a long breath and shut your eyes.

ALICE: There's no use trying. I just *can't* believe impossible things.

WHITE QUEEN: Poor girl, you probably haven't had much practice. When I was your age, I always did it for half an hour each day. Why, sometimes I've believed as many as six impossible things before breakfast. But we have talked enough, my dear. It is time for you to move on to the next square.

ALICE: Will I see you again, Your Majesty?

WHITE QUEEN: By and by, perhaps. One never knows in chess. But we must part for the moment. You go that way, and before you know it you'll be in the next square.

ALICE: I do hope I meet somebody nice there.

WHITE QUEEN: Why, what a silly girl you are. You'll meet the nicest one of all: Humpty Dumpty!

MUSIC: *Gay theme.*

NARRATOR: Sure enough, when she reached the next square, there was Humpty Dumpty, perched on his wall. Humpty Dumpty himself! Alice could hardly believe it. She ran forward with her arms outstretched, for she felt that at any moment he might fall and break into a million pieces.

ALICE: It *is* Humpty Dumpty, it is! And how exactly like an egg he is.

HUMPTY: It's very provoking to be called an egg—very.

ALICE: I said you looked like an egg, sir. And some eggs are very pretty, you know.

HUMPTY: Some people have no more sense than a baby. Tell me your name and your business.

ALICE: My name is Alice.

HUMPTY: It's a stupid enough name. What does it mean?

ALICE: Must a name mean something?

HUMPTY: Of course it must. Now *my* name means the shape I am—and a very good shape it is, too. With a name like yours, you might be any shape.

ALICE: Why do you sit here all alone?

HUMPTY: Because there's nobody here with me. Did you think I didn't know the answer to that riddle? Ask another.

ALICE: Don't you think you'd be a lot safer on the ground?

HUMPTY: What tremendously easy riddles you ask! Of course I don't think so. If I ever did fall off—which there's no chance of—but *if* I did, the King has promised me. . . .

ALICE (*Promptly*): To send all his horses and all his men.

HUMPTY: Shame on you. You must have been eavesdropping to know that.

ALICE: I haven't, indeed! It's in a book.

HUMPTY: Ah, that's different. They may write such things in a book if they like. Now let's get back to the last remark but one.

ALICE: I'm afraid I can't quite remember it.

HUMPTY: In that case it's my turn to choose a new subject. So here's a question for you. How old did you say you were?

ALICE (*Brightly*): Seven years and six months.

HUMPTY: Wrong! You never said a word about it!

ALICE: I thought you meant "How old *are* you?"

HUMPTY: If I'd meant that, I'd have said it. Seven years and six months. An uncomfortable sort of age. If you'd asked my advice, I'd have said, "Leave off at seven." But it's too late now.

ALICE: But one can't help growing, you know.

HUMPTY: One can't, perhaps, but two can. Now it's your turn to pick a subject.

ALICE: That's a very nice belt you have on. Or rather, necktie. Or is it a belt? That is, it looks like a tie . . .

HUMPTY: It is a very provoking thing when a person doesn't know a belt from a necktie. It's a necktie, my child. The White Queen gave it to me as an unbirthday present.

ALICE: I beg your pardon, but what is an *un*birthday present?

HUMPTY: A present given when it isn't your birthday, of course.

ALICE: Oh. I like birthday presents best.

HUMPTY: You don't know what you're talking about. There is only one day in the year when you may get a birthday present, but three hundred and sixty-four days when you might get an *un*birthday present. There's glory for you.

ALICE: I don't know what you mean by glory.

HUMPTY: Of course you don't—till I tell you. I meant, "There's a nice knock-down argument for you."

ALICE: But glory doesn't mean "a nice knock-down argument".

HUMPTY: When *I* use a word it means just what I want it to mean: neither more nor less. But this is all impenetrability. By which, of course, I mean that we had better change the subject and it would be just as well if you'd mention what you're going to do next, as I suppose you don't mean to stand here all the rest of your life.

ALICE: You're so good at explaining things, I wonder if you could explain the poem "Jabberwocky" to me.

HUMPTY: I'm not very good at explaining poems, I'm afraid. But I can *repeat* poetry. Shall I recite a poem for you now?

ALICE: That would be very nice.

HUMPTY: "In winter, when the fields are white, I sing this song for your delight." Only I don't sing it.

ALICE: I see you don't.

HUMPTY: If you can *see* whether I'm singing or not, you've very sharp eyes. "In spring, when woods are getting green, I'll try and tell you what I mean." There now, wasn't that lovely?

ALICE: Is that all?

HUMPTY: That's all. Goodbye.

ALICE: Oh. I suppose, then, that I must go. Goodbye, till we meet again.

HUMPTY: I shouldn't know you again if we *did* meet. You're so exactly like other people.

ALICE: The face is what one goes by, generally.

HUMPTY: That's just what I mean. You have the same face everybody has—two eyes, nose in the middle, mouth under. Now, if both eyes were on one side of your face . . . or if your mouth were at the top. . . . But it's too late to do anything about that now. So goodbye till we *never* meet again. It's been very nice talking with you.

ALICE: Thank you, sir. But before I go, can you tell me in which direction I am next to move?

HUMPTY: Why, straight ahead. That's the way Pawns always move. Bishops, you know, move on an angle. And Knights, why, they move three squares at a time.

ALICE: Yes, I know.

HUMPTY: Speaking of Knights, at this very moment the White Knight is in the middle of his move. If you run straight ahead, you may catch up with him.

ALICE: How wonderful to meet a real Knight! Thank you very much, Humpty Dumpty, for a lovely conversation.

HUMPTY: Not at all, my dear. Impatience!

ALICE: I suppose that means something different, too?

HUMPTY: Of course it does. Impatience always means goodbye. Impatience, Alice. Impatience!

MUSIC: *Rollicking theme.*

NARRATOR: Alice waited a moment, but as Humpty had closed his eyes, she said goodbye once more and quietly walked away. She couldn't help thinking to herself about Humpty Dumpty.

ALICE: Of all the unsatisfactory. . . .

NARRATOR: But she never finished the sentence. At that very moment a heavy crash shook the forest from end to end. Poor Humpty Dumpty! Alice had no time to think further about his fate, however, for by now she had reached the next square. And sure enough, just as Humpty had predicted, there was the White Knight. How kindly he looked as he rode up on his white horse.

KNIGHT: It was a glorious victory, wasn't it? I can even take one more person prisoner.

ALICE: I hope it won't be me, sir. I don't want to be anybody's prisoner. I want to be a Queen.

KNIGHT: So you will, when you've crossed the next brook. I'll see you safe to the edge of the wood—and then I must go back, you know, for that's the end of my move.

ALICE: Thank you very much. Perhaps I shouldn't mention it, sir, but I notice there are a great many curious objects fastened to your horse's saddle.

KNIGHT: Ah, yes—all my inventions. I see you're admiring the little box. It's my own invention to keep sandwiches in. You see I carry it upside down, so that the rain can't get in.

ALICE: But the things can get *out* that way. Did you know the lid was open?

KNIGHT: I didn't know it. Well, the box is of no use without them. I'll just hang it on this tree. Can you guess why?

ALICE: No, sir, I can't.

KNIGHT: In hopes that some bees may make a nest in it. Then I should get the honey.

ALICE: But you have a beehive—or something like one—tied to the saddle.

KNIGHT: Yes, and it's a very good beehive, too. But not a single bee has come near it yet. And the other thing is a mousetrap. I suppose the mice keep the bees out—or the bees keep the mice out.

ALICE: It isn't very likely, is it, that there would be any mice on a horse's back?

KNIGHT: Not *very* likely. But if they *do* come, I don't choose to have them running all about. It's best to be prepared for everything. That's why the horse has those anklets 'round his feet.

ALICE: What are *they* for?

KNIGHT: To guard against the bites of sharks. It's an invention of my own. I say, I hope you have your hair well fastened on.

ALICE: Why—only in the usual way.

KNIGHT: That's hardly enough. You see, the wind is so very strong here. It's as strong as soup.

ALICE: Have you invented a plan for keeping hair from being blown off?

KNIGHT: Not yet. But I have a plan for keeping it from *falling* off. First, you take a stick. Then you make your hair creep up it, like a vine. The reason hair falls off is because it hangs down. Things never fall upward, you know. It's my own invention. You may try it if you like.

ALICE (*Dubiously*): Perhaps I will . . . someday.

KNIGHT: My newest invention is a way of getting over a gate. You see, I said to myself: The only difficulty is with the feet, for the head is already high enough. So first I put my head on the gate—then the head's high enough. Then I stand on my head—and that makes the feet high enough. And then I'm over, you see.

ALICE: Yes, I suppose you would be over when that was done.

KNIGHT: Well, here we are at the end of my move. I must leave you now.

ALICE: But what am I to do next?

KNIGHT: You've only a few yards to go. Down the hill and over that little brook, and then you'll be a Queen. But you'll stay and see me off first, I hope. It would encourage me so.

ALICE: Certainly, if you'd like me to.

KNIGHT: Goodbye, then. Remember, just over the brook, and you've reached the Eighth Square.

NARRATOR: Alice waited until the kindly old White Knight had turned his horse around. Then they shook hands, and he trotted off. Alice waved until he was out of sight, then turned and ran down the hill. A very few steps brought her to the edge of the brook, and before she could think, she was flying across it. In a moment, she had come to rest on a lawn as soft as moss, with little flower beds dotted about it here and there.

ALICE (*Delightedly*): The Eighth Square at last! How lovely! Oh, how glad I am to get here. And what is this on my head? It feels—it feels as though—it *is!* A crown, a crown, my very own crown. I've reached the Eighth Square. I have become a Queen!

MUSIC: *Gay theme.*

NARRATOR: At last she was a Queen—the most important piece in the whole game of chess. She looked around proudly, and was amazed to discover the Red Queen and the White Queen sitting close to her, one on either side. She wanted to ask if the game was over, but thought it might not be polite. So, instead, she said:

ALICE: Please, would you tell me—

RED QUEEN (*Interrupting*): Speak when you're spoken to.

ALICE: But if everybody obeyed that rule, and if you spoke only when you were spoken to, and if everybody else waited till *they* were spoken to, nobody would ever say anything at all.

RED QUEEN: Ridiculous! Why, don't you see, child. . . .

ALICE: I'm not a child any more. I'm a Queen.

RED QUEEN: Nonsense. You aren't a Queen until you've passed the examination.

ALICE: I'm sure I didn't mean. . . .

RED QUEEN: That's just what I complain of. You *should* have meant. What is the use of a child without meaning? Even a joke has meaning, and a child is of more importance than a joke. You couldn't deny that, even if you tried with both your hands.

ALICE: I don't deny things with my hands.

RED QUEEN: Nobody said you did. I said, you couldn't if you tried. But let us get on with the examination. White Queen, ask the first question.

WHITE QUEEN: Can you do Addition, Alice?

ALICE: Oh yes, I was very good at Addition in school.

WHITE QUEEN: Then tell me what one . . . and one . . . and one . . . and one and one (*Very fast*) and one and one and one and one add up to.

ALICE: I don't know. I lost count.

RED QUEEN: She can't do Addition. How about Subtraction? Take nine from eight.

ALICE: I can't take nine from eight because. . . .

WHITE QUEEN: Can't do Subtraction, either. Can you do Division? Divide a loaf by a knife—what's the answer to that?

ALICE: I suppose—

RED QUEEN: Bread-and-butter, of course. You can't do sums at all!

ALICE (*Angrily*): Can either of *you* do sums?

WHITE QUEEN (*Ashamed*): No, I can't, though Red Queen is very good at them. But I'll tell you a secret. I can read words of one letter!

RED QUEEN: Let us try useful questions. How is bread made?

ALICE (*Confidently*): I know that. You take some flour. . . .

WHITE QUEEN: Where do you pick the flower? In a garden or a hedge?

ALICE: It isn't picked at all. It's ground.

WHITE QUEEN: How many acres of ground? Don't leave out so many things.

RED QUEEN: That's enough of useful things. Let us try languages. What is the French for fiddle-dee-dee?

ALICE (*Protesting*): But fiddle-dee-dee's not English.

RED QUEEN: Who ever said it was?

ALICE (*Defiantly*): If you tell me what language it is, I'll tell you the French for it.

RED QUEEN: Queens never make bargains.

ALICE: I wish Queens never asked questions.

WHITE QUEEN (*Yawning*): Oh dear, I am sleepy.

RED QUEEN (*Yawning*): Yes, so am I. We shall have to postpone the examinations.

ALICE: Until when?

RED QUEEN: Until a year from next Thursday.

ALICE: But that isn't fair! I've succeeded in getting as far as the Eighth Square. I don't want to have to wait until next year to become Queen.

WHITE QUEEN: But you don't have to wait until next year. My backward memory tells me that you didn't pass the examination until the third time around—*three* years from half-past last Monday.

ALICE (*Almost in tears*): But it isn't fair. I've worked so hard to become Queen, getting all the way from the Second Square to the Eighth. I listened to Tweedledum and Tweedledee have their foolish quarrel. I nearly lost my temper trying to fix the White Queen's shawl. I had to listen to Humpty Dumpty's nonsense, and admire the White Knight's worthless inventions. I've answered your horrid questions and been bullied about by you, but no matter what I do it doesn't seem to please you. And now you say I must wait three years before I become Queen.

RED QUEEN: Tut, tut, my dear. Queens never lose their tempers.

ALICE: I can't stand this any longer. And as for *you*, Red Queen, you're the cause of it all.

RED QUEEN (*Disturbed*): Alice! What are you doing?

ALICE: I'm shaking you, that's what I'm doing. I'm going to shake you and shake you and shake you. I only wish I could shake some sense into you. I'm going to shake you until you turn—until you turn into an animal. I'm going to shake you until you turn into a cat!

RED QUEEN: No, no, no!

ALICE: Yes, yes, yes. I'm going to shake you—and shake you—and shake you. (*She sounds sleepy.*) Going to turn you into a kitten . . . shake you . . . and turn you . . . and shake you . . . and turn you . . . into a kit- ten . . . into a kitten.

MUSIC: *Dream-like music, played softly enough so that* Alice *can be heard speaking above it.*

ALICE (*Sleepily*): Into a kitten! I'm going to shake you into a kitten!

SOUND: *Cat purrs.*

ALICE (*Awake*): Why—why, Dinah! It's you! I did shake her into a kitten. I did, I did—and it's you. I—I'm home again. Yes, home in my own house, by the fire. Oh, Kitty, I've had the most marvelous dream. I dreamed I went into Looking-Glass House. And the Red Queen was there—and the White Queen, too. I saw Humpty Dumpty, and the White Knight, and Tweedledum and Tweedledee—and oh, Kitty, how strange it all was. And how real it all was to me then—but now I can see that I didn't really step through the Looking-Glass after all. It was a dream—it was all a wonderful, wonderful dream, Kitty. A dream!

LOOKING-GLASS CHARACTERS (*Softly*): Alice! Alice!

ALICE: Where are those voices coming from? It *was* a dream. I *know* it was a dream.

Looking-Glass Characters *(Their voices more distant):*
  Alice.
Alice: Or—or was it?
Music: *Happy theme.*

THE END

The Kidnapping of David Balfour

(from *Kidnapped*)

by Robert Louis Stevenson

Characters

ROBERT LOUIS STEVENSON
MR. CAMPBELL
DAVID BALFOUR
TWO MEN
A WOMAN
JENNET CLOUSTON
EBENEZER BALFOUR
CAPTAIN ELIAS HOSEASON
RANSOME, *a sailor*

SOUND: *Wind and ocean's roar.*
MUSIC: *Bagpipes playing martial air.*
STEVENSON: Of all the books that I have ever written, the one that is perhaps remembered best—the one of which I am possibly most fond myself—is the story which I set down in the form of memoirs—memoirs of one David Balfour, a young Scot who experienced many adventures. He was cast away on a desert isle, endured a journey in the wild Highlands, made the acquaintance of Alan Breck Stewart and other notorious outlaws, and

suffered hunger, thirst, great heat and extreme cold. I'd like to offer you now just a taste—a sampling of Davie's many adventures. Won't you come along with me? I'll be more than pleased to tell you the story of how his adventures began, for my name is Robert Louis Stevenson, and I *wrote* Davie's story—"Kidnapped."

Music: *Bagpipe music.*

Stevenson: It was a bright morning early in the month of June, the year of grace 1751, when eighteen-year-old David Balfour took the key for the last time out of the door of his father's house. The sun began to shine on the summit of the hills as he went down the road; and by the time he had come as far as the manse, the blackbirds were whistling in the garden lilacs, and the mist that hung around the valley at the time of dawn was beginning to die away. Mr. Campbell, the minister of Essendean, was waiting for him by the garden gate, good man! He asked David if he had breakfasted; and hearing that he lacked for nothing, took David's hand in both of his own and clapped it kindly under his arm.

Campbell: Well, Davie, lad, I will go with you as far as the ford, to set you on the way.

David: Thank you, Mr. Campbell. That will be so kind of you.

Campbell: Tell me, Davie—are ye sorry to leave Essendean?

David: Why, sir, if I knew where I was going, or what was likely to become of me, I would tell you candidly. Essendean is a good place indeed, and I have been very happy here, but then, I have never been anywhere else. Since both my father and mother are dead, there is nothing to keep me here, though to speak the truth, if I thought I had a chance to better myself where I am going, I would go with a better will.

CAMPBELL: Ay? In that case, I must tell you what I know. When your mother was gone, and your father began to sicken for his end, he gave me in charge of a certain letter which he said was your inheritance. He told me to give it to you, and send you with it to the house of Shaws, not far from Cramond.

DAVID: Why the house of Shaws, Mr. Campbell? Do you ken that?

CAMPBELL: That is your family name, lad: David Balfour of Shaws. It's an ancient, honest, reputable clan, too—though nowadays a bit gone to seed. And the letter—which I now give over to you, lad—is written in your father's own hand.

DAVID: Hm. It's addressed to the hands of Ebenezer Balfour, Esquire, of Shaws. (*Happily*) Why Mr. Campbell! All this time I believed myself to be simply the son of a poor country man in the Forest of Ettrick. And instead, I belong to a great house! Mr. Campbell, if you were in my shoes, would you go?

CAMPBELL: Of a surety, lad, that would I, and without pause. If the worst comes to the worst, and your high relations should put you to the door, you can turn around and come back.

DAVID: That can I, and will I, if need be.

CAMPBELL: Well, Davie—here is the gate, and I leave you. God be with you, young man, setting out on your own in this hard world. May He keep ye from harm. And—and, Davie, lad—don't forget us poor folk of Essendean, whom you grew up with, for we love you, boy, and long that someday we may be right proud of you.

DAVID: I shall try to make you so, Mr. Campbell. Thank you for your kindness and your care and your blessing. Goodbye, good friend.

CAMPBELL: Goodbye. God bless you. Goodbye, David Balfour of Shaws!

MUSIC: *Adventurous theme.*

STEVENSON: And so David set out, and after two days' journey, reached Cramond parish, the location of his family estate—the estate of whose existence he had only just learned. Wherever he went, he asked specific directions of the townspeople. The answers he received were all similar, and all puzzled him.

1ST MAN: The house of the Shaws? Turn to the right at the Red Cock Inn. But—but what does a fine young lad like you want with that old terror, Ebenezer Balfour of Shaws?

WOMAN (*After a pause*): That's right, laddie, straight ahead. But I'm warning you: don't go up there unless you have to. He's a nasty one, is old Ebenezer Balfour!

2ND MAN (*After a pause*): Ebenezer Balfour's? Go on up that hill. But let me warn you: if you get too near the place, he's liable to fire on you! Take care!

STEVENSON: In spite of these frightening warnings, David continued on. Once again he desired directions, and this time stopped a young, dark-haired woman.

DAVID: Excuse me, ma'am. Can you direct me to the house of Shaws?

JENNET (*Bitterly*): Aye, lad, you are right before it. Look there: Do you see that ruin, all black and jagged? There, where no smoke rises from the chimney, where no road leads to the door, where there is no semblance of a garden? There?

DAVID: Yes, ma'am, I do.

JENNET: Well, lad, that's it.

DAVID: That! That awful place which is not even finished?

JENNET (*Angrily*): That—aye, that is the house of Shaws! Blood built it; blood stopped the building of it; blood shall bring it down. See here! I spit upon the ground! Black be its fall! If ye see the lord, Ebenezer Balfour, tell him what ye hear; tell him this makes the twelve hundred and nineteenth time that Jennet Clouston has called down the curse on him, his house and stable, man, guest, and master, wife, miss or bairn—black, black be their fall! I, I, Jennet Clouston, curse them. Black be their fall!

MUSIC: *Eerie theme*.

STEVENSON: To say that David was disheartened would be to put the case mildly. Perplexed by the words of the villagers—especially those of Jennet Clouston—and unfavorably impressed by the appearance of his family house, he would have turned around and returned to Essendean if it had not been for his curiosity and courage. So, undaunted, he went up to the uncompleted castle known as the House of Shaws, walked past the dark windows, and knocked at the great, nail-studded door. In a minute, a window on the second floor opened, and an old man with a blunderbuss appeared.

EBENEZER (*From a short distance*): Whoever ye are, watch out for me gun. 'Tis loaded! What is your business?

DAVID: I have come here with a letter to Mr. Ebenezer Balfour of Shaws. Is he here?

EBENEZER: From whom is it?

DAVID: That is neither here nor there.

EBENEZER: Well, ye can put it down upon the doorstep and be off with ye.

DAVID: I will do no such thing. I will deliver it into Mr. Balfour's hands, as it was meant I should. It is a letter of introduction.

EBENEZER: Who are ye, yourself?

DAVID: I am not ashamed of my name. They call me David Balfour.

EBENEZER: David—David Balfour! Is your father dead, then? Ah, of course he is dead; and that'll be what brings ye chapping to my door. Well, man, be patient a moment. I'll let ye in.

MUSIC: *Strange theme.*

SOUND: *Squeaking door, opening slowly.*

EBENEZER: Ach, come in, lad, come in.

SOUND: *Door closing.*

EBENEZER: Now, then, let's see the letter.

DAVID: That you shall not. The letter is for Mr. Balfour, not for you.

EBENEZER: And who do ye think I am? Give me Alexander's letter.

DAVID (*Amazed*): You know my father's name?

EBENEZER: It would be strange if I didn't, for he was my born brother; as little as ye seem to like either me or my house, I'm your born uncle, Davie, my man, and you're my born nephew. So give us the letter, and sit down. But first, tell me: do you ken what's in it?

DAVID: You see for yourself, sir, that the seal has not been broken.

EBENEZER: Ay, but what brought ye here—besides to give me the letter, I mean? Ye'll have had some hopes, no doubt?

DAVID: I confess, sir, when I was told that I had kinsfolk well-to-do, I did indeed indulge the hope that they might help me in my life. But I am no beggar; I look for no favors at your hands, and I want none that are not freely given. For as poor as I appear, I have friends of my own that will be blithe to help me.

EBENEZER: Hoot-toot! Don't fly up in the snuff at me. We'll agree fine yet. I'm just as glad I let you in. But it's late, lad, and you'll be tired. Come awa' now to your bed.

This way. We can talk in the mornin'. Here. This is the door.

SOUND: *Creaking door opening.*

DAVID: What a dank smell!

EBENEZER: I wish ye a pleasant night, boy.

DAVID: Will you not give me a light to go to bed with?

EBENEZER: Hoot-toot! There'll be a fine moon soon. Lights in a house is a thing I don't agree with. I'm uncommon 'feared of fires. Good night to ye, Davie, my man.

SOUND: *Squeaking door closed.*

STEVENSON: And so, with neither lamp nor lantern, David Balfour was locked for the night in a great dark chamber in the mysterious House of Shaws. His mind was troubled by the many events of the past few days and by the strange old man, Ebenezer Balfour, who laid claim to being Davie's uncle. Gradually, though, the lad fell asleep, and after a fitful night, awoke to find himself in a sun-filled room. As his uncle had not yet unlocked the door, David looked around, and casually picked up a book from one of the shelves, and began to thumb through the pages. When his hand turned to the fly-leaf, though, his mind was puzzled.

DAVID: What's this? An entry on the fly-leaf? Why—it's an inscription, and in my own father's handwriting, too. "To my brother Ebenezer on his fifth birthday." That's strange. The script is a fine, manly, firm hand—such as my own father wrote all the years of my life. Yet the inscription says this book was given on Ebenezer's *fifth* birthday. Oh, there must have been some mistake. If Ebenezer owns this great house and all of the Balfour estate, he must have been the older son. Therefore my father was younger than five when he wrote this inscription. But that cannot be, for the handwriting is so firm, so mature. Perhaps Father was an exceptionally quick student, but still . . . There must be a solution to this mystery somewhere and I'm bound if I won't find it. Everything here is so strange, so melancholy, and so mysterious!

MUSIC: *Eerie theme.*

STEVENSON: David did not get an opportunity to question his uncle till several nights later.

EBENEZER: I hope ye have had enough supper, lad.

DAVID: Yes, sir, I have. Uncle Ebenezer, there's something I wish to ask.

EBENEZER: Yes, lad?

DAVID: Was my father very quick at his books? I mean, did he learn his reading and writing at a very early age?

EBENEZER: Alexander? Not him! I was far quicker mysel'! Oh, I was a clever chappie when I was young. Why, I could read as soon as he could.

DAVID (*As if to himself*): As soon as *he* could? But that implies that my father was the elder! What does all this mean? (*Aloud*) Were—were you and my father twins, Uncle Ebenezer?

EBENEZER (*Suspicious, angry*): What makes ye ask that?

DAVID (*Coldly, calmly*): What do you mean? Take your hand from my jacket. This is no way to behave.

EBENEZER (*With effort*): Oh, no, Davie—Davie, no. Don't be angry with me, I meant no harm. It's just—you shouldn't speak to me about your father. That's where the mistake is. He was all the brother I ever had, ye see. And to prove to ye that I bear ye no hard feelings, I have something for ye. There's a wee bit o' silver that I promised ye when ye were born. Oh, nothing much, ye understand—but a promise is a promise. So, if you'll just step outside and see what kind of a night it is, I'll get the money out for you.

DAVID (*Good-naturedly*): All right, Uncle Ebenezer.

SOUND: *Door.*

EBENEZER (*Musing, to himself*): That boy is getting too inquisitive. I'll have to be doing something about it. But what? Well, this little silver will convince him that I'm his friend and mean him no harm. It'll be easier then, and well worth the price. (*Calling out*) All right, Davie, lad, come back.

SOUND: *Door.*

DAVID: It's growing dark rapidly, Uncle. A storm is brewing in the east.

EBENEZER: Here, Davie, man, is the silver I promised ye. Forty pounds!

DAVID (*Pleased*): Thank you, Uncle Ebenezer.

EBENEZER: That'll show you! I'm a queer man, but my word is my bond. And, you know, blood is thicker than water, and there's proof of it.

DAVID: I am grateful, sir.

EBENEZER: Not a word! No thanks; I want no thanks. (*Craftily*) But, er . . . tit for tat, Davie. Tit for tat.

DAVID: I am ready to prove my gratitude in any reasonable degree.

EBENEZER: Well, lad, as ye see, I'm old, and will need help in care of the house and the garden.

DAVID: That will I give you willingly, Uncle.

EBENEZER: Well, then, let's begin. Here. Here's the key of the stair-tower at the far end of the house. Ye can only get into it from the outside, for that part of the house is not finished. Go up in there, and at the top of the stairs, ye'll find an old chest. Bring it down to me.

DAVID: Can I have a light, sir?

EBENEZER: Ye know better than to ask me that, lad. No lights in my house!

DAVID: Very well, sir. Are the stairs good?

EBENEZER: They're grand. There are no bannisters, so

keep close to the house wall. (*Evilly*) But the stairs are *grand* underfoot.

MUSIC: *Adventurous theme.*

SOUND: *Wind, thunder and lightning softly in background.*

STEVENSON: So out went David Balfour into the night. The night had fallen blacker than ever, and the wind was moaning in the distance, while great rolls of thunder tumbled in the skies, and from time to time a flash of lightning illuminated the area in a crackling instant of white splendor. Minding his uncle's words about the bannisters, David kept close to the house, feeling his way up the invisible stairs. Up, up and up he climbed, slowly, torturously—not being able to see a thing. Suddenly, when he had reached a great height, there was a blinding flash of lightning, and the skies opened.

SOUND: *Thunder and steady rain.*

STEVENSON: Instinctively, Davie covered his eyes with his hands, but not before he had had a chance to see that just at the very place on which he was standing, the stairway stopped!

DAVID: So that's what my uncle meant when he said that this part of the house was unfinished! There are no more stairs—just a great drop! That lightning flash came just at the right time to save me, thank God! But, *why—why* should my uncle send me here? Why does he hate me so that he must send me on an errand that is sure to mean certain death? What is the meaning of all this mystery, this hate, and this horror?

MUSIC: *Frightening theme.*

STEVENSON: Shaking more with fright than with cold, drenched more with sweat than with rain, David began to inch his way down the treacherous stairs. When he was halfway down, there was another flash of lightning, by which he saw his uncle, standing below on the ground. At the sound of the crash, old Ebenezer Balfour turned and went into the house, a fearful expression on his face.

DAVID: Did he think that crash the sound of my body falling? Or was it that in the thunder he heard God's voice, denouncing murder? Whatever it was, he seemed to be seized by a panic of fear. Why else would he leave the door ajar? The noise of the rain is great; he will not hear me enter the kitchen. I think Uncle Ebenezer is in for a surprise!

MUSIC: *Eerie theme.*

EBENEZER (*Murmuring madly*): There's an end of that. He's dead, he's dead!

DAVID (*Coldly*): Who is dead, Uncle Ebenezer?

EBENEZER (*With a cry of fright and terror*): David! Are ye alive? Oh, man—my heart! I faint! Quick—the blue phial in the cupboard! My heart! Save me!

DAVID: Here is the blue phial. Drink it down.

EBENEZER (*Weakly*): Give it me. Heart—medicine. There. That's better. Oh, David, what a fright ye gave me. Are ye alive?

DAVID (*Angrily*): That I am, small thanks to you. Why have you lied to me, Uncle? What is the reason that you hate me so? Why do you seem to watch me, spy on me, yet fear me so? Why do you dislike it when I hint that my father and you were twins? Is it because it is true? Why did you lie about making a promise to give me money when I was born? Oh, I know you made that story up: only a fool would believe it. Why did you give me money to which I had no claim? Why did Jennet Clouston rain curses on our house and name? And last of all, why did you try to kill me? Why did you send me on an errand that should have meant certain death? Why? Why? Answer me, Uncle Ebenezer, answer me!

EBENEZER (*Weakly, yet coldly*): Bear with me, David. I'll tell you all tomorrow morn. As sure as death . . . I will.

MUSIC: *Eerie, mysterious theme.*

STEVENSON: This time it was David who locked his uncle in a chamber for the night. The next morning he released him and the two ate a silent breakfast together, each keeping constant watch upon the movements of the other.

DAVID: Well, Uncle? No words for me?

EBENEZER: I—I have had enough porridge and ale for now, David.

DAVID: Have you nothing *more* to say to me? It will be time, I think, to understand each other. You took me for a country bumpkin, with no more mother-wit or courage than a porridge-stick. I took you for a good man, or no worse than others at the least. It seems we were both wrong. What cause have you to fear me, to cheat me, and to attempt my life—

EBENEZER (*Affably*): Now, Davie, Davie—I promised I would make all clear to you today, and I shall. Just give me time.

DAVID: Time, time! That's all I have given you! I want my answer, Uncle Ebenezer.

EBENEZER: Very well, then. You shall have it. Now, I know you will not believe *me*. But will you believe Rankeillor, the lawyer in town? He is as honest a man as ye will ever meet, and is highly respected by all in these parts. He kenned your father. I have to go down to town today, anyway, to arrange some things with Captain Elias Hoseason, and we could visit Lawyer Rankeillor then.

DAVID: Elias Hoseason? Who is he?

EBENEZER: Captain of the trading brig, the *Covenant*. He sails to the Americas today, and I have business with him. After I see him and you see the town, we will go to Rankeillor's, and you shall understand everything. I give you my solemn word.

DAVID: Very well, Uncle Ebenezer. I may be a fool for saying "Yes," but I am not afraid of you. Let us go into town.

MUSIC: *Adventurous theme.*

HOSEASON (*A robust, hearty voice*): Ah, Balfour, I was beginning to think ye might not come.

EBENEZER: Never would I let you down, Captain Hoseason. We are too good friends for that.

HOSEASON: That we are. But, say—who is the young fellow?

EBENEZER: This is my nephew, David Balfour. Davie, Captain Hoseason.

HOSEASON: How do you do, laddie? Any friend of Balfour's is a friend of mine, eh, Ebenezer?

EBENEZER: To be sure, to be sure.

DAVID: You keep your room uncommon hot, sir.

HOSEASON: It's a habit I have, Mr. Balfour. I'm a cold-rife man by nature; I have a cold blood, sir. There's neither fur nor flannel—no, sir, nor hot rum, will warm up what they call the temperature. It's the same with most men who've been sailing the tropic seas. But, laddie, there's no reason for you to suffer in it. Your uncle and I have business to talk over. You'd rather go down to see the town, I'll wager. There are ladies in this very inn—oh, ho! Or perhaps you'd like to have a look at my ship? Have you ever been on a ship, laddie?

DAVID (*Excited*): No, indeed, sir. I surely would like that.

HOSEASON (*Calling aloud*): Ransome, you young scamp! Come here!

RANSOME: Yes, sir?

HOSEASON: This is young David Balfour. Show him around the ship for a while.

RANSOME: Yes, sir.

DAVID: Thank you very much, Captain.

HOSEASON: Not at all, boy. Not at all. And when my business is done with your uncle here, I'll let you know.

DAVID: Very well, then. Goodbye now.

HOSEASON: Goodbye.

EBENEZER (*Slowly*): Goodbye . . . David . . . Balfour.

MUSIC: *Mysterious theme.*

SOUND: *Waves and sea gulls.*

HOSEASON: (*Fading on*): Ah, Balfour, here you are.

DAVID: Captain Hoseason!

HOSEASON: What do you think of my ship, the *Covenant?*

DAVID: Where is my uncle?

HOSEASON (*Laughing*): Calm down, laddie. Calm down. 'Twill be a long time before you see him again.

DAVID: What—what do you mean?

HOSEASON: Ransome! Shaun! Come tie this young man up!

DAVID: What does all this mean? Where is my uncle?

HOSEASON: Ay, that's the point!

DAVID: You—you mean I've been—kidnapped!

HOSEASON (*Laughing loudly*): You're a smart one indeed, laddie. Aye, you've been kidnapped. (*Sharply*) Tie this boy up, men. And throw him in the hold!

DAVID (*Struggling*): No! No!

HOSEASON: Oh, fight will you? Knock him out, Mr. Shaun. Knock him out cold.

SOUND: *Hard blow of a fist. Then, wind. The voices in the following scene should be unearthly, ghostly—as though traveling over the miles on the wings of the wind.*

CAMPBELL: God be with you, Davie Balfour.

HOSEASON: Aye, laddie, you've been kidnapped.

JENNET: Black be the fall of the House of Shaws. Black be their fall!

EBENEZER: I'm your born uncle, Davie, and you're my born nephew.

1ST WOMAN: He's a nasty one, is old Ebenezer Balfour.

EBENEZER: You shouldn't speak to me about your father.

JENNET: Black be their fall!

HOSEASON: Aye, laddie, you've been kidnapped!

SOUND: *Howling wind.*

MUSIC: *Adventurous theme.*

STEVENSON: And in that manner was our young hero taken prisoner. But what you have just heard is only the beginning of many, many exciting adventures which befell the youthful captive. And if you read my book, you will learn how Davie encounters outlaws, takes part in a mutiny, escapes death many times, endures the fury of the elements, and ultimately returns to his native land after a number of other adventures to solve the mysteries of his Uncle Ebenezer, of the House of Shaws, and of his own true heritage, all as a result of that terrible day in 1751, when young David Balfour . . . was kidnapped!

MUSIC: *Dramatic theme.*

THE END

The Man Without a Country

by Edward Everett Hale

Characters

TWO CHORUSES
PROSECUTING COUNSEL
DEFENSE COUNSEL
PRESIDENT OF THE COURT
PHILIP NOLAN
MRS. GRAFF
THREE SAILORS
YOUNG OFFICER
CAPTAIN VAUGHAN
DANFORTH
2ND CAPTAIN
THREE SOLO SPEAKERS

1ST *and* 2ND CHORUSES (*Speaking in unison with slightly exaggerated emphasis*):
   Breathes there the man, with soul so dead,
   Who never to himself hath said,
   This is my own, my native land!
1ST CHORUS: This is my own, my native land!
2ND CHORUS: This is my own, my native land!
1ST *and* 2ND CHORUSES (*After a slight pause*): From the *New York Herald,* August 13, 1863.

1st SOLO: Nolan. Died, on board U.S. Corvette *Levant,* Lat. 2° 11′ S., Long. 131° W., on the 11th of May, Philip Nolan.

1st CHORUS: Philip Nolan? Who was Philip Nolan?

2ND CHORUS: Philip Nolan. . . . The man without a country.

1st CHORUS: Ah, yes. The man without a country. It all began—when?

2ND CHORUS: In 1807, when young Philip Nolan, lieutenant in the United States Army, was tried at a court-martial.

1st CHORUS: The charge?

2ND CHORUS: Conspiracy to commit high treason.

PROSECUTING COUNSEL: May it please the Court, Nolan is a traitor to the United States.

DEFENSE COUNSEL: May it please the Court, Nolan, as a soldier, has given valiant service to the United States.

PROSECUTING COUNSEL: He has defiled the United States! He deserves nothing of the United States.

DEFENSE COUNSEL: He is innocent. He deserves mercy of the United States.

SOUND: *Gavel being rapped three times.*

PRESIDENT OF THE COURT: Philip Nolan, you stand accused of treason against the United States, a conspirator in the Aaron Burr plot. Have you anything to say which will show that you have always been faithful to the United States?

NOLAN (*Impetuously*): *This* the United States and *that* the United States! For a week, throughout this trial, I've heard nothing but the United States. I say *Damn* the United States! I wish I may never hear of the United States again!

1st CHORUS: Let him be sentenced. . . .

2ND CHORUS: Let him be sentenced. . . .

PRESIDENT: Prisoner, hear the sentence of the Court. The Court decides that you should never hear the name of the United States again.

SOUND: *Muffled drum roll.*

1ST *and* 2ND CHORUSES: From that moment, September 23, 1807, till the day he died, May 11, 1863, Philip Nolan never again heard his country's name. For that half-century and more, he was a man without a country.

1ST CHORUS: Nolan was delivered to the Naval Commander at Orleans, and put aboard a ship bound for an extensive cruise in foreign waters.

2ND CHORUS: At the same time, the Naval Commander at Orleans was handed a letter of instructions:

2ND SOLO: Sir. You will receive from Lieutenant Neale the person of Philip Nolan, late a lieutenant in the United States Army. You will take the prisoner on board your ship, and keep him there with such precautions as shall prevent his escape.

3RD SOLO: The gentlemen on board will make any arrangements agreeable to themselves regarding his society. He is to be exposed to no indignity of any kind, nor is he ever unnecessarily to be reminded that he is a prisoner.

2ND SOLO: But under no circumstances is he ever to hear of his country or to see any information regarding it.

3RD SOLO: It is the intention of this government that he shall never again see the country which he has disowned. Before the end of your cruise, you will transfer him to another outgoing naval vessel, together with these instructions.

2ND SOLO: Respectfully yours, W. Southard, for the Secretary of the Navy.

1ST *and* 2ND CHORUSES: And so it came about that Nolan began the first voyage—the first of what was to be a lifetime of voyages.

1ST CHORUS: He was treated as a gentleman always . . .

2ND CHORUS: But no one would answer his requests for news of his native land.

1ST CHORUS: Though they didn't know the reason, even the common sailors were forbidden to mention the topic to Nolan.

2ND CHORUS: They called him Plain Buttons, because he was dressed in the regulation army uniform, shorn only of its brass buttons, because they showed the insignia of the country he had disowned.

1ST CHORUS: At first, Nolan treated the whole matter as a jest.

NOLAN (*Lightly*): Well, what's the news from home, my lads? I saw the packet boat delivering letters this morning. (*Pause*) Won't answer me, eh? Well, no matter. I don't suppose I'd find your news all that fascinating.

2ND CHORUS: Later, he became bitter.

NOLAN (*Raging*): Must all my books be censored? Must all my newspapers be scissored? Must I have this eternal silence because once, as a lad, I made a foolish blunder?

1ST *and* 2ND CHORUSES: Once, he even tried to trick an old friend into giving him news.

1ST CHORUS: The vessel on which he was then staying—it must have been 1808—was anchored in the harbor of Naples.

2ND CHORUS: A dance was being held on board for members of the American community then living in Italy.

1ST CHORUS: Philip Nolan was a guest at the party.

2ND CHORUS: As was a woman he had known, years before, in Philadelphia.

SOUND: *Dance music of the period, softly in the background.*

NOLAN: I hope you have not forgotten me, Miss Rutledge. Shall I have the honor of dancing with you?

MRS. GRAFF: I am no longer Miss Rutledge, Mr. Nolan. But I shall dance all the same.

NOLAN: And do you enjoy it, living here in Naples?

MRS. GRAFF: It is pleasant enough, I daresay. But I shall be pleased when my husband's tour of duty here is expired, and we may go back.

NOLAN: Ah, then, you miss Philadelphia? Tell me. What do you hear from home?

MRS. GRAFF (*Coldly*): Home! Mr. Nolan! I thought you were the man who never wanted to hear of home again!

1ST CHORUS: The woman coldly withdrew herself from the man's arm, and strode away.

2ND CHORUS: Nolan's face flushed as though he had been slapped. Turning on his heel, he walked from the salon and returned to his quarters.

1ST CHORUS: It was the last time he ever tried to learn anything of the land he had left behind.

1ST *and* 2ND CHORUSES: 1812 . . . 1815 . . . 1818. . . .

NOLAN: Well, my friends. A beautiful day, isn't it?

1ST SAILOR: That it is, sir. Care to join us in a pipe?

NOLAN: No, thanks. But I'll sit with you a bit. Pray, don't let me disturb your conversation.

2ND SAILOR: Oh, we were just reading aloud, sir. We like to do that, whenever we get a new book on board, you know. Helps to pass the time.

NOLAN: An excellent idea! What book is it today?

1ST SAILOR: It's a poem, sir, by Walter Scott. "The Lay of the Last Minstrel."

NOLAN: I don't believe I know it. I'll listen, if I may.

3RD SAILOR: Better yet, sir, why don't you do the reading? You're a powerful reader, sir—a sight better than any of us. It would be a treat to hear you.

NOLAN: Very well. I can't promise much success on poetry

I've never seen before, but I'll give it a try. Is this the place where you left off?

1ST SAILOR: That's it, Mr. Nolan.

NOLAN (*Clears his throat*):

"Breathes there the man, with soul so dead,
  Who never to himself hath said,
  This is my own, my native land!
  (*Coughs slightly, then continues*)
  Whose heart hath ne'er within him burn'd,
  As home his footsteps he hath turn'd,
  From wandering on a foreign strand!
  (*Pauses*)

"For him . . . (*Pauses*) For him no minstrel raptures
    swell;
  High though his titles, proud his name,
  Boundless his wealth as wish can claim,
  Despite those titles, power, and pelf,
  The—the wretch—the wretch concentered all in
  self. . . ."

SOUND: *Splash.*

1ST CHORUS: His eyes smarting with tears, Nolan stopped.

2ND CHORUS: He gave a wild look at the seated sailors—
and pitched the book into the sea.

1ST *and* 2ND CHORUSES (*After a slight pause*): 1820 . . .
1830 . . . 1840 . . .

1ST CHORUS: It happened, once, that the vessel on which
Nolan was staying overtook a small schooner laden with
African slaves.

2ND CHORUS: The vessel's Captain, Vaughan by name, ordered the schooner boarded and the slaves freed.

YOUNG OFFICER: We've unchained the poor wretches, Captain, but they're still in a terrible way.

VAUGHAN: I should think they'd be glad to know they're

free, and will be put ashore at our next port, instead of
being sold into bondage.

YOUNG OFFICER: That's just the trouble, sir. There's no
way to make them understand that they *are* free, for
none of us speaks Portuguese, which is their language.

NOLAN: *I* speak Portuguese, Captain Vaughan. Shall I go
as interpreter?

VAUGHAN: Splendid, Nolan! Go aboard the schooner and
make the men understand what we propose.

1ST *and* 2ND CHORUSES: Soon Nolan was back from his errand . . . but the Captain saw at once that all was not
well.

VAUGHAN: Did you tell them that we will set them free at
the next port, Nolan?

NOLAN (*With difficulty*): I did, sir. But they say that is not
enough.

VAUGHAN: What is it that they want?

NOLAN: They say, "Take us home. Take us to our own
country. Take us to our own houses . . . to our own
wives . . . to our own children." They say . . . that a
man who is uprooted from his home, and is not allowed
to return to it . . . is as much a slave as if he were
shackled with chains for all his days.

VAUGHAN (*Slowly*): Go back to them, Nolan, and tell them
it shall be as they wish. We will take them home.

YOUNG OFFICER (*Lightly*): They must have made quite an
impression on Nolan, sir. Did you see how strange he
looked as he delivered the message?

VAUGHAN: Let that show you what it is to be without a
family, without a home, and without a country. And if
you are ever tempted to say a word or to do a thing that
shall put a bar between you and your family, your home,
and your country, pray God in His mercy to take you
that instant home to His own heaven.

NOLAN (*As though at a slight distance*): Yes, listen to him, boy! Listen to what the Captain tells you, and believe him! (*Bitterly*) Oh, if anybody had said that to me when I was of your age!

1ST *and* 2ND CHORUSES: 1845 . . . 1855 . . . 1860 . . .

DANFORTH: You asked me to come to your cabin, Mr. Nolan?

NOLAN (*In an aged voice*): Yes, Danforth. I'm—I'm dying.

DANFORTH: I'll fetch the ship's doctor at once, sir.

NOLAN: No. . . . No . . . it's not a doctor I want. I'm too far gone for that. Besides, I have little enough wish to prolong my life.

DANFORTH: Then what can I do for you, sir?

NOLAN: You can tell me—everything, Danforth.

DANFORTH: I don't understand, sir.

NOLAN: Tell me . . . about my country. Tell me . . . about the United States.

DANFORTH: But—but it is forbidden, sir.

NOLAN (*Beseechingly*): I am dying, man! Have you no pity? Have you no mercy? Look, here is my prayerbook. Let it fall open at your touch, and see where the pages open themselves. Look! Read where they have opened.

DANFORTH (*Reading*): "For ourselves and our country, O gracious God, we thank Thee, that notwithstanding our manifold transgression of Thy holy laws, Thou hast continued to us Thy marvellous kindness."

NOLAN: Yes! For ourselves *and our country!* That is the prayer I have read on my knees every night for the past fifty years. And see, here on the flyleaf, I have drawn a map of the United States from memory, filling in the new states from surmise and conjecture. Oh man, man, I am dying! You must—tell—me—everything!

DANFORTH (*Moved*): Mr. Nolan, I will tell you everything you ask about. Only, where shall I begin?

1st CHORUS: And so the young officer began telling his nation's history to the old man they called Plain Buttons.

2ND CHORUS: It was no easy task, condensing fifty years' history into the span of a single night.

1st CHORUS: When the morning light filled Nolan's cabin, young Danforth saw that the old man's life was indeed drawing to a close.

NOLAN: God bless you, Danforth! To know—finally to *know* how it has gone with the United States. Thank God it has all gone well.

DANFORTH: Will there be anything else, Mr. Nolan?

NOLAN (*Quietly*): Look in my Bible, Danforth, when I am gone. There is a note there for the captain.

1st CHORUS: May 11, 1863.

2ND CHORUS: On board the U.S. Corvette *Levant*.

DANFORTH: Captain. Lieutenant Nolan is dead.

2ND CAPTAIN: Ah, so it finally happened. Poor man!

DANFORTH: There was a note for you in his Bible—next to the text, "They desire a country, even a heavenly: wherefore God is not ashamed to be called their God: for He hath prepared them a city."

2ND CAPTAIN (*Musing*): "They desire a country, even a heavenly. . . ."

DANFORTH: The note, sir.

2ND CAPTAIN (*Reading*): "Bury me in the sea; it has been my home, and I love it. But will not someone set up a stone for my memory at Fort Adams at Orleans, that my disgrace may not be more than I ought to bear? Say on it:

1st *and* 2ND CHORUSES: "In Memory of Philip Nolan, Lieutenant in the Army of the United States. He loved his country as no other man has loved her; but no man deserved less at her hands."

THE END

Enoch Arden

by Alfred, Lord Tennyson

Characters

ANNIE LEE
PHILIP RAY
ENOCH ARDEN
MRS. CRAVEN
MRS. LANE
NARRATOR

NARRATOR: On a windswept cliff overlooking a tiny sea-side village, three happy youngsters were at play one afternoon—three youngsters whose futures were bound up irrevocably with one another, whose lives were to be crossed and recrossed with each other's again and again. Their tale is one of youth and age, of gaiety and solemnity, of happiness and heartbreak. It has been set down for all men to read and contemplate, by the immortal Alfred, Lord Tennyson. This is a story of deathless love, the tale of Annie Lee, of Philip Ray, and of their selfless friend, Enoch Arden.

SOUND: *The crash of a breaking wave and surf.*

ANN (*As a child, laughing*): Come on, Philip. Climb up here to the top of the cliff! Enoch, hurry! It's beautiful up here. You can see the whole ocean!

PHILIP (*As a child, soft-spoken*): We're coming. You ran ahead so fast!

ANN: Don't be silly, Philip. There, give Enoch a hand over the edge.

ENOCH (*As a child, deep-voiced*): I can make it by myself, any day!

ANN: Look, Enoch, Philip. Isn't it beautiful?

PHILIP: The whole ocean, spread out before us like a carpet!

ENOCH: How high this cliff is! It's like a castle!

ANN: I am the beautiful Princess who lives in the castle. Enoch, you and Philip must be my lords-in-waiting.

ENOCH: If you're to be a Princess, Annie, you must have a crown and a cape.

PHILIP: This old fishnet can be Annie's cape.

ANN: One of you must gather dried seaweed for my crown. How wonderful to be a Princess. Look over there! That sailing vessel! See how tiny it looks.

ENOCH: Some day I shall sail away on such a vessel, far across the blue sea.

ANN: Sail away and leave us, Enoch?

PHILIP: Why? Why not be content at home, and be a miller? That's what I'm going to be!

ENOCH (*Scornfully*): Yes, Philip, just like you to be a miller. I shall be an adventurous sailor, and bring home presents from faraway lands, for Annie, who shall be my little wife.

PHILIP: Nay then, Enoch. Annie shall be *my* little wife.

ENOCH: A miller's wife? Princess Annie? (*Laughs*)

PHILIP: What sort of husband would you be, you that talk of sailing ever away from home?

ENOCH: A better husband than you, Philip.

ANN: Enough, enough, both of you. Do not quarrel for my sake. I shall be little wife to both, and the three of us will live forever as the best of friends, with the whole ocean spread before us. Philip, Enoch, I'll race you to the sand dunes yonder. (*Laughing*) Last one there's a one-legged sailor!

MUSIC: *Delightful theme.*

NARRATOR: With the passing of time and the washings of the tide, life continued for the three little friends, and to the old village busybodies, like Mrs. Craven, it seemed to take less time for them to grow up than it takes for the wind to fling a netful of salt spray against a flapping sail. Though they had reached their late teens, Annie, Philip and Enoch were still as close as they had been as childhood playmates. Where one was, there would be the other two, or if not there, seldom far away.

SOUND: *Church bells tolling in the distance.*

MRS. CRAVEN: Ho there, Philip Ray. Where be you off to in such a hurry?

PHILIP (*A young man now, serious but not solemn*): I'm looking for Annie Lee, Mrs. Craven, and Enoch Arden.

MRS. CRAVEN: Why, they went a-climbing up the cliff, along with the rest of the young folk of the village, 'most an hour ago. They've all gone out a-harvesting the hazelnuts, you know. Why didn't you go along, too, lad?

PHILIP: My father is sick-a-bed, and he needed me to fix his supper.

MRS. CRAVEN: Ah, poor man, your father. Well, Philip, better late than never as they say. Run along to the cliffs, yonder. I'm sure you'll find Annie and Enoch—and the rest o' them, too—out a-lookin' for the hazelnuts.

MUSIC: *Romantic theme.*

NARRATOR: Off bounded Philip, in the direction indicated by Mrs. Craven. When he reached the cliff, he saw the merry groups of young people, laughing and dancing as they gaily harvested hazelnuts. On he ran, looking for his two dearest friends. At last he saw them up ahead, in a clump of trees, and ran towards them. Before Enoch and Annie had seen him, their words reached Philip's ears, and he stopped silently behind a tree, listening to their conversation.

SOUND: *Surf pounding softly in background.*

ANN (*Now about seventeen, a sweet-voiced girl*): Enoch, here's a whole pile of them! Why, we must be the first to discover this grove of trees!

ENOCH (*About nineteen, deep-voiced; now, serious*): Annie—

ANN: Why, Enoch! What's wrong? You look so strange!

ENOCH (*Hastily*): Oh, nothing's wrong, it's—

ANN: Then why do you look so oddly?

ENOCH: Come here, Annie. Sit down here, next to me.

ANN (*Tentatively*): The others will wonder what's become of us. We ought to—

ENOCH: Just for a moment, Annie.

ANN: Yes, Enoch?

ENOCH: Annie—for the past few years, I've had an idea in mind—an idea that you could help me with.

ANN: An idea, Enoch?

ENOCH: You see, I've been saving all my money—to purchase my own boat, you know, and—and to make a home. I've been learning the business of sailing and fishing, too, Annie.

ANN: Yes, I know. A luckier or a bolder fisherman, one more careful in peril, doesn't breathe for leagues along the coast, Enoch. Everyone knows that.

ENOCH: I've been thinking it over, and—well, I have my eye on just the right fishing boat, and I've already picked out a house for us to live in, Annie.

ANN: A house—for *us* to live in?

ENOCH (*Miserably*): Don't you know what I'm trying to

tell you, Annie? Can't you help a fellow out? I'm not a genius when it comes to using my tongue—

ANN: Oh, you're doing just fine, Enoch.

ENOCH: Then—then you'll say "Yes"? I do love you, so very much, Annie. I do want you so very much to be my wife, Annie. Will you marry me?

ANN: Enoch, Enoch, yes, I will. Yes, I will, my darling.

ENOCH (*Softly*): Mrs. Enoch Arden, you'll be, Annie. Mrs. Enoch—

SOUND: *The crash of a tree branch.*

ANN (*Startled*): What was that?

ENOCH: A branch—probably dead—it fell, that's all.

ANN: No, Enoch! Look! It was a man!

ENOCH: He's running away from here.

ANN: Enoch, it was Philip! Call him back, Enoch!

ENOCH (*Calling*): Philip! Philip! Come back! He doesn't hear.

ANN: He hears, Enoch, but he won't turn back, for all that. Is this how it's to end? By gaining one, I lose the other?

ENOCH: Don't cry, Annie. If it's me you love, it can't be helped.

ANN: Do you remember how, as children, the three of us would play up here—here, on this very cliff? You and he would fight, even then, over which would win me as a bride. I would say "Don't quarrel, Philip and Enoch, I'll be little wife to you both!" But it cannot be. It's you that I love, Enoch Arden, you. Look, the sun is setting. How beautiful it is! See, the ocean has turned crimson with fire!

ENOCH: It's late. (*Softly, tenderly*) Come home, Annie. Come home, my love.

MUSIC: *Romantic theme.*

NARRATOR: So Enoch and Annie were married. For seven

years good fortune smiled upon them, and never had there ever been a happier couple in the whole village. Philip, who had never quite given up his love for Annie, spent less and less time with the Ardens, until at last, he barely saw them for weeks at a time. Then, after seven full years, without word or warning, misfortune came to live at the home of Enoch Arden.

MRS. LANE (*An old gossip*): Good day to you, Mrs. Craven. Have you heard the news?

MRS. CRAVEN: News? What news?

MRS. LANE: About Enoch Arden—and about his wife, Annie, too, poor creatures.

MRS. CRAVEN: Is it a misfortune? Bad news?

MRS. LANE: Aye, bad news it is indeed. More misfortune than any one house should have to bear—especially such a happy house as theirs, which has had nothing but *good* fortune these last seven years, since they two were married.

MRS. CRAVEN: Don't beat about the bush, Mrs. Lane. Tell me! What has happened?

MRS. LANE: First, Enoch was clambering up a mast down in the harbor—on one of his fishing boats. Yesterday it was, and by Heaven if he didn't fall to the deck by mischance, breaking several bones.

MRS. CRAVEN: Mercy! What a dreadful thing to have happened!

MRS. LANE: As if that weren't enough, in the same evening, Annie, his wife, bore him a third child—but not a well babe, as the other two before him were. Nay, nay. A sickly, frail little babe it is, like to be a cripple all its life!

MRS. CRAVEN (*Sighing*): Ah, me, such a calamity! Ah, it seems that misfortune has come to stay in the home of Enoch Arden.

MUSIC: *Unhappy theme.*

NARRATOR: In those unhappy times, no one was more concerned than Enoch himself.

ENOCH (*Older than before, careworn*): Annie—Annie, dear. Are you awake?

ANN (*More serious than before*): Yes, Enoch, awake with my thoughts.

ENOCH (*Hesitantly*): There's something I must tell you, Annie—something I meant to tell you awhile ago, and should have told you before now.

ANN: Is something wrong, Enoch?

ENOCH: Not wrong, exactly. It's about us—you and me, and the children. I'm worried about you, Annie. Times have been bad, lately, and the money hasn't been coming in regularly.

ANN: We'll get by, Enoch.

ENOCH: It's not enough that we get by, Annie. I've got dreams—dreams for you, and the young 'uns. I want them to have a better raising than we ever had. I want you to dress in pretty clothes, and not homespun. I want to find doctors for the laddie, so that perhaps he can be made well and strong. I want—

ANN: I want those things too, Enoch, but I don't worry about them. All will come in good time. We can wait.

ENOCH: No, Annie. Times are bad and getting worse. The fleet has been failing this last sixmonth. So I've—I've signed on as boatswain on a China-bound vessel.

ANN: Enoch! No, Enoch, I won't let you!

ENOCH (*Patiently*): It's no use, Annie. We can't afford to go on this way. I've sold our boat, and left the money in the village at the store, so that you'll have all the provisions you and the children will need while I'm gone.

ANN: Sold the boat already? Enoch, when do you sail?

ENOCH: We sail tomorrow.

ANN (*In despair*): Tomorrow! No, Enoch, no—you musn't!

ENOCH: There's no other way, my love. It's only for a while. I'll be back before you've had the chance to miss me.

ANN: I know, husband, that when you've made up your mind to a thing, there's no purpose in my trying to change it. If you must go, my darling, then go in safety, and return in speed. Remember us while you are gone.

ENOCH: You'll be with me every moment, Annie—you and the babes. This voyage, by the grace of God, will bring fair weather yet to all of us. Keep a clean hearth and a clear fire for me, for I'll be back, my girl, before you know it. I'll bring gifts for you and the children. The baby, the poor, weakly, little one—and I love him all the better for it, God bless him—he shall sit upon my knees, and I will tell him tales of foreign parts, and make him merry, when I come home again. Come, Annie, come, cheer up before I go.

ANN: Enoch, you are wise; yet for all your wisdom, well know I that I shall look upon your face no more. I'll give you a lock of the crippled one's hair; it will bring you good fortune and fond memories.

ENOCH (*Tenderly*): Annie, my girl, cheer up, be comforted. Look to the babes, and till I come again, keep everything shipshape, for I must go. Fear no more for me, or if you fear, cast all your cares on God; that anchor holds. Is He not yonder in those uttermost parts of the morning? If I flee to these can I go from Him? And the sea is His; the sea is His: He made it.

ANN: All that you say is so. Yet in my woman's secret heart of hearts, I know I'll never see you more—never in this world, Enoch Arden.

SOUND: *A sudden gust of wind, then immediately into* . . .

MUSIC: *Dramatic theme.*

NARRATOR: So Enoch Arden went to sea against the wishes

of his wife, Annie. Months went by without word from him, then a year. The year rolled into two, and the two into five. Annie tried to carry on without giving up faith but there were lonely days and tearful nights when it was very hard for her to be brave. Then, Death paid its first visit to the Arden cottage. The little crippled son flickered like a candle, and died.

SOUND: *Soft wind in background. Then, knock at door.*

ANN (*Woodenly*): Come in.

SOUND: *Door opening.*

ANN (*Surprised*): Philip!

PHILIP (*Older than before*): Your pardon, I pray, for intruding on your grief, Annie. I just heard down in the village about—well, about the baby. I hurried as fast as I could.

ANN: That was kind of you, Philip. After all these years— never once setting foot across our threshold—

PHILIP (*Hurriedly*): I thought that—well, that seeing as how Enoch was away, there might be something for which you needed a man to assist you.

ANN: Thank you kindly, Philip, but there's nothing to be done that I cannot do. I've arranged the funeral for the child myself—'twill be a simple service.

PHILIP: I'll come, Annie—if I may, that is. I used to watch the little fellow at play. I—well, I was always fond of children, you'll recall.

ANN: Yes, Philip, that I do recollect.

PHILIP: Then, Annie, if there's nothing I can do for you, I'll say good night to you. Rest well, I pray you.

ANN (*Softly*): Thank you. Good night, Philip Ray.

SOUND: *Door shuts.*

MUSIC: *Unhappy theme.*

NARRATOR: In its relentless way, time moved on.

MRS. CRAVEN (*Chatting aimlessly*): Ah yes, Mrs. Lane,

that's just the way it goes. The wind passes from the South and goes to the North, and no one knows why or wherefore. It's the same with time.

MRS. LANE: Time! Believe me, Mrs. Craven, that's the Lord's own gospel. Why, who would believe the things that time has brought to pass—aye, the things that you and I have seen occur in this village, in our own day! I can remember things ten year ago, fifteen year ago, twenty year ago—aye, as if 'twere yesterday.

MRS. CRAVEN: So can I! Do you recollect the day that Enoch Arden was married—him as has been vanished this past ten year? Who would have thought, on such a happy day, that such a misfortune would fall to him and his.

MRS. LANE: Poor Mrs. Arden, poor Annie! Have you seen her these last few days at all? Tired as a woman o' ninety-nine, she looks. Gone is the bloom from her cheek, all gone the beauties of youth. No wonder: taking care of her children all alone these past ten years, without a word from her husband.

MRS. CRAVEN: Ah, poor Enoch Arden is long since at the bottom of the sea, I'm afeared. Everyone admits it—everyone save Annie herself. She still has faith that Enoch Arden lives.

MRS. LANE: It's that alone that prevents her from accepting Philip Ray. Lovesick as a cat, he is, and has been these many years, since the three o' them grew up together. When Annie married Enoch, nary a word did Philip say, but he remained a bachelor, all the same.

MRS. CRAVEN: For her own sake, then, I say Annie had better come to her senses. Face the fact that Enoch's dead, and take Philip, who's as good a man as ever crossed a village stile.

MUSIC: *Active theme.*

SOUND: *Children playing happily in background.*

PHILIP (*Tenderly*): Listen, Annie. How merry the children are down yonder in the wood. (*Pauses*) Tired, Annie?

ANN (*Sighing*): Tired?

PHILIP (*Urgently*): The ship was lost, *the ship was lost!* No more of that self-torture, Annie. Why should you kill yourself and make them orphans quite?

ANN (*Unhappily*): I thought not of it, but—I know not why—their voices make me feel so solitary.

PHILIP (*Tenderly*): Annie, there is a thing upon my mind, and it has been upon my mind so long, that though I know not when it first came there, I know that it will out at last.

ANN: Philip—

PHILIP: Nay, let me speak. Annie, it is beyond all hope, against all chance, that he who left you ten long years ago should still be living. I grieve to see you poor and wanting help, but I cannot help you as I wish to do unless—perhaps you already know what I would have you know. Annie, I wish you for my wife. I would prove a father to your children. I do think they love me as a father, and I am sure that I love them as if they were mine own. And I believe, if you were my wife, that after all these sad, uncertain years, we might be still as happy as God grants to any of his creatures. Think upon it, Annie. We have known each other all our lives, and I have loved you longer than you know.

ANN (*Softly*): Philip, you have been as God's good angel in our house. God reward you for it. But can one love twice? Can you be ever loved as Enoch was? What is it that you ask?

PHILIP: I am content to be loved a little after Enoch.

ANN: Dear Philip, wait a while. If Enoch comes—but

Enoch will not come—yet wait a year. A year is not so long. Surely I will be wiser in a year. Wait a little!

PHILIP (*Sadly*): Annie, as I have waited all my life, I well may wait a little.

ANN: Nay, I am bound: you have my promise—in a year. Will you not bide your year as I bide mine?

PHILIP: I will bide my year.

MUSIC: *Melancholy theme.*

ANN (*Softly, in prayer*): Dear Father—my Enoch, is he gone? Give me a sign, O Lord, for my heart is heavy, and I know not what to do. Here, I grasp the Holy Book, and open to a page. Let the verse whereon my finger falls be as a sign. Let me find Your guidance in the text, O Lord. "Under a palm tree." What means this? I seem to see Enoch, sitting on a height beneath a palm tree, over him the sun. He is happy, he is singing "Hosanna in the highest": yonder shines the Sun of Righteousness, and these be palms whereof the happy people strewing cried "Hosanna in the highest." Then he is dead, my Enoch is dead. There is no reason why Philip and I should not marry. If I do wed him, let it be at once.

MUSIC: *Peaceful theme.*

NARRATOR: So Annie took Philip, the friend of her childhood, for a husband. They were happy together, and with the birth of a child, the roses came back to Annie's cheeks, and the laughter back to the hearts of the children. Several years more passed, and Philip and his family lived a life of golden contentment. Then, one dark and rainy night, an unkempt, aged, broken stranger passed through the village, and knocked on the door of the Lane Inn, looking for a night's lodging.

SOUND: *Howling wind and rain. Then, knock on door.*

MRS. LANE: Just a minute there, whoever ye be. I'm coming, I'm coming.

SOUND: *Door.*

MRS. LANE: Yes? What might you want, old fellow?

ENOCH (*Much aged and broken*): Is this Mr. Lane's house? I was told that you supplied food and lodging to travelers. I've come to spend the night.

MRS. LANE: Mr. Lane has been dead these nine years come Michaelmas. I am his widow, God rest his soul, and I can welcome you to my lodging house, such as it might be. Come in, old stranger—come in out of the rain and wind, and I'll fix you a bite to eat and a cup of tea.

SOUND: *Door closing.*

ENOCH: That would be very good of you. I'm sorry to disturb you so late.

MRS. LANE: No trouble at all. It's just that we've fallen on hard times hereabouts, and I haven't had many lodgers of late. I didn't expect to hear a knock at the door— especially on such a bad night. Here now, sit down and have a bite of this. The tea will be ready in a minute.

ENOCH: Thank you, thank you kindly, Mrs. Lane. You say the town has come to bad times?

MRS. LANE: Aye, aye—nary a house but has been touched by trouble these past years. Ah, it all began with Enoch Arden's going away from home.

ENOCH (*Carefully*): Enoch—Enoch Arden, did you say?

MRS. LANE (*Laughing, confidingly*): But of course you wouldn't know, seeing as you're a stranger in these parts, eh? But if you've the appetite for a tale, there's one that'll fetch your interest.

ENOCH: Aye, tell me about this—this Enoch Arden.

MRS. LANE: Sir, he was a sailor, with the prettiest wife you can imagine—name of Annie—and three children. The eldest a boy, the second a girl, and the youngest a crippled laddie.

ENOCH: A cripple, you say?

MRS. LANE: One fine day, Enoch out and sets sail for China aboard a great sailing vessel, and never a word is heard from him again. After a short time, the youngest child —the sickly one, you know—passed on, poor thing.

ENOCH: What? The cripple dead?

MRS. LANE: Aye, dead and buried and gone to his rest, poor child. Life was hard on poor Annie Arden—and if it weren't for Philip Ray, the Lord alone knows how she'd have managed.

ENOCH: Who was Philip Ray?

MRS. LANE: Why, he was an old suitor of Annie's, who had grown up as Enoch's best friend. Since his mill was prospering, he saw to it that the children were sent to a proper school, for he said that that was Enoch's dearest wish. After ten years, when Annie finally realized that her husband was dead and beneath the raging seas, why, she allowed Philip to begin his courting. A year later, they two were wed.

ENOCH (*Stunned*): Wed—Annie wed to Philip?

MRS. LANE: Aye, and the best thing it was for her, too. At first, they say, her heart wasn't in her new marriage, but with the coming of another babe, well, she became the happiest wife in the village. Her two oldest children look on Philip as their father, and a more contented family you couldn't find in all the countryside. It just goes to prove that all works out for the best in the end.

ENOCH: It's a strange tale you tell. A strange and fascinating tale. Is it—is all of it true?

MRS. LANE (*Proudly*): Every word!

ENOCH: I should—I should like to see these lucky and

happy people, Mrs. Lane. Could you take me to their home?

MRS. LANE: Why, most surely that I can. Tomorrow morning I'll—

ENOCH: No, tonight. We must go tonight!

MRS. LANE: Tonight! It's raining out; you'll catch your death. It's easy to see that you're old in years, and have been tired out by your travels.

ENOCH: Nonetheless, it must be tonight. I have money; I'll pay you well.

MRS. LANE: Yes, sir. If you're sure you want to go. I'll just get a shawl and my lantern. (*Short pause*) Pull up your collar, sir, and button your coat. 'Tis a bad storm we're having this night!

MUSIC: *Dramatic theme.*

SOUND: *Rain and wind in background.*

MRS. LANE: There, sir—do you see that light? That's the house!

ENOCH: Good. Wait here, Mrs. Lane. I wish to go up to the window, and peek in. I shall be right back. (*Short pause. Then to himself*) How bright the fire burns! There—on the right of the hearth—'tis Philip. On the other side, 'tis my—'tis Annie. My wife no more. The baby on her knee, hers, yet not mine. My children, tall and beautiful, mine no longer. Oh, God, how has this come to pass? How? How?

SOUND: *Howling wind and rain.*

ENOCH (*In a feverish whisper*): How? How?

MRS. LANE: There, there, old sir—'tis all right. You're back in my house. Ah, I knew the storm was too much for you. Why did you insist on going out in it, just after some old village story?

ENOCH: Tell me, Mrs. Lane—this miller's wife that I have seen. Has she no fear that her first husband lives?

Mrs. Lane: Aye, aye, poor soul, fear enow! If you could tell her you had seen him dead, why that would be her comfort.

Enoch: Woman, I have a secret—only swear before I tell you—swear upon the Book not to reveal it till you see me dead. That will be very soon, I fear. Swear, on the Book.

Mrs. Lane (*Frightened*): Aye, by the Holy Bible, I swear it.

Enoch: Did you know Enoch Arden of this town?

Mrs. Lane: Know him? I knew him far away, but not to speak to. Aye, aye, I mind him now, coming down the street. Held his head high, did Enoch Arden, and cared for no man, he.

Enoch (*Slowly, sadly*): His head is low, and no man cares for him. I think I have not three days more to live. I am the man.

Mrs. Lane: You Arden? You! Nay! Sure he was a foot higher than you be!

Enoch: My God has bow'd me down to what I am; my grief and solitude have broken me; nevertheless, know you that I am he who married—but that name has been twice changed—I married her who married Philip Ray.

Mrs. Lane: Lord save us!

Enoch: Sit, listen, while I tell you of the shipwreck, the years of wandering in foreign lands, alone, unloved— (*Coughs*) But I am slipping fast. There is so little time.

Mrs. Lane (*Pleading*): See your bairns before you go! Eh, let me fetch them to you, Arden. I'll run all the way, I'll—

Enoch: Woman, disturb me not now at the last, but let me hold my purpose till I die. Sit down again; mark me and understand, while I have power to speak. I charge you now, when you shall see her, tell her that I died blessing her, praying for her, loving her; save for the bar between us, loving her as when she laid her head beside my own. Tell my daughter, whom I saw so like her mother, that my latest breath was spent in blessing her and praying for her. And tell my son—(*Coughs*) that I died blessing him. Say to Philip I blessed him, too; he never meant us anything but good. There is but one of my blood who will embrace me in the world to be: my little crippled son. This lock of hair—so carefully preserved—is his. She cut it off and gave it to me the day I sailed, and I have borne it with me all these years, and thought to bear it with me to my grave. But now my mind is changed, for I shall see him, my babe, in bliss. When I am gone, give her this (*Coughs*), for it may comfort her. (*Coughs*) It will, moreover, be a token to her, that I—am—he.

MRS. LANE (*Alarmed*): Mr. Arden! Mr. Arden! (*In a shocked whisper*) Dead! Listen to me, hear me, miserable man. All that you have bade me do, I shall perform. I shall pray for the rest and happiness of your soul, poor man. Rest easily, rest peacefully. We shall remember you, Enoch Arden.

MUSIC: *Tragic theme.*

THE END

The Swiss Family Robinson

by Johann Wyss

Characters

SAILOR
SEA CAPTAIN
WOMAN PASSENGER
JOHANN ROBINSON
ELIZABETH, *his wife*
FRITZ, *about 14* ⎤
ERNEST, *about 11* ⎥ *their sons*
JACK, *about 10* ⎥
FRANZ, *about 8* ⎦
JENNY MONTROSE
CAPTAIN LYMAN
NARRATOR

NOTE: *As ten years pass during the course of the story, different actors may play the sons in the second half of the play from those taking the roles at the beginning.*

SOUND: *Clanging of a ship's bell, in a steady rhythm.*
SAILOR (*Calling*): Man the lifeboats! Man the lifeboats! The ship is sinking! She's struck a rock, and she's going down fast! Soon it'll be every man for himself. Man the lifeboats!

SOUND: *Ship's bell, clanging quickly in agitation.*

NARRATOR: If there is any cry that can fill a heart with terror, it is that of a sailor calling "Man the lifeboats! The ship is going down!" So it was that dark and stormy night on which our story begins. Hundreds of miles from her destination, a little vessel filled with passengers and cargo bound for a new colony in the New World, struck a hidden rock on the ocean's floor, sprung a leak, and foundered. When it was clear that there was no other choice, the vessel was abandoned. In the darkness, the boats were lowered, and the passengers and crew scrambled aboard. The sailors fell to the task of rowing. Occasional flashes of lightning illuminated the poor deserted vessel. To all who sat in the boats, it was a sorry sight. But none felt the tragedy more than the captain himself.

SOUND: *The roar of ocean, in background, for duration of scene.*

SAILOR: Don't look back at her, Captain. That's my advice. It's a hard thing to see a ship go down.

CAPTAIN: Aye—and such a good ship as she is.

SAILOR: We must be grateful we've escaped with our lives.

WOMAN: He's right, Captain. We must not look back. We must look forward.

CAPTAIN: I can't help it, ma'am. As long as she is in sight, I can't take my eyes from her.

SOUND: *Crack of lightning and boom of thunder.*

CAPTAIN (*Excitedly*): Did you see her that time? It looked —it looked as though there were still people on her!

SAILOR (*Excitedly*): Aye, Captain! Poor wretches—whoever they may be.

CAPTAIN (*Urgently*): Hand me my telescope from under the seat. (*Pause*) That's it.

WOMAN: But it's dark again. You can't see anything anymore.

CAPTAIN: I mean to be ready with it in case there's another flash of lightning.

WOMAN: Poor things—I wonder why they did not get away. Do you suppose there is yet a lifeboat on board?

CAPTAIN: No, ma'am, there can be none. I, myself, saw the last of them lowered into the sea. We are in it.

SOUND: *Crack of lightning and boom of thunder.*

WOMAN: Did you see them that time?

CAPTAIN: I—I believe I did see people on her! Poor things.

SAILOR: Could you make out who it was, Captain?

CAPTAIN: No—only that there were two grown people, and what seemed to be a pack of children: four of them, I think.

SAILOR (*Thinking aloud*): Two grown people and four children . . .

WOMAN (*Excitedly*): That would be the good minister from Switzerland and his family. What was their name? Robinson!

CAPTAIN: Yes, ma'am, I expect you're right. Poor devils. I'm afraid this dark night will see the end of the Swiss Family Robinson.

MUSIC: *Dramatic theme.*

NARRATOR: But the Swiss Family Robinson—for indeed, it *was* that family that was stranded on the disabled vessel —did not take nearly so dim a view of things as did the captain. It was with a calm voice that the father of the family, Johann Robinson, a minister by calling, an educated man by training, and an adventurer by nature, addressed his wife and four fine sons.

JOHANN: My dear ones, you must not be terrified. We must have trust in the good Lord.

ELIZABETH (*In a gentle voice*): You are quite right, my dear. Boys, it is wrong of us to be afraid.

FRITZ: But it—it is very hard to be brave, Father, in a situation like this.

JOHANN: Of course, Fritz. That's what bravery means.

ERNEST: Are we going to drown, Father?

JOHANN (*Laughing*): No, no, my boy. Nothing of the kind.

FRITZ: But what will become of us?

JOHANN: My family, all is not lost—not by any means. The last time there was a flash of lightning, I saw quite clearly some land not far away.

ERNEST: Where, Father?

JOHANN: There, to the left. I should say we are no more than several hundred yards from the shore at this very moment.

ELIZABETH: If the land is that way, why did all of the boats make off in the other direction?

JOHANN: It is my opinion that the captain had allowed the vessel to get off course. It was because of his unfamiliarity with these waters that the ship struck a rock. In the darkness, the lifeboats pulled off whichever way the tides carried them.

ERNEST: We must hope that those poor people in the boats find their way to the land you saw.

ELIZABETH: We must indeed, Ernest.

JACK: But what good does it do us to know that we are near shore? We cannot swim in the dark; and by morning, the ship will have sunk to the bottom.

JOHANN: That is not so, little Jack. Have you not noticed that the vessel has remained practically stationary for the last half-hour?

ELIZABETH: Why, yes, now that you mention it, Johann. I believe you are right.

JOHANN: I believe that this ship has wedged itself tightly

between the rocks on which she first struck. And if that is so, we can take courage, my dear family. Although our good ship will never sail again, she is so placed that our cabin will remain above water, and tomorrow, if the wind and waves abate, I see no reason why we should not be able to get ashore.

FRITZ: Oh, Father, if only you are right!

ELIZABETH: We must find some food and take a good supper. It will never do to grow faint by fasting too long. We shall require our utmost strength tomorrow.

FRANZ: God will help us soon now, won't He, Father?

JOHANN: We cannot know God's will, my little Franz. We must have patience and wait His time.

ELIZABETH: God has kept us safe for now, children. Let us be thankful for that.

JOHANN: You speak wisely, my dear wife. Come, children. Let us pray.

MUSIC: *Stately hymn, in and under.*

NARRATOR: And so it was that the Swiss Family Robinson stayed the night on the deserted ship. As the sun rose the next morning, it looked down on a calm and quiet sea. The family awoke feeling as refreshed as if they had spent the night in the finest hotel in Europe. After morning prayers, the family besieged the father with questions.

FRITZ: How are we ever to get off this boat, Father?

ERNEST: And how will we get to the land?

ELIZABETH: Surely we can't just leave this vessel here, Johann, with all her valuable cargo. We must find a way of getting these goods to shore, for we shall need as many supplies as possible.

FRANZ: Will there be savages on the shore, Father? Or pirates?

JACK: What country is it that we see yonder? Do you know?

JOHANN (*Laughing*): One at a time, my family, one at a time. So many eager questions!

ELIZABETH: You cannot blame the children, Johann. We are all anxious to know what you propose to do.

JOHANN: Well, then, this is my plan. Each of you must go and hunt about the ship. Anything that is easily carried, and which may be of use to us when we reach the shore, should be brought together in one great pile here.

FRANZ: But how are we to *reach* the shore, Father?

JOHANN: Ah, that is *my* concern. I have a plan, though, that I think should work. While you are all busy searching the ship, I shall be hard at work devising our escape.

ERNEST: Hurrah! Hurrah for Father! He's going to save us!

JOHANN (*Laughing*): That won't be possible if we stand here chatting all day. Be off with you! We have work to do.

MUSIC: *Lively theme.*

NARRATOR: And so, with a light heart and a firm will, each of the members of the marooned family went off to see what he could find that might be of use when they reached the shore. Later, they all gathered to show their treasures.

FRITZ: Look, Father. Here are guns, a shot belt, a powder flask, and plenty of bullets.

JACK: Those will come in handy if we have to protect ourselves from pirates.

JOHANN: More likely we will need them to provide food for ourselves when we reach the shore. It is good that the older boys have been taught to hunt. It will be a useful skill.

ERNEST: And see what I have brought, Father. Here are

nails, an ax, and a hammer. And here are more tools: pincers, chisels, and drills. I found a whole box of carpenter's things.

FRANZ: Look at all these funny curved needles I found, Father. Do you think they will be of use? They're very sharp.

JOHANN: Most useful indeed, Franz. But they are not needles. Those are fishhooks, and I can't think of anything more handy for a family stranded on the seashore. We shall not go hungry while we have these. You have chosen well.

ELIZABETH: Will you praise me, too, dear husband? I have nothing to show, but I can give you good news. Some useful animals are still alive. A cow, a donkey, two goats, six sheep, a ram, and a fine sow. And lots of poultry. I was just in time to save their lives by taking food to them.

JOHANN: You have done well, indeed, dear wife. It would be a sorry thing if, in our anxiety to save ourselves, we were to forget God's more helpless creatures.

FRITZ: And what of you, Father? What have you been doing while we were all on our scavenger hunt?

JOHANN (*Proudly*): I have been building!

ERNEST: Building? A ship, Father? Or a raft?

JOHANN (*Laughing*): It is neither a ship nor a raft, and yet it is both.

FRANZ: What do you mean?

JOHANN: Come over here, my children, and see for yourselves.

SOUND: *Footsteps.*

ELIZABETH: Why—it is merely a lot of barrels cut in half and tied together. How on earth is such a contraption going to save our lives and get us to the safety of the shore?

JACK (*Excitedly*): I know! I know! We will each get into one of the barrels and float to our destination. That's a capital idea, Father. I have often floated along the old mill pond at home in just such a tub.

JOHANN: You have guessed it exactly, Jack!

ERNEST: Oh, what fun!

ELIZABETH: I don't know if I would call it fun, Ernest. You forget that your poor old mother doesn't know how to swim.

JOHANN: You need have no fear of that, my wife. These barrels will keep us afloat perfectly well.

FRITZ: But how shall we manage to steer? We cannot simply float to land, Father. What if the tide is against us?

JOHANN: Good thinking, Fritz. I am glad to see you have your wits about you. I have thought of that. You see, I found these three old oars lying about the deck. They shall do perfectly.

FRANZ: Why have you made so many tubs, Father? There are only six of us, and there are many more barrels.

JOHANN: We must take with us as many of the animals as possible, my son.

ELIZABETH: You don't mean to say, Johann, that you plan on adding the weight of a cow to our own, in that tiny little craft!

JOHANN: No, my dear, we shall not take the cow just yet. But the chickens certainly shall go with us. If we cannot find food for them on shore, they, at least, will be able to provide food for us. And I think a goat and a sheep would not add too great a load. The geese and ducks, of course, we shall set free, for being water animals, they will fare even better than we.

JACK: I say three cheers for Father. It's a marvelous plan.

JOHANN: Now, my beloved ones, with God's help we are about to effect our escape. Let the poor animals we must leave behind be well fed, and put plenty of fodder within their reach. In a few days we may be able to return and save them likewise. After that, collect everything which may be of use to us. And then, let us be off!

BOYS (*Ad lib*): Hooray! We're going for a sail! (*Etc.*)

MUSIC: *Gay theme.*

NARRATOR: The little family set to work, doing everything the father had suggested. Within a short time they were ready to embark on their great adventure. There was no need to coax the boys into the crudely made float of barrels. The animals were a different matter, though. And it was most difficult of all to convince Elizabeth Robinson that she, too, would fare safely.

ELIZABETH (*Timidly*): Oh, I shall never muster up enough courage to get into one of the barrels.

FRITZ: But, Mother, dear, it's so easy.

ERNEST: And so comfortable!

JACK: And such fun!

ELIZABETH: No, no, I simply cannot do it.

JOHANN: But, my dear, you cannot expect us to leave you behind! Come along, and put your trust in our Heavenly Father.

ELIZABETH (*Bravely*): You are right, husband. We must trust in the Lord. Hold onto your seats, boys. Here comes your poor old mother.

MUSIC: *Light theme.*

NARRATOR: And so the small band of sailors set out on their homemade craft. At first the current proved too strong for them. Around and around in circles they wheeled, until the boys were red from laughing—and the poor mother was white from dizziness. At last they managed to gain the knack of using their oars, and with the father giving instructions to the two older boys, the little craft made steadily for the shore. Almost before they knew it, they had reached a peaceful cove. Grateful beyond words, each one stepped briskly onto the quiet beach, and together the little family bowed their heads in thanksgiving. When their prayers were finished, they rose and looked around them. What they saw was a spot lovelier than they had ever imagined.

SOUND: *Surf and bird calls in background.*

ELIZABETH (*Breathlessly*): It's—it's beautiful.

JOHANN (*Softly*): The Lord has indeed led us to a most lovely place.

FRITZ: Look, Father, how white the sand is—and how clear and quiet the water is upon the beach.

JACK: And those trees over there in that grove. Such brilliant green foliage. And, Father, look! They're loaded with fruits and nuts and blossoms!

ERNEST: Did you ever see so many birds? And see all the different kinds! I know them from my schoolbooks. Parrots and parakeets, flamingos and thrushes, swallows, gulls, sparrows—and many I've never seen before.

FRANZ: And the air is so fresh! The sun is so warm!

ERNEST: Oh, Mother, it's like an enchanted island in a storybook. Father, where do you suppose we are? What is the name of this island?

JOHANN: I am sure I do not know, my son. From the look of the place, no civilized man has ever been here. It is my opinion that we have found an island never before known to man.

JACK (*Jubilantly*): Our very own island! An island all for our own!

FRITZ: Oh, Father, do let us give it a name.

ERNEST: Yes, Father, do! What shall we call it?

JOHANN: Why not name this place in honor of our homeland, my sons?

BOYS (*Ad lib*): Yes, yes! A wonderful idea. (*Etc.*)

JOHANN: Let us call this island that we have found: New Switzerland.

BOYS (*In unison*): New Switzerland.

ELIZABETH (*Softly*): A very good name it is, too. But, you know, I almost think it already *has* a name, for it reminds me so much of a place that we have all read about often.

JACK: What place is that, Mother?

ELIZABETH: The Garden of Eden.

MUSIC: *Happy, peaceful theme.*

NARRATOR: And so it was that the beautiful and peaceful island became the new home of the Swiss Family Robinson. Although the boys were anxious to go exploring at once, their first activity was to raise a tent on the beach, to serve as a house. Using the bits and pieces that they had salvaged from the wreck, and all the ingenuity and learning at their command, they soon had erected a fine and pleasant dwelling place.

FRANZ: What shall we call our new house, my brothers?

JACK: I know! Let's call it Tentholm.

FRITZ: That's certainly an appropriate name, Jack. And we can call the cove where we arrived Safety Bay, for it truly afforded us safety and salvation from terrible misfortune.

ERNEST: What do you think of the new names, Father?

JOHANN: They are well and wisely chosen, Ernest. But if you boys are intent on giving names to all the places you come to, and all the new things you find, your imaginations will soon be exhausted. It is my belief that many more new and wonderful and exciting things await our exploration and discovery.

FRITZ: Do you think we will be good explorers, Father?

JOHANN: That depends upon how carefully you observe each thing that you find, and how well you make use of it.

It is no virtue to discover those things which God has created; but to discover the purpose for which He intended them, that is truly to be desired. And we must make that our aim.

ERNEST: We will, Father, surely.

JOHANN: If we all do that, then even should we never leave this place, we shall be rich, indeed, and our lives shall be full, useful, and happy.

FRITZ: That is exactly what I feel they *will* be, Father. Somehow I have a premonition that we shall all be happier than we have dreamed possible in our New Switzerland.

MUSIC: *Bright theme.*

NARRATOR: Young Fritz's words were truer than he could know. Each day on the island the family explored and wandered and observed. And each day they found that all the plants and animals, all the flowers and birds, every rock and stone and leaf could be put to some purpose. They learned to make ropes by twisting and braiding heavy vines. They discovered clear water—the sweetest they had ever tasted—in the stems of tropical plants. They experimented with methods of cooking and preparing the wild plants they picked and the wild animals they killed; and many a delicious meal was made of broiled kangaroo, wild potatoes, fried penguin, fresh guava, and roasted acorns.

Fortunately, they were able to make several return trips to the deserted ship wedged on the rocks; and into the funny little boat of sawed-off barrels went everything they could find which might be of use. All the livestock were saved, as well as tools and clothing, so that life was made easier and more pleasant for them. But their greatest satisfactions came from discoveries on the island itself—and every day brought better ones than before.

FRANZ: Father, look at these funny green berries I found in the Monkey Grove this morning. What do you suppose they can be? They are so sticky, I can't believe they are of much use.

JOHANN: You are wrong, my son. These are waxberries, and when we have gathered more of them, we shall be able to make candles.

JACK: Father, do you suppose we will have any use for these dried sticks? I picked one up to shoo some birds away from our garden, and noticed this sticky syrup dripping from the end.

JOHANN: You have made an important discovery, Jack. Those "sticks," as you call them, are sugar canes. Believe it or not, they're better than candy!

FRITZ: Father, I have found a large bed of oysters not far from here, but I don't think they're edible. They're much larger than the ones in Safety Bay, and each one has a little white stone inside.

JOHANN: Ah, my son, you do not yet know the value of those little white stones. Here in New Switzerland they are useless. But we must gather them and put them aside. If we ever return to Europe, they will make us rich indeed, for they are rare and valuable pearls.

ERNEST: Look, Father, at what I have here. A ball such as the men in Switzerland used to use for playing ninepins.

JOHANN: Let me see it, Ernest.

ERNEST: Some monkeys threw it down from a treetop. Do you suppose that monkeys know how to play ninepins, Father?

JOHANN (*Laughing*): No, no, my son. This is a rare and wonderful fruit, inside of which is a sweet fluid, much like milk. This is a coconut!

MUSIC: *Gay theme.*

NARRATOR: And so the days rolled by, each day filled with wonder, adventure, and surprise, each evening filled with gratitude, well-being, and prayer. Several months after their arrival on the island, the family had come to love New Switzerland as if they had been born there.

JOHANN: Dear children, I want you to know how proud of you I am. Each of you has pitched in and done his best to make life pleasant and rewarding. You have grown stronger in body, keener in mind, and straighter in spirit since we came to settle in this place. We must be grateful to the Lord for the great kindness He has shown.

ELIZABETH: It's true, Johann. I have never seen our four sons in finer spirits.

FRITZ: Who wouldn't be in fine spirits, Mother? Having all of New Switzerland to roam in, and living here in our happy dwelling at Tentholm—what more could anyone ask?

JOHANN: It is about the place where we live, Fritz, that I wish to speak. You see, we must leave it soon.

ELIZABETH: Leave Tentholm, Johann, where we have been so happy?

JOHANN: Soon it will be winter. This place is too open in the cold weather. And so I have built us a new home.

FRITZ: So that was what you have been doing every afternoon!

ERNEST: We wondered why you so often slipped away.

JACK: What is our new home to be like, Father?

JOHANN: It is the nicest place you've ever seen—built high into a tree.

ELIZABETH: Are we really to live in a tree? But how? We cannot fly!

JOHANN (*Laughing*): That will not be necessary, for I have

built steps into the tree's trunk. There we shall be sheltered from the elements, as well as from any wild animals that may be lurking about. But before we move from Tentholm, we must make one more trip out to the ship.

FRITZ: Why, Father? We have not left a single thing of value there.

JOHANN: If the wreck were left there when the winter comes, the winds and waves would surely sink her, or carry her out to sea. It is my plan, therefore, to blow her up with dynamite. Surely, then, some of the planking would drift into our harbor, and we should have the use of it.

ERNEST: That sounds like an excellent plan, Father.

ELIZABETH: It is, indeed, but I shall be sad to see the last of the brave ship that carried us from Switzerland. As long as we can see her, torn apart though she is, there seems to be hope that one day we will be found, and may return to the civilized world.

JOHANN (Gently): We must not hope for that, dear Elizabeth. If it be God's will that we be rescued from our island home, He will take care of it. And I, for one, am not so sure that I wish to return to civilization. What has civilization to offer us?

ELIZABETH: You are right, Johann. We have all the necessities we require. The gardens are flourishing; our livestock has multiplied. The children are healthier and happier than they have ever been. As for me, when I have my family about me, I could not ask for more.

ERNEST: Hurrah for Mother!

JOHANN: It is decided, then. Tomorrow we shall make one more trip—the last—to our dear old friend, the wrecked sailing ship. And then, on to Falconhurst.

JACK: Falconhurst? What is that, Father?

JOHANN: Did you think only you boys were good at naming things? That is what I call the tree house I have built. Falconhurst: our new home.

MUSIC: *Lively theme.*

NARRATOR: And so it was decided. The Swiss Family Robinson liked their new home in the trees even better than dear old Tentholm. And as the days rolled into weeks and the seasons changed, even the last vague glimmering of desire for a return to civilization vanished. They were all wholly satisfied with their way of life in New Switzerland. Winter passed, and then spring and summer. One year drifted effortlessly into the next, and they were barely aware of it. The four sons, who had been small boys when they first set foot on New Switzerland, were now grown young men. Ten years had passed.

SOUND: *Surf in background.*

JOHANN: Ten years, Elizabeth. Only think: We have been in New Switzerland for ten years.

ELIZABETH (*Quietly*): It does not seem possible that so much time has passed since we first stepped onto the beach of Safety Bay. How happy we have been, Johann.

JOHANN: Yes, dear wife. As King David said, "We spend our years as a tale is told." God has indeed blessed us.

FRITZ (*Excitedly*): Father! Father! Only hear what has happened!

ELIZABETH: Gently, Fritz, gently. Why so out of breath?

JOHANN: What is it, my son?

FRITZ: Only wait until you hear. I was out fishing, when an albatross tried to snap away some of my fish. Thinking to scare it away, I struck the bird with a piece of bamboo, and it fell to the deck of our homemade kayak.

ELIZABETH: There is nothing so very unusual about a dead albatross.

FRITZ: The bird was not dead, but only stunned. And when I examined it, I noticed a rag tied to its leg. This I removed, and to my astonishment found English words written on it. This was the message: "Save an unfortunate Englishwoman from the smoking rock."

ELIZABETH: The smoking rock? That must mean the volcano. We have not been near there in years.

JOHANN: Can it be that there is another living person on this island about whom we know nothing? What did you do, my son?

FRITZ: I tore a strip from my handerchief, Father, and on it wrote: "Do not despair. Help is near." I tied the new message to the albatross' other leg, and as though it could read my mind, it flew straight up into the sky, and off toward the volcano.

ELIZABETH: Can it be that this unfortunate woman has tamed the albatross, and taught it to return to her?

JOHANN: Why not? Have we not trained many of the wild animals ourselves?

FRITZ: Oh, Father, may I have your permission to make the sea journey to the part of the island where the volcano is? If there is another person living on the island, we must do all we can to save her.

JOHANN: Quite right, my son. You must go at once. God bless you and preserve you, my boy—and may He bring you success on this errand.

MUSIC: *Lively theme.*

NARRATOR: Fritz's adventure did meet with success. Six days later, his kayak glided into Safety Bay, with a beautiful young woman as a passenger. The family embraced her warmly as though they were all old friends. When greetings had been exchanged, the young woman gladly told her story.

JENNY: My name is Jenny Montrose. Three years ago, the

ship on which I was sailing—the *Dorcas*—was wrecked, and all aboard, save only myself, went down. Since that time, I have lived on this island, always hoping that someone would rescue me one day. How will I ever be able to repay you?

ELIZABETH: No, no, my dear. You must not think of repaying us. It is a joy to be able to speak with one of my own sex after so long. And my husband and sons will benefit from having a visit from you. Their manners, I fear, have become a bit rusty. Whatever we have is at your disposal. And if you care to live with us, please consider Falconhurst your home.

JENNY: How kind of you. I—I shall always remember—how warm—and—sweet—(*Her voice breaks.*)

ELIZABETH: There, there. Don't cry, my dear daughter. You are at home. You have come to friends.

MUSIC: *Happy theme.*

NARRATOR: And so Jenny Montrose became a member of the Swiss Family Robinson. The whole family adored her, and with Jenny in their midst, the seasons practically flew by for them. It seemed that the quiet idyll at New Switzerland would never change, when one day, about a year later, guns were heard in the harbor. Instantly the family ran to the crest of a hill, where Father Johann raised his telescope to his eye.

JOHANN: It is a British ship, my little family, lying at harbor not far from Safety Bay. There can be no doubt that they are signaling us. Run quickly, Fritz, and raise the flag on the flagpole in the bay. They will be sure to come ashore when they see it. Come, let the rest of us put on our best clothes and make ready to greet them.

NARRATOR: Sure enough, a half-hour later a small boat could be seen moving toward Safety Bay. When it reached the harbor, the Swiss Family Robinson was waiting to greet the sailors. The Captain himself stepped onto the beach with outstretched hand.

CAPTAIN LYMAN: I am Captain Lyman, of Her Majesty's Navy. I thank my good fortune that I have found residents upon a coast generally deemed uninhabited.

JOHANN: Welcome, Captain Lyman. I am Johann Robinson, once a minister in Switzerland, but for ten years resident in this place. This is my family, and our young friend, a countrywoman of yours. We all welcome you to New Switzerland.

MUSIC: *Lively theme.*

NARRATOR: At last it had come—long after the hope of it was forgotten: the chance to return to civilization. When he had heard their adventures, Captain Lyman told them he would be happy to take back to Europe any of the islanders who wished to go. It was a hard decision, and the Swiss Family Robinson thought long and seriously on it. At last the day arrived when the captain would ask for their answer.

CAPTAIN LYMAN: My good friends, the time will be soon at hand when my ship must set sail. Have you decided whether your family will accompany me or not? We will be happy to have you; but I could not blame you for wishing to stay here in this enchanted spot forever.

JOHANN: My sons are old enough to decide for themselves, Captain. And Miss Montrose, of course, must make her own choice. Let each speak for himself. As for my wife and me, we have decided that we will not return. We will remain for the rest of our days in New Switzerland.

ERNEST: Long life and happiness to those who make New Switzerland their home. For I intend to be one of them.

JACK: And Ernest is not the only son who will stay. I, too, will remain.

JENNY (*Plaintively*): Won't somebody wish long life and prosperity to those who go away? I shall be sad to leave New Switzerland and return to my family in England if none wish me Godspeed.

FRANZ (*Cheerfully*): Godspeed then, Miss Jenny. I, too, am bound for England, for I wish to have an education before I return to New Switzerland.

JENNY (*Quietly*): And what of you, Fritz? Do you go, or stay?

FRITZ: You know that where you are, Jenny, I shall be, too. Captain Lyman, are you prepared to arrange a marriage ceremony?

ELIZABETH: What's this? What's this?

JENNY: It is agreed between us, dear Mother Robinson. My dearest wish is that Fritz and I may be married with your blessings, here in the place we all love so well.

JOHANN: You have chosen well and wisely, Fritz.

FRITZ: Thank you, Father.

JOHANN: I think we have all chosen well.

ELIZABETH: Yes, Johann, all have chosen well, and for wise reasons. It does not matter whether one goes or stays. Each must do what is best for him. I know that for all of us one place alone shall live in our hearts as "home." And that is our dear island, New Switzerland.

FRANZ *and* FRITZ: Hurrah for New Switzerland!

JOHANN (*Laughing*): Let us return your blessing. Hurrah for England!

CAPTAIN LYMAN: I say, bless you *all!* Hurrah for the Swiss Family Robinson! (*Laughter*)

MUSIC: *Lively, happy theme.*

THE END